AF813369

Anti-Europeanism

Marco Baldassari · Emanuele Castelli ·
Matteo Truffelli · Giovanni Vezzani
Editors

Anti-Europeanism

Critical Perspectives Towards the European Union

Springer

Editors
Marco Baldassari
The European College of Parma Foundation
Parma, Italy

Matteo Truffelli
Department of Humanities, Social Sciences and Cultural Industries
University of Parma
Parma, Italy

Emanuele Castelli
Department of Law, Politics and International Studies
University of Parma
Parma, Italy

Giovanni Vezzani
Center for Studies in European and International Affairs
University of Parma
Parma, Italy

ISBN 978-3-030-24427-9 ISBN 978-3-030-24428-6 (eBook)
https://doi.org/10.1007/978-3-030-24428-6

© Springer Nature Switzerland AG 2020
This work is subject to copyright. All rights are reserved by the Publisher, whether the whole or part of the material is concerned, specifically the rights of translation, reprinting, reuse of illustrations, recitation, broadcasting, reproduction on microfilms or in any other physical way, and transmission or information storage and retrieval, electronic adaptation, computer software, or by similar or dissimilar methodology now known or hereafter developed.
The use of general descriptive names, registered names, trademarks, service marks, etc. in this publication does not imply, even in the absence of a specific statement, that such names are exempt from the relevant protective laws and regulations and therefore free for general use.
The publisher, the authors and the editors are safe to assume that the advice and information in this book are believed to be true and accurate at the date of publication. Neither the publisher nor the authors or the editors give a warranty, expressed or implied, with respect to the material contained herein or for any errors or omissions that may have been made. The publisher remains neutral with regard to jurisdictional claims in published maps and institutional affiliations.

This Springer imprint is published by the registered company Springer Nature Switzerland AG
The registered company address is: Gewerbestrasse 11, 6330 Cham, Switzerland

Foreword

Against Europe: The Changing Patterns of Euroscepticism Over Time

The contributions of this collective volume explore the many differentiated forms of Euroscepticism or anti-Europeanism. The phenomenon is not new. Since its inception, the European construction has triggered opposition, suspicion and controversies.[1] It started already in the 50s at the time of the European Coal and Steel Community launched by Robert Schuman and Jean Monnet. The British government reacted to the offer by stating that it was inconceivable to place two fundamental segments of their economy under the control of a technocratic authority. The same distrust was expressed all along the 50s in the UK but the coming to power of de Gaulle in France in 1958 made many people fear that the EEC would die even before coming to life. Actually, it did not happen as de Gaulle was convinced that the new venture would be of considerable help in his titanic effort to transform a backward and closed economy dependent on his colonial empire into an open and competitive one. But he was and remained a deeply convinced nationalist using Europe as «the rescue of the nation state» to use the Alan Milward's words.

For many years, France was perceived as the bad guy of the game, refusing further integration, closing the door to Britain finally conscious of its isolation, using the «empty chair» crisis to impede the Commission to expand its powers, protesting against the creeping «federal» jurisprudence of the European Court of Justice (ECJ). And this was not only a matter of politics: the bureaucracy was reluctant to implement the policies it disliked, while the Conseil d'État was rejecting the possibility to rely on the interpretation of European law by the Luxembourg Court. It is difficult to qualify this attitude as being anti-European

[1] I have developed further these arguments together with G. Mocavini. «*Resisting European Integration: the Variegated Forms of Anti-EU Protest*», in Giuliano Amato and alii (eds), The History of the European Integration, Hart Publishing, 2018, London.

since the principle of merging some powers at the supranational level was not contested. But at the same time, there was without any doubt a reluctance to consider the European Economic Community (EEC) more than an institution for regional cooperation run by and for sovereign states. It would be considered by today standards as a strong form of Euroscepticism.

The resignation of de Gaulle which made possible the access of the UK had a double effect. First, it redistributed the cards in attributing the role of the «reluctant partner» in the play to the newcomer. Secondly, it introduced new visions about what Europe could and should be. British ideas and interests were not at odds with the continental ones, but they were certainly not identical. On the political side, the British had to swallow a very bitter pill (whose consequences are under the eyes at time of Brexit). They had to accept through contorted formulas that European law would be superior to British rules and, in order to legitimate such a legal, political and mental revolution, relied for the first time upon a referendum in order to get the approval of the British people. For the very first time, a form of popular sovereignty was introduced aside of the sovereignty of the parliament, the central pillar of the whole system. The consequences of these two parallel sources of legitimacy have come to light in the two past years of the Brexit saga.

The place and strength of this conception of power spilled over in the debate about the legitimacy of EEC decisions. David Marquand, in an academic journal contribution, analysed the flaws of the institutional system and in particular the weak legitimacy of an assembly made of representatives indirectly selected by national parliaments. He stated that there was a «democratic deficit», two catch-words which have become the lag of all those rejecting too much integration as well of those dissatisfied with the actual functioning of the institutions and advocating further integration. In sum, «democratic deficit» was a kind of universal critique of the EEC but obviously much more vigourously used by Eurosceptics or those hostile to the European construction. In other words, the criticisms were based on the necessity to safeguard state sovereignty and national democracy. However, from the 70s to the Maastricht treaty in 1992, the opposition to the furthering of the European construction was swept away by the bizarre tango danced by two odd partners, Jacques Delors and Margaret Thatcher. Delors, a dedicated pro-European, was keen to deepen the economic and social integration of the continent and to anchor France in the process (he had known too well as Mitterand's Minister of Finances how illusory was the seduction of a national and divergent economic policy). On her side, Margaret Thatcher was more or less in the state of mind of de Gaulle in 1958: no appetite for Europe but a rational assessment that the EEC could be a powerful leverage for the transformation of Britain. The convergence and compromise between different interests and strategies allowed a formidable expansion of powers and transformation which cumulated in 1992 in spite or because of the 1989 earthquake. The Economic and Monetary Union was completed in 2002, and the draft of a European Constitution was conceived as the final touch to this ambitious project.

However from 1992, one did not pay enough attention to the mounting criticisms against the creeping expansion of EU powers in fields belonging to the core of state competences as well as to the potential deleterious effects of a hasty enlargement to ten new members. Those who understood better the implications of the change were the British authorities which stated that «wider was wiser». The statement was perfectly fine as far as the market expansion was concerned; it was more doubtful in the field of integration, but the British elites were perfectly aware of the implied consequences. The enlargement reinforced their vision of a Union which should not be a federation (the «F» word according to the colourful Schmitter's expression), which should not be «an ever closer union». Instead, the Union should evolve within the red lines drawn by Eurosceptic governments and tolerate as many opt-outs as requested by reluctant participants. In other words, «Euroscepticism» was not only an expression of parties or social groups but an entrenched alternative vision within the institution itself. As André Fontaine stated apropos of international relations in the 60s, there was only «a single bed for two visions».

The evidence that the member states and their respective public opinions were divided on the future of the collective enterprise came to the fore in 2005 when the Dutch and French referenda objected to the European Constitution. The rescue of the Treaty in a more low-profile agreement with more or less the same content added to the frustration of those objecting to the practice of «integration by stealth». Populist movements mushroomed everywhere and exploited in ways varying with the peculiarities of each polity any possible difficulty at the national level as a consequence of the defects and flaws of the EU. It became the ideal scapegoat for every problem in the way the Italians shout abuse at their national government (Piove. Governo ladro !- It rains, the government is a thief !). The EU was becoming the target for all possible blames linked to European policies (or not !). The trend was amplified by the 2008 financial and economic crisis, and then by the massive inflow of migrants in 2015–16. At that point, the European Union became the focal point of fierce criticism and blame from all angles and points of view: the lawyers deplored the complexity, the rigidity and the cumbersomeness of the institutions; the economists underlined the flaws and risks of failure of the Euro as well as its impact on the divergences between member states; the policy-makers put the blame on the technocratic approach prevailing in Brussels; the populists claimed that the European Central Bank, the ECJ and other technocratic elites were responsible for austerity, poverty and growing inequalities and the loss of national sovereignty as well as the expropriation of the people's power.[2]

The past 25 years have been characterized by a dual transformation of the anti-European feelings. First, they have grown in extension and dimension. While initially the anti-European movements were vocal in a few countries and exerted usually a marginal influence on the functioning of member states as well as on the EU system, they are by now present in every country, are often part of coalitions and hold the government in several eastern countries as well as one of the founding fathers of Europe, Italy. Their line of attack is different from the past too. While

[2] Yves Mény, Imparfaites démocraties, Protestations populaires et vagues populistes, Presses de SciencesPo, Paris, 2019; (italian version: Popolo ma non troppo- Il malinteso democratico, Il Mulino, Bologna, 2019).

initially the EEC and then the EU were criticized for not conforming to the principles of representative democracy, the critique today is radically different and is in line with similar blames expressed at the national level: the peoples of Europe both at the national and European level have been deprived of their rights as unique source of legitimacy by corrupted, technocratic, global elites caring only for their own self-interests. For the populists, the ideal democracy is not anymore a well-functioning representative democracy but a democracy of the people. And since there is nothing such as a European people, power has to be returned to the peoples constituting the 28 nations of Europe.

The populist movements have not (yet?) taken over the power in Brussels, but their fight against integration has had deleterious effects at all levels of government. Nationally, they have been able to influence dramatically the public debate and the political agenda even when they failed to win a majority. As a consequence, most of the national party systems which had prevailed since the Second World War are in pieces. The social democratic parties are in decline nearly everywhere. Great Britain, the only country where Euroscepticism went as far as exiting, is still in the middle of a constitutional and political crises. Two prime ministers have been forced to resign, and no solution to the Brexit saga is still in sight to date in June 2019.

In this chaotic and confused muddle, there are however some signs of hope. First, the populist movements so efficient at destroying are much less efficient at managing and governing. The Austrian coalition has lost ground after a scandal involving the vice-prime minister. Italy's coalition is in deep crisis, and none of the most critical issues that the country is facing have been addressed. Britain has been characterized as a deeply divided country: a split opinion, a split party system, a split country. Populism will appear more and more not as the solution but as the problem.

Furthermore, the hot debates of the past years have been largely transformed from being exclusively national to a pan-European conversation about the future of the Union. Habermas' dream of a European public space is not yet there, but it is in the making. Nothing important taking place in a European country is foreign to the others. In addition, the controversies have moved away from the discussions over the membership of the Union (being in or out) to the conflicting views about allocation of powers or the content of policies. Brexit has been the exception and at the same time the embodiment of the difficulties and problems related to the exit strategy. It has cooled down a lot of wishful thinking to the extent that nearly all populist movements claim that their objective is not to leave the Union but to build up a «different» Union.

«*Les jeux ne sont pas faits*». We can expect that the years to come will be a bumpy road. The most dramatic scenario would be another financial or monetary crisis that the EU would have the greatest difficulty to tame. But, if the worst does not happen, it can be expected that Europe will appear for what it is, i.e. an imperfect but indispensable organization for the sake of peace, prosperity and capacity to face the tremendous challenges of the third millennium. It takes time to integrate countries with divergent ideas, interests and visions, and on my fronts, the EU is much more integrated than the USA in 1860; i.e. 70 years after its foundation and even today, the EU offers to its members and citizens a more homogeneous and extensive range of civil, political and social rights than its American counterpart. On the economic side, the dismantling of the Union would simply mean becoming a colony of either the USA or China. As somebody put it «There is no alternative».

Paris, France
May 2019

Yves Mény

Acknowledgement This volume is the outcome of an international workshop organized in November 2017 at the University of Parma and financed by the Center for Studies in European and International Affairs (CSEIA—www.cseiaparma.it).

CSEIA CENTRO STUDI IN AFFARI EUROPEI E INTERNAZIONALI

Contents

Introduction

Marco Baldassari and Giovanni Vezzani

1 Multiple Crises and Oppositions in Europe

It is largely recognized that the EU is currently facing the most difficult crisis since its origins. Multiple and diverse internal and external shocks have turned the unification project—which should have brought a progressive convergence based on functional integration—into a less ambitious intergovernmental bargaining. The European motto of an "ever a closer union" is suffering a lack of effectiveness, while Europe is crossed by different fractures. The latter seem to represent something more than mere epiphenomena and tend to assume a structural significance. The first of them concerns the divide between debtors and creditor states (north/south fraction, i.e. "core" and "periphery" countries), which reflects the macroeconomic unbalances and tensions that are present in the Eurozone. The second refers to the Brexit, which dramatically questioned the irreversibility of a widened Europeanization process as a gradual path towards a largely shared supranational dimension. Thirdly, the East/West divide is represented by the *rassemblement* of the Eastern European Countries (the so-called Visegrad Group), which appears to be more and more reluctant to accept any kind of "open borders" discourse and the rule of law, based on the free circulation of persons, mutual respect and dignity of human beings. The dispute over migrants redistributing quotas is another disruptive signal that has led some important scholars and practitioners in the field of EU studies to talk about "disintegration", "differentiation", "decline" of the Europeanization process (Zielonka 2018; Krastev 2017).

M. Baldassari (✉)
European College of Parma, Parma, Italy
e-mail: m.baldassari@collegioeuropeo.it

G. Vezzani
CSEIA (Center for Studies in European and International Affairs),
University of Parma, Parma, Italy
e-mail: gio.vezzani@gmail.com

© Springer Nature Switzerland AG 2020

M. Baldassari et al. (eds.), *Anti-Europeanism*,
https://doi.org/10.1007/978-3-030-24428-6_1

In addition to the above-mentioned major fault lines, contemporary European societies and institutions are going through a long-lasting and growing process of depoliticization. From this perspective, society is increasingly conceived as a spreading web of market forces or a sum of individualist monads maximizing their private interests or gains, while institutions are understood as belonging to a neutral or technical domain, with their own proper (bureaucratic) functioning rules, and in this way they tacitly avoid the question of recognizing possible conflicting political alternatives (Mouffe 2018). The post-ideological governance has absorbed the democratic life into a hank of conglomerated norms, practices and procedures which *de facto* impedes a real dialectic between civil society, the public sphere and institutions. This process has turned the classical and liberal modern "left/right" cleavage into an "élite/people" division—introducing a new (?) polarization within society—which from an historical point of view could also be described with the expression "Polanyi moment": that is, the idea that globalization trends, as well as the financialization of the capitalist system, are bringing contemporary societies towards a critical threshold in terms of the sustainability of overall fluxes (goods, capitals, persons, etc.) (Polanyi 1944). The 50s and the 60s of the last century have been considered the glorious years of the Keynesian economic model, which represented the democratization of the capitalism system, thanks to the construction of modern welfare state system. This model, which was built up in order to mitigate the conflicting claims coming from the working class and social movements, entered into an irreversible crisis in the middle of the 70s. Then, the neoliberal counter-revolution brought gradually the divorce between capitalism and democracy, which exploded in its virulent contradiction with the financial crisis of 2007–2008. After this "thirty years' pact" between the capital and the labour forces (the mid-40s until the mid-70s), we witnessed approximately other thirty years of neo-liberalism based on liberalization and dismantling of social and pension schemes and strong public health frameworks as well as flexibilization of the job market (from the mid-70s to the first decade of the Twenty-First Century). The counter-revolution that characterized this second phase re-set the balance in favour of the capital revenue rather than salaries and better working conditions. "Reclaiming the State" is therefore a sort of protection (Fazi and Mitchel 2017) against the self-regulated market forces of the neoliberal counter-revolution which started in the middle of the 1970s and entered into crisis in 2007–2008. It is plausible to maintain that the current situation is one in which, "the old is dying and the new cannot be born; in this interregnum, a great variety of morbid symptoms appear", to recall Antonio Gramsci's definition of "crisis" (Gramsci 1971).

In this context, the book draws a panorama of different critical perspectives towards the EU, from diverse points of view, including an in-depth analysis of the political dimension from multiple angles, such as the changes of the party systems in the member states and the emersion of new movements and agents during the crisis of the last decade, but taking into account also the structural problems (and the incompleteness) of the European institutional framework and the vexed question of the identification (or invention) of salient identities and of the role of culture in European societies and in the EU. These debates have been constructively analysed from different approaches and standpoints by considering anti-Europeanism not as purely negative and disruptive trend, but rather as a theoretically interesting and potentially fruitful political phenomenon, a sort of force field for different theories, concepts and ideas coming from disciplines as different as political science, political philosophy and comparative politics. Having considered that, first of all we must consider that Europe is deeply embedded in the evolution of the capitalist system and it is part of the neoliberal process. The European Union, in particular, was a strategic field in which different powers, conflicts, class struggles, intra-state and interstate relations moved across the continent and shaped in different manners the sovereignties of the member states. The European Union, since it has been always a conflicting plurality, was always a battlefield of different approaches, theories, doctrines as well as pragmatic solutions, bargaining and institutional compromises. It was the result of the mediation, through a concrete and pragmatic cooperation that tended to avoid the "fatal" word "unification", or "United States of Europe" in order to make the integration process more acceptable, silent and natural. Even though leaders and the head of state and government, during the history, did not forget to mention the "federative moment" (at least with a rhetorical aim), the proper unification theme remained undercurrent. Since diversity, plurality and conflict are the keywords to understand the features of the European construction, we should consider Euroscepticism as a fully fledged approach that contributed to shape the relation among the nation states. Far to be a mere refusal or a brutal rejection, it contains a variety of forms and positions that deserve to be analysed, grouped and studied and the present volume tries to sketch and to take into consideration, from different perspectives. Of course, the phenomenon grew in its dimension after the multiple crises and depoliticization process that we previously mentioned and, more in general, with the crisis of democracy that hit the state as well as the new forms of post-sovereign governance like the EU, but it would be wrong to consider anti-Europeanism simply a recent product of the economic instability. Anti-Europeanism, as well as Euroscepticism and Eurocriticism, had always accompanied the evolution of the EU construction and has been part of it. We can just briefly mention here the Gaullist pessimism towards supranational European institutions, especially the Commission, which brought the so-called empty chair crisis, in 1965, with the withdrawal of the French representatives, not to say about the position by Margareth Thatcher in the 80s, when she firmly declared "I want my money back", invoking the "rebate" problem, concerning the English contribution to the EU financing. It is worth mentioning that there was also a "federal Euroscepticism", which on the contrary criticized Europe from a different angle, by stressing the accent on the mere functional and technical drift, removing the question of the political unification. In this case we have a form of scepticism towards the EU institutions which is not reducible to sovranism. Therefore, since Euroscepticism is a very heterogeneous and complex attitude, it is quite difficult to bracketing the anti-Europeanism into a simple left/right division (Leconte 2010). This volume, therefore, points out that Euroscepticism, far from being a mere contingent and theoretical oppositional phenomenon, is instead a structural part of the European integration process itself, inescapably intertwined with the politicization and re-articulation of fault lines and cleavages both within the

EU and within the member states. If we consider the EU as a strategic field of power relations rather than as a pure system of norms (like a strict juridical approach might suggest), or as a mere process of negotiation between sovereign states, it becomes clear that it is precisely from the dialectic relation between the European and the anti-European discourses that a common public opinion (what Juergen Habermas described as *Weltinnen Politik*. (Habermas) may arise.

Throughout the different contributions, the book also tries to scrutinize the relation between anti-Europeanism and populism. This link should not be conceived derivatively, as if one term would stem from the other. In other words, these two phenomena should be kept distinct and considered in their specificities. Opposing attitudes towards Europe represent an extremely diversified field, characterized by a variety of political positions, ideologies, parties, movements, campaigns, etc. The first effort of this collective volume has been to avoid any pre-comprehension of populism as a necessarily regressive phenomenon, a degeneration of democracy or a pathological condition for European societies. We moved from the methodological assumption that the "appeal to the people" and the vagueness of the populist message should not be stigmatized a priori. In the same vein, we avoided to treat the rhetorical dimension of the public debate uniquely as a form of false discourse or ideological manipulation. It is true that the demagogic satisfaction of the uncritical popular needs due for electoral purposes could be a form of deconsolidation of democracy (the Italian word "clientelismo" captures this concept), which means treating votes as a compensation for a promised benefit. Nevertheless, one should not overlook the fact that the emersion of populist movements is not only reducible to demagogy. Populism is rather as a twofold and open modus operandi in contemporary politics. It represents a form of disaffection for traditional politics, as well as for traditional centre liberal (both left and right wing) parties, due to the centrality of the free market forces in their social conception. At the same time, populism is a style and an attitude that could be adapted to very different circumstances, and it may also be conceived in a constructive and institutional way rather than in disruptive and radically oppositional terms. As Nadia Urbinati argued, the ambiguous/inaccurate use of the word "populism" could lead to think that politics is based either on the defence of the status quo or on the support of populist claims, which are therefore put outside the institutional arena of power. But populism is not only an oppositional form of mobilization: it is also a strategy of power (Urbinati 2014). Democratic politics does not essentially consist in building majorities and governments, but it also rests on dialectical political competition between groups, which nowadays cannot be plausibly reduced to the classical bipolar system historically experienced in the centre liberalist period. Populism is not an ideology, and therefore we do not argue in this book that it should be confined or assimilated to the extreme right, or a sort of new edition of neo-fascism. It could be conceived either as a flawed democratic reaction, which could lead to illiberal form of government, or, in some cases, a genuine response against a neoliberal anti-democratic governance (Mudde and Rovira Kaltwasser 2017). Populism could be also considered in different ways as a sort of mentality and attitude, or a logic to construct the people, a political will or collective identities. The forms of oppositions to the European discourse can be traced back also from this "populist reason", to use the expression coined by Ernesto Laclau. The alter-Europeanism, or a critical attitude towards the EU, needs, for example, to establish a frontier between "We" and "They", declaring an enemy of the people (the élite) and forming a chain of different popular claims that could generate a democratic process subverting a consolidated regime. In this case, populism is a synonymous of radical democracy (Laclau 2005). Mainstream interpretations of populism tend to reduce the phenomenon to something potentially doomed to authoritarian regression. According to this view, populism would inevitably entail an attitude based on the rejection of pluralism. Therefore, mainstream analysis tends to oppose the differentiation of society, intrinsically good, to a (false) homogeneous organic community, artificially generated by the populist discourse. In this regard, populism could easily fall within the conservative or right-wing domain. On the contrary, Yves Surel and Yves Mény recognized that populism cannot be considered as a relatively stable and coherent trend of the new radical right and that it does not correspond to a political family, but rather to a dimension of the discursive and normative register adopted by political actors. Populism is a set of resources available to a plurality of actors, in a more or less systematic way (Meny and Surel 2001). The risk of the liberal mainstream interpretation is to understand populism uniquely as a "regressive" phenomenon and anti-Europeanism as a by-product of this regression. According to this questionable interpretation, any form of Europeanist discourse is projected towards modernity and progress, whereas populism is linked to old concepts such as the "state" and "sovereignty", which have been overcome by the cosmopolitan dimension and the globalized open society.

This volume does not aim at collecting all different positions regarding Euroscepticism or to present an exhaustive list of case studies. It is neither an all-encompassing theoretical analysis, nor a comprehensive vision about the European Union and its crisis. It contains different contributions on multiple topics, whose *fil rouge* is to reconsider "Opposing Europe" positions (both in a theoretical way and in a empirical way) from a multifaceted, cross-border framework. In doing that, the authors developed, from different angles, both quantitative and qualitative analyses. The book is divided into three parts. The first is devoted to theoretical approaches and quantitative analysis on Euroscepticism and populism. The focal goal of this part is to provide a general conceptual framework of the subject. The second part focuses on the notion of crisis and neoliberal Europe. The above-mentioned multilayered crisis is a cause and not a consequence of the raise of populist movements consequently, the Europe-crisis nexus is analysed in strong connection with populism, even though it must not be reduced to causal determination. Finally, the third part is devoted to taking into consideration some specific cases.

The first part of the volume is devoted to the theoretical approaches and quantitative analysis. Francesco Nicoli's essay precisely recasts the question of antagonism within the ambivalence between the crisis of democracy and the populist reaction. Was populism the force that led to the crisis of democracy? Or was instead the deconsolidation of democracy that brought the populist phenomenon? "While Euroscepticism has been classically framed as a reaction to elitism and to a project of integration that has never really been supported "by the people", recent studies have also started to think about Euroscepticism as the "Europeanized" apparition of a wider cosmopolitan-communitarian cleavage" (cfr: *infra*). In this regard, Euroscepticism must be considered a European manifestation of a global cosmopolitan and communitarian divide which is leading to structural adjustments in the party systems after a phase of "de-alignment" from the previous left/right cleavage. In this case, the "EU will face a shift from 'permissive consensus' to 'constraining dissensus' but it risks to move towards a widespread 'constraining consensus', where not only populist and nationalist parties, but also democratic forces would oppose further integration". Nicoli argues that "the emergence of polarized, political counter-movements constitutes an unavoidable stage of integration, marking a transformative leap in the nature of European integration".

Anti-Europeanism read through the lens of the Euro crisis is tackled by Constantin Schäfer and Martin Gross. In their investigation on how Euroscepticism in the public opinion and party systems of EU member states has developed since the 1990s, they analyse to what extent the Euro crisis has affected specific support for the EU regime and diffuse support for the process of European integration, as well as the party systems' positions on European integration. Even if the debt crisis in Europe has led to a strong rise in output-related Euroscepticism in many countries, this did not bring as a consequence the rejection in toto of the unification process or to "exit" strategies from the Eurozone. "Moreover, party systems have only partly adapted to popular Euroscepticism during the Euro crisis" Schäfer and Gross argue.

The ambivalence of the populist moment is stressed also by Najimdeen Bakare, who suggests to use a "constructivist prism" to understand the phenomenon: "The strength of contemporary European populism can be fairly explicated through a constructivist prism. In addition to contributing to socialization breakdown, populism has demonstrated how socially constructed narratives can redefine democracy".

Having defined the theoretical approaches and some quantitative elements of problems related to populism and Euroscepticism, the second part of the volume is devoted to Europe in times of crisis and to recent examples of fractures in the EU. Marco Baldassari argued that the shift towards an institutionalized differentiated integration will bring a progressive depoliticization of economy and will give rise to disruptive forces. A serious gap of legitimacy is generating popular disaffection which deals, in a broader sense, with a deconsolidation of the classical liberal and representative democratic framework. Since the social market economy remains the key doctrine of any further strengthening of the economic and monetary unions, the Euro crisis will contribute to exacerbate the fractures between core and peripheral countries.

Valeria Tarditi and Davide Vittori also tackle the political consequences of these relevant economic aspects. They carried out an analysis based on the examination of social democratic and radical parties in Spain and in Italy. In particular, the changing positions of these parties regarding Europe were critically considered. The "Faustian pact" that induced social democratic parties to give full unconditional support to European integration impedes to propose an alternative or a project launching a new European discourse based on values different from neo-liberalism. This brings the problem of solidarity and how refunding the European project with more cooperative bases and not only through augmenting competitive behaviour.

Kathrin Rheinl tackled the multiple facets of European solidarity and its effect on EU critical attitudes in times of the European financial and migrant crises, showing that solidarity does indeed affect attitudinal Euroscepticism. European citizens more likely oppose European integration once it comes along with cross-country burden sharing. Finally, the contribution by Kristina Khutishvili aims to discuss current challenges of populism and nationalism by using the apparatus of political philosophy. Three important philosophic categories, such as identity, responsibility and dialogue, are scrutinized as having explanatory power while reflecting on current collisions. By showing their interrelated character, the author underlines the issue of speechlessness and multilateral lack of communication between people and the establishment, different intellectual groups.

The third part of the book critically addresses some of the dimensions involved in the Eurosceptic (or overtly anti-European) discourses. Three different cases are taken into account from different approaches (including the normative–philosophical perspective), so that it becomes possible to cope with some of the multifaceted forms of opposition to European integration. Despite the evident heterogeneity of the phenomena considered, the three chapters jointly highlight the relevance and the different uses of cultural identitarian claims in formulating political arguments and claims against the EU. For some actors, culture and identity represent the main framework within which positions in favour of or against the idea of Europe can be moulded. As Giovanni Vezzani's chapter demonstrates, in some cases religion (Islam in particular) can be presented as the mark of a supposed non-European or even anti-European identity. Europe's "Other" is thus constructed as an irreducibly and radically adversarial subject. However, Vezzani argues that even the critical deconstruction and denunciation of Islamophobic narratives are not sufficient, per se, to ground a credible and effective alternative. In his view, the development of a plausible common conception of citizenship should balance centripetal and centrifugal forces, in order to provide at the same time a stable commitment to liberal democratic institutions and the fair inclusion of members of minority groups. Building on John Rawls's "idea of public reason", Vezzani contends that both a common political identity and shared evaluative standards are required for European citizens to be able to reconcile stable and just political institutions and the "fact of reasonable pluralism". In this way, public reason becomes the pivotal element of an inclusive and yet distinctively liberal democratic conception of citizenship, which is based on the "criterion of reciprocity" as its moral–political cornerstone.

Considering immigration and the EU itself as two among the most divisive issues in present-day debate in Europe, Benedetta Carlotti and Stella Gianfreda empirically investigate the positions of the Northern League and the Five Star Movement (two differently populist and Eurosceptic parties which formed a governmental alliance after the last Italian elections in March 2018) about these topics. By applying computer-assisted discourse analysis to an original data set of 533 parliamentary speeches delivered in two distinct institutional arenas (the Italian and the European Parliament) and taking into considerations different sub-dimensions for each of the two matters, Carlotti and Gianfreda claim that Northern League tends to frame its opposition towards the EU and immigration on the basis of cultural identitarian and sovereigntist arguments, while the Five Star Movement takes advantage of the two issues to strengthen its anti-elitist positions. Interestingly, they found that while the Northern League is inclined to present the EU in terms of a threat to national sovereignty and cultural identity, the Five Star Movement seems to be more concerned with stressing the lack of democratic accountability of élites at the EU level.

In his contribution, Maurilio Pirone considers the process of European integration from the viewpoint of contentious non-institutional actors. Especially, the author considers "Blockupy" and "neo-municipalism" as two instances of social movements which combine some form of opposition to EU's policies with a strong pro-European commitment. While both movements tend to assume a markedly transnational character, they are also both engaged in a heated confrontation around the policies implemented by the EU in the economic and social field. Pirone investigates the connections between the local, the national, the transnational and the properly European levels in order to locate these new kinds of mobilization processes and the demands arising from them. In these two experiences—Pirone argues—Europe emerges as a "transnational area cooperation from below as well as of contentious politics", while the EU's institutional framework seems inadequate to reabsorb such bottom-up social movements.

Let us conclude with some remarks from the standpoint of political philosophy. The main result emerging from this multidisciplinary analysis of the growing importance and vigour in public debates of such positions as souverainism, neo-nationalism and populism in the aftermath of the economic crisis and the Brexit process is that the EU and the political struggles and claims concerning it cannot be above (or below) political philosophical reflection. If, as it can be certainly affirmed, the EU's institutions have "deep and long-term social effects and in fundamental ways shape citizens' character and aims, the kinds of persons they are and aspire to be" (Rawls 2005: 68), then it should be evident that both European institutions, policies and processes and the most relevant demands and forms of opposition concerning them must undergo philosophical scrutiny (see, for instance, Rawls and van Parijs 2003). There is no doubt that debates in support of or in opposition to the EU, its institutions and its reform proposals deal with both fundamental dimensions of justice, namely the *distribution* of economic, social and symbolic resources and the *recognition* of cultural and political identities (Maffettone 2013: 18). While this book was not mainly concerned with directly addressing such pivotal political philosophical questions of justice from a normative perspective, it may contribute to pave the way to further advancements in that direction.

References

Fazi, T., & Mitchel, W. (2017). *Reclaiming the state: A progressive vision of sovereignty for a post-neoliberal world*. London: Pluto Press.

Gramsci, A. (1971). *Selection from the Prison notebooks* (Quaderni del carcere n.3). Intl Pub Co Inc.

Krastev, I. (2017). *After Europe*. Philadelphia: University of Pennsylvania Press.

Laclau, E. (2005). *On populist reason*. London: Verso Books.

Leconte, C. (2010). *Understanding euroscepticism*. London: Palgrave.

Maffettone, S. (2013). *Un mondo migliore. Giustizia globale tra Leviatano e Cosmopoli*. Roma: LUISS University Press.

Meny, Y., & Surel, Y. (2001). *Democracies and populist challenge*. London: Palgrave MacMillan.

Mouffe, C. (2018). *For a left populism*. London: Verso Books.

Mudde, C., & Rovira Kaltwasser, C. (2017). *Populism: A very short introduction*. Oxford: Oxford University Press.

Polanyi, K. (1944). *The great transformation. The political and economic origins of our time*. Boston: Beacon Press.

Rawls, J. (2005). *Political liberalism. Expanded edition*. New York: Columbia University Press.

Rawls, J., & van Parijs, P. (2003). Three letters on the law of peoples and the European union. In *Revue de philosophie écononomique* (vol. 7, pp. 7–20).

Urbinati, N. (2014). *Democracy disfigured: Opinion, truth and the people*. Cambridge: Harvard University Press.

Zielonka, J. (2018). *Counter-revolution: Liberal Europe in retreat*. Oxford: Oxford University Press.

Theoretical Approaches and Quantitative Analysis

Democratic Deficit and Its Counter-Movements: The Eurocentric–Eurosceptic Divide in Times of Functional Legitimacy

Francesco Nicoli

1 Introduction

The long wave of Populism and Euroscepticism, which began in Europe during the Euro crisis and is currently widespread, requires to re-assess how legitimacy is provided in multilevel polities. In this chapter, I offer a novel understanding of multilevel legitimacy, which can be used to explain not only the European, but also the global shift towards populist and sovereignist politics. Indeed, the rise of such nationalist and communitarian parties is a global trend, as witnessed by the election of Donald Trump in the USA, by the strength of leaders such as Vladimir Putin or Victor Orbán in Eastern Europe and by the success of the Brexit referendum. The global dimension of the phenomenon has created momentum for a novel assessment of the domestic implications of globalization. The European Union, however, is arguably the political organization most sensitive to the striking back of nationalism. On the one hand, the EU is a political community in the making, thus vulnerable to nationalism due to the mismatch between national political authority and Europeanized functions. On the other hand, the Union exists over a delicate constitutional balance between its two foundational principles: the aim of achieving an "*ever-closer Union*", and the acknowledgement that a true "European People" does not yet exist; hence, the different peoples of Europe must be "*united in diversity*". While the Union's institutions and political life are characterized by this inherent tension, the re-emergence of nationalist politics threatens such constitutional compromise. The structural weakness of the Union is further activated by the multiple crises ("polycrises") it has faced in the last decade (Fabbrini 2015; Nicoli and Zeitlin 2019), weakening the Union's output legitimacy without strengthening the democratic mandate of its leadership.

Against this background, this chapter aims to contribute to two bodies of literature. On the one hand, it provides a novel contribution to theories of political legitimacy in

F. Nicoli (✉)
University of Amsterdam, Amsterdam, Netherlands
e-mail: f.nicoli@uva.nl

© Springer Nature Switzerland AG 2020

M. Baldassari et al. (eds.), *Anti-Europeanism*,
https://doi.org/10.1007/978-3-030-24428-6_2

multilevel polities by introducing the concept of functional legitimacy. On the other hand, it contributes to the literature investigating structural causes of the renewed politicization in Europe from a theoretical perspective, discussing the conditions under which the politicization/polarization dynamics can become a beneficial, rather than a destructive, element of the European system. To these ends, Sect. 2 of the chapter assesses the broad problem of legitimate political institutions in a globalized world; in doing so, it provides a new theory of functional legitimacy in multilevel polities. Section 3 discusses how political, national and cultural identities, which represent the main elements of constitutionally protected diversity in the multilevel European system and interact with functional legitimacy. Next, Sects. 4 and 5 discuss, in the light of the functional legitimacy theory, the emergence and dynamics of politicization in multilevel systems, with particular attention devoted to the surfacing of a new cosmopolitan–communitarian cleavage. Finally, Sect. 6 discusses the dynamics of integration when domestic politicization and functional legitimacy are considered jointly.

2 Modelling Functional Legitimacy

To set the stage for a comprehensive assessment of the politicization of European integration, a new general theory of functional legitimacy is introduced here, building upon, and moving beyond, earlier works by Easton, Scharpf, Majone and many others. Let us start by a simple consideration: European integration and globalization alike generate shifts in competences and authority allocation, which may result in mismatches that can harm the capabilities of communities to achieve meaningful democratic rule. Some have proposed a linear understanding of this problem: in a simple perspective (for instance, Rodrik 2012), a primarily economic integration leads to the emergence of a mismatch between economic freedom and national democratic representativeness, creating a source of built-in democratic deficit. Such a mismatch can be addressed in two ways: either by complementing economic integration by scaling-up supranational political and regulatory competences, or by addressing the capability shortages of nation states by scaling integration back. While this narrative is surely compelling, one may wonder whether it may be, perhaps, too linear in its explanation of the phenomenon of politicization of supranational integration. After all, as noted by several scholars (Majone 1999; Bundesverfassungsgericht 2009: 252; Nicoli 2017a), not all policy fields are made equal: some areas (for instance, technical regulations or standards) could be integrated easily with no harm to the democratic sustainability of a political system (even in the eyes of populists or nationalists, as shown in Fig. 3).

In fact, a nonlinear understanding of supranational legitimacy requires the matching of Majone's (1999, 2014) theory of insulation/participation with Scharpf's (1997, 2009) input/output legitimacy model. According to Majone, in order to deliver effective regulatory policies some functions (mostly regulatory) are carried out better by institutions that are "insulated" from the political system, while other policies

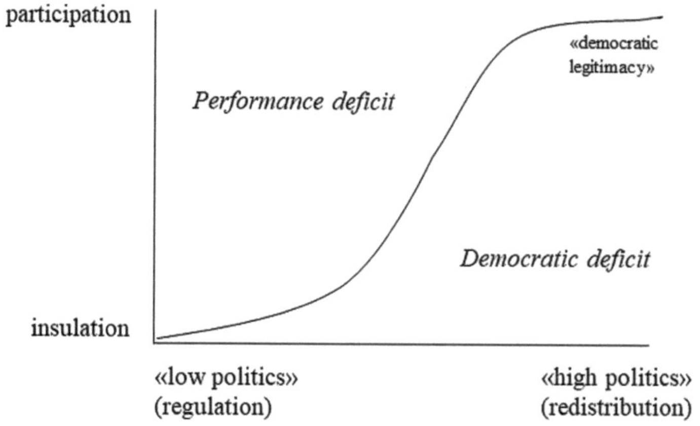

Fig. 1 Functional–democratic legitimacy

(typically redistributive policies[1]) require democratic decision-making processes. Majone's approach is well complemented by Scharpf's conceptualization of legitimacy as "input" and "output", whereby input legitimacy is provided (in a democratic system[2]) by an effective electoral process, while output legitimacy is provided by successful policy-making, leading to widespread beneficial outcomes. Building on Majone (1999, 2014) and Scharpf (1997, 2009), I argue that, as long as integration concerned functions perceived as non-redistributive, output legitimacy alone was largely sufficient; this is because democratic decision-making is required only in certain key fields, while regulatory policies can be dealt within insulated institutions without any harm to democracy (for an extensive discussion, see Nicoli 2017a).

The fundamental dynamics of such system is represented in Figs. 1 and 2. Building on Majone (1999, 2014), the Bundesverfassungsgericht (2009) and Genschel and Jachtenfuchs (2016), we can assume a continuum between pure regulatory powers and redistributive/core state powers/redistributive competences (horizontal axis in Figs. 1 and 2).[3] Building on Scharpf (1997), we can assume a continuum between participation and insulation: the higher the degree of participation (i.e. of democratic

[1]But in this chapter, we refer, more broadly, to "core state powers".

[2]In the scope of this chapter, a sufficient conceptualization of political legitimacy can be obtained by combining Weber, Scharpf/Easton and Dahl's understanding of legitimacy. The input/output legitimacy distinction proposed by Scharpf and Easton represents a starting point. Input legitimacy, however, does not equate with democratic rule. Following Weber's (1919) conceptualization, input legitimacy can be divided into three subcategories: constitutional, traditional, and charismatic legitimacy. Finally, we can define democratic legitimacy as the sub-subcategory of constitutional/legal legitimacy delivered by constitutional systems that correspond to Dahl's (1989) definition of *polyarchic democratic systems*. One shall note that polyarchic democratic legitimacy is the only form of input legitimacy that ensures that failures in delivering output legitimacy do not necessarily imply opposition "to the system", as widely discussed later in this chapter.

[3]For instance, the setting of technical standards may constitute an example of pure regulatory competence, while decisions on income tax rates would be pure redistributive competence.

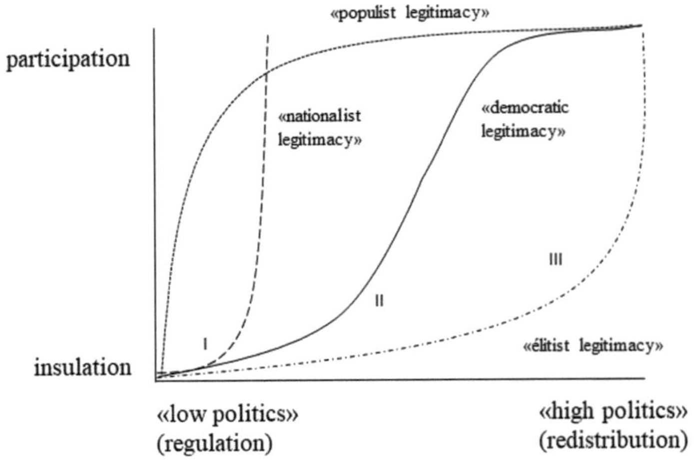

Fig. 2 Functional–democratic legitimacies compared

governance, for instance representative or direct democracy), the stronger the quality of the input by democratic means. Similarly, the higher the degree of insulation (i.e. decisions taken on the basis of expertise), the greater the expected output through successful policies. This is represented on the vertical axis of Fig. 1. Let us therefore consider the two continuums—from participation to insulation and from low politics (i.e. mostly regulation) to high politics (i.e. redistribution and other core state powers). In the former case, we would find—close to *perfect* insulation—other forms of delegation, progressively more dependent on political control, the more we move up on the axis. At some point, towards the upper part of the axis, we would find classical representative democracy and, further up, instruments of direct democratic control such as referenda or emerging forms of *e-democracy.* In other words, the continuum from participation to insulation is rather non-controversial. The horizontal axis is, on the other side, more controversial. Even if we can agree conceptually that *some* policies are *rather* more regulatory than redistributive, and others are rather more redistributive than regulatory, different individuals probably have different views on a given policy's nature over this balance.[4] Individual determinants such as education, but also beliefs, values and personal experience, ultimately determine whether a given policy is considered "low" or "high" politics; this will be further discussed in the next section.

In fact, Fig. 1 provides a more complex understanding of the functional legitimacy dynamics discussed in the previous paragraph. By combining Scharpf and Majone's

[4]A typical case, in the European context, has been monetary integration (Nicoli 2017a: 391). For a very long time, monetary policy was considered and implemented, as a redistributive policy. European integration in the field was possible only in a (historically narrow) window of time when, due to the failures of neo-Keynesian monetarism in the 1970s and 1980s, a shared belief concerning the regulatory nature of monetary policy (i.e., only regulating the rate of inflation) emerged. Such a consensus disappeared less than 20 years later, but the institution maintains its insulated characteristics.

theory, we can figure out the key elements of a theory of functional legitimacy: the nature of the function (redistributive or regulatory) determines the nature of legitimacy (input or output) required. It may follow that the institution under observation finds itself in legitimacy disequilibria: excessive participation (e.g. through direct democracy instruments) to deal with functions that do not actually require it (e.g. technical regulations) would do more harm than benefit to legitimacy, because they would create a clear "performance deficit" in policy fields where excesses of representation provides no legitimacy gains. Figure 1 gives a graphical representation of such systems: a performance deficit is associated with a lack of output legitimacy, while a democratic deficit is associated with a lack of input legitimacy.

The function in the centre of Fig. 1 identifies the area where policies are fully legitimated; it is assumed to be S-shaped, because it is reasonable to expect that the more we move towards the integration of redistributive policies (or core state powers), the more input legitimacy is needed (and the other way round). At some point, as long as we maintain that individuals do hold democratic values, a need for input legitimacy will arise if an international organization acquires sufficient redistributive/core state powers. Therefore, for this condition to be satisfied, the level of democratic decision-making provided by the system must fall on the legitimacy function. If it falls below, the system suffers from some degree of democratic deficit. If the system does not require input legitimacy, it must be legitimised on the output side. However, as suggested by Majone (1999) and Moravcsik (2002), protection from the influence of politicians is often a condition for effective regulatory policies: agencies are often able to deliver better results if they are insulated from constant political pressure. So, in order to have an effective output legitimacy, the more we move towards regulative and non-essential policies, the more insulation (and less electoral decision-making) is needed. Again, agents may hold different beliefs on the degree of insulation needed in a given point, but we can assume that all agents (including the most die-hard direct-democracy supporters) are likely to believe that, at a certain point, insulation will be needed to achieve output legitimacy. For this condition to be satisfied, the level of non-electoral decision-making must be on their legitimacy function. If it falls above, the system is experiencing a "performance deficit": in other words, the outcomes of integration are structurally downplayed because of the excessive levels of political pressure, and output legitimacy is not achieved.

3 Functional Legitimacy and Individual Beliefs: Identities, Ideologies and Allegiances

Now, it is reasonable to assume that different agents (with different identities and utility functions) have very different legitimacy functions (Fig. 2). This is dependent on two main issues: first, different individuals have different preferences on the continuum between representation and insulation; second, different individuals interpret the regulatory/redistributive nature of a policy differently.

For instance, genuine elitists are likely to support much more insulation than supporters of direct democracy, which would likely see no insulation at all. At *prima facie*, it is clear that the main danger for any supranational political system is represented by nationalist sentiments (Fig. 2). No matter the degree of representation/participation delivered at supranational level, nationalist legitimacy will still consider the spilling over of high politics/redistributive functions at supranational level as a source of democratic deficit. Now, contemporary discussion on identities as a proper "dimension" of politics finds its roots in the communitarian/liberal debate that characterized the North American political philosophy in the late 1970s, in the *No Demos* debate in Europe in the 1990s, and in the renewed interest on welfare chauvinism in the early 2000s. Since Hooghe et al. (2002), Kriesi et al. (2006, 2008), and Kriesi (2012) put forward the idea that phenomena such as Euroscepticism were anchored in structural changes of Western societies (and are therefore "here to stay", either embedded in new positions within existing parties, or by generating dedicated issue parties), this idea has gained traction. On a similar pathway, Zürn and de Wilde (2016) and Hooghe and Marks (2018) build on the "new dimension" literature in their interpretation of the original Lipset and Rokkan (1967) cleavage model, suggesting that Euroscepticism is the European manifestation of a global cosmopolitan/communitarian divide that it is leading a restructuring of the party system after a phase of "de-alignment" from the previous left/right cleavage.

While many of these issues are discussed later in this chapter, under this perspective we can consider that allegiance and political identities are, at least to some extent, *endogenous* to the perception of, and satisfaction with, one's economic security: globalization and European integration, producing new winners and new losers, generate a change in political allegiances and identities. Similarly, higher education levels increase trust in expertise-based decision-making (typically adopted by non-majoritarian institutions), expanding the area of those policies that can be object of "delegation" to technical decision-making and moving the individual's legitimacy function to the right. Hence, the understanding concerning the number of fields that can be regulated by non-majoritarian institutions varies greatly between different individuals, where high-income and high-education individuals have higher likelihood of both (a) seeing their interests represented in non-majoritarian institutions and (b) not perceiving the mere existence of such supranational institutions as a threat to democracy. On the other hand, nationalists are likely to oppose supranational redistribution, regardless of the degree of democratic control they would be able to exert on it. National identity constitutes an important constraining factor, since it determines, ultimately, the range of possible forms of integration. Insofar as the individual has to take conscious action, it will reward (and identify with) systems and institutions that have (perceiving) benefitted him/her, while punishing institutions and systems that have harmed his/her economic security; similarly, individuals will tend to identify more with the supranational society if they perceive they benefit from it, as postulated already by Haas (1958/2004) and recently tested in Nicoli and Merler (2018). Hence, the new cleavage should be observable globally, but be marginally stronger in the

European context (in respect to other non-European democracies). Indeed, as shown among others by Schafer and Gross later in this volume, utilitarian attitudes have been key in driving Euroscepticism during the Euro crisis (Schafer and Gross 2018). This utilitarian element is reinforced by a structural component, whereby sociotropic factors, depending on fundamental changes in the structure of the economy and of global interactions, play an important role.[5]

But what does considering identities and allegiances endogenous to the process of integration imply, since the latter produces winner and losers? The main implication of identity endogeneity is, in fact, that a degree of output legitimacy is still needed to prevent the emersion of nationalist sentiments, even when the system moves towards more redistributive functions (or high politics, or core state powers). In other words, output legitimacy remains important even when the system is grounded in stronger democratic institutions, because by producing widespread benefits and therefore creating allegiance towards the supranational system, output legitimacy reduces the likelihood that *nationalist groups* become dominant in a given country. Generating allegiances and identification with the new system is a necessary condition, since a prevalence of nationalist sentiments would render supranational democratic institutions not sufficient. This is because nationalist legitimacy—as depicted in Fig. 2—is not affected by the degree of supranational representation/participation and tends to see all forms of international cooperation as democratically illegitimate, regardless of the degree of participation they entail. Furthermore, notwithstanding the endogenous nature of allegiances and identities, Fig. 2 suggests that as long as integration advances over the pattern modelled by "elitist legitimacy", not only will the EU face a shift from "permissive consensus" (point I in Fig. 2) to "constraining dissensus" (Hooghe and Marks (2009)—point II in Fig. 2), but it risks moving towards a widespread "constraining consensus" (point III) where not only populist and nationalist parties, but also democratic forces, would oppose further integration.

4 Dealing with Democratic Deficit: The Politicization Gap and Its Counter-Movements

Having assessed how democratic legitimacy is provided in multilevel supranational organizations, the specific case of the European Union is now analysed. While the process of politicization of the public life and of the institutions of the European Union has fascinated many scholars, it has hardly provoked excitement in the public at large until recent years. The European multiple, simultaneous crises [or "polycrises" as in Nicoli and Zeitlin (2019, forthcoming)], however, have contributed to

[5]While there is not a lack of works on the "winners and losers" of globalization, its application to European-wide, longitudinal electoral data sets in the context of the European crises is relatively recent [see for instance Hernández and Kriesi (2016), Nicoli (2017b), Nicoli and Reinl (2018)]. Furthermore, socioeconomic factors are perceived as "uniting" elements: the Euro crisis has led to a process of convergence of both identities (Nicoli and Merler 2018) and preferences for integration (Nicoli 2018a).

change this picture: from anti-austerity protesters to opportunistic politicians, Europe has witnessed a growing rhetoric against the "unelected bureaucrats" allegedly taking decisions instead of "the people". In other words, the *spilling over* of integration (due to crisis-induced functional pressures) into "core state powers" (Bundesverfassungsgericht 2009: 242; Genschel and Jachtenfuchs 2016) shifts integration "to the right" of Figs. 1 and 2, towards high politics and redistributive functions. Hence, even for genuine democrats, it creates a need for input legitimacy which was not there before. In Fig. 1, the effect of crisis-led integration corresponds to a shifting of the Union to the right side of the diagram, moving—as a consequence of institutions and policies introduced in response to the crisis—from a situation of "performance deficit" (by definition, a crisis) to a situation of democratic deficit (Majone 2014; Nicoli 2017a). The democratic deficit (i.e. the lack of spaces for contestation at supranational level) produces two (democratic) counter-movements: domestic politicization and institutional politicization (see, for instance, Zürn (2019), Schmidt (2019); both forthcoming). It is now worth recalling Schmidt's (2006: 223) "politicization gap". While the European Union institutions deal with *policies without politics*, national political systems retain *politics without policies*. This gap provides a manoeuvering space that political agents (both domestically and supranationally) tend to narrow by politicizing European integration in two directions. On the one hand, politicization manifests itself in the re-emersion of a domestic debate on the allocation of competences across the levels of the multilevel polity (debates being led, typically, by nationalist demands to return competences to the national governments). Further, domestic politicization takes the form of a struggle to prevent the implementation of (seemingly illegitimate) EU-wide policies, at times by going as far as attempting to decrease the level of integration altogether (and bringing "the policies" back to a domestic level). This process is inherently *constraining* towards European integration and takes place mostly at a national level.

On the other hand, politicization appears as a drive to inject "the politics" into the supranational governance, *à la fois* expanding the autonomy of supranational actors by increasing their input legitimacy, and/or by loosening the constraints on their (autonomous) action; such process *enables* European institutions to expand their capacity of discretionary action, bringing politics to the supranational level. The academic debate on politicization, outlined in the next section, has therefore clustered around these avenues of research. A first strand investigates politicization as a domestic reaction to the process of integration, stemming from the lack of spaces for contestation at supranational level. The second avenues for research explore the evolution of representative institutions, in particular the emergence of the European Parliament, seen as the main arena for democratic representation at EU level, but also the changing role of the Commission in the light of increasing politicization.

Domestic Politicization First, scholars have addressed politicization as a "bottom-up" process, taking place within national political systems often characterized by "*politics without policies*" (Schmidt 2006). Yet, democracies are resilient systems because their electoral process allows for an effective change of the course of action of the government when political outcomes are not aligned with the preferences of the majority. In other words, a functioning democracy disperses the anti-systemic potential of performance deficits by channelling the political opposition generated by such deficit *within* the system, rather than *against* the system. Nevertheless, since the newly integrated "core state powers" are held in non-majoritarian institutions and are regulated at a constitutional or quasi-constitutional level, the opportunities for opposition *in the system* are greatly reduced, hence expanding the scope for opposition *to the system* rather than *in the system* (Mair 2007). The domestic politicization counter-movement is driven by the lack of European arenas of policy contestation, matched with the preservation of domestic political space; fundamentally, it aims at solving the democratic deficit of the EU by shifting competences back to the national level. Hence, domestic politicization is characterized by a growing "constraining dissensus" towards European integration, as argued by Hooghe and Marks (2009, 2018) as well as Kriesi et al. (2006) and Kriesi (2012, 2016). Among them, Zürn and de Wilde (2016) interpret such growing "negative" politicization as the emergence of a new "cosmopolitan/communitarian" cleavage that tends to replace (in Hooghe and Marks' (2018) view) or build upon (in Kriesi et al. 2006, Kriesi 2012) the traditional left/right divide. Negative politicization scholarship has also generated a myriad of studies on Euroscepticism both in the public opinion and in electoral processes, where Hooghe and Marks' "constraining dissensus" theory becomes the most evident (Serricchio et al. 2013; Hobolt and de Vries 2016; Hernández and Kriesi 2016; Nicoli 2017b). Along with studies on negative politicization in the public opinion and in electoral processes, others have attempted to look at negative "élites" politicization in the governance process, for instance in the implementation and contestation of the country-specific recommendations in the European Semester (van der Veer and Haverland 2018).

Institutional Politicization The second avenue of politicization research addresses the issue of supranational capacity build-up. While Majone (1999) and Moravcsik (2002) have argued that, as long as the EU deals primarily with regulatory policies, the EU does not need politicisation and can better pursue its goals by remaining "insulated" from party politics, the lack of salience of European policy for mass politics has been often referred to as one of the most worrying features of the EU (Schmidt 2006). Among others, Kriesi (2016: 1) recognizes insulation as a typical de-politicization strategy. Yet Majone (2014) had acknowledged that, in the wake of the crisis, an integration of redistributive policies has taken place, and thus, politicisation should follow to avoid the emergence of a democratic deficit. The association between authority transfer and politicization, originally postulated by Schmitter (1969) and brought forward again by Wilde and Zürn (2012), finds support in Hutter et al.'s (2016) findings, which associate politicization with increased authority of European institutions. Scholarship on the accrual of authority and autonomy on politicization of institutions looks, mostly, at the European Parliament and at the European Commission. Research on the politicization of the EP has taken two directions. On the one hand, many have analysed how the conflict and cleavages within the Parliament itself have evolved from being based on national interests into bringing the traditional right/left divide into European politics (Hix et al. 2007; Hix and Marsh 2011; Hix and Høyland 2013). From this perspective, some have suggested the strengthening of the European Parliament's powers in order to limit the alleged EU democratic deficit: by fostering the powers of democratically elected representatives, the interest in, and salience of, European-wide decisions would increase in the public at large, leading to politicization. On the other hand, others have explored how the European Parliament has used its budgetary and control powers to enact several forms of "competence creeping", acquiring an even larger influence than the delegated power attributed to it by the treaties, for instance Meissner and Schoeller (2018). The strengthening of the discretionary autonomy of the Commission, as well as the Commission's (and its president) incremental self-understanding as a "politicized executive" of the EU, has also been studied by Christiansen (1997, 2001). More recently, this research has focused the link between the Commission and the Parliament, especially in the light of the *Spitzenkandidaten* process (Dinan 2015; Deckarm 2017; Braun and Popa 2018; Braun and Schwarzbözl 2019). Indeed, since 2015, the calls for a more "legitimized" (i.e. politically legitimized) governance have multiplied, culminating perhaps with the long-standing French proposal for a Eurozone Parliament, reiterated by Hollande in 2016 and Macron in 2017, or for the direct election of the President of the European Commission through a reinforced *Spitzenkandidaten* process, as suggested by Jean-Claude Junker and the European Political Strategy Centre (2017).

5 Politicization as Manifestation of a Transformative Leap

The two politicization counter-movements seem to take, *prima facie*, opposite directions: institutional politicization addressing supranational capabilities and their build-up, and domestic politicization leading to the emersion of contesting parties. However, the (dis)integrative potential of the two counter-movements is best understood together as a joint, intertwined process that addresses (in two different arenas) the politicization gap generated by integration, leading to a new polarization in the political system. In this section, building on long-standing scholarship, I argue that the emergence of polarized, political counter-movements constitutes an unavoidable stage of integration, marking a transformative leap in the nature of European integration.

Let us first consider domestic politicization. Understanding domestic politicization as being exclusively led by constraining parties is probably reductive, since party systems are a complex phenomenon. In fact, the political life of many member states is increasingly characterized by a growing polarization between "open", pro-European attitudes (hence, parties), and "closed", Eurosceptic attitudes (and parties), nor should this come as a surprise for scholars of European integration. For instance, while Neofunctionalist theories have often relied on "bounded rationality" to conciliate a rational choice approach and the open-ended, "unintended" logic of a spillover-led integration process, Neofunctionalist scholars themselves have been accused of lacking sufficient foresight in predicting the pace of integration. Yet, for many shortcomings of the Neofunctionalist scholarship, it is beyond doubt (although, perhaps, beyond widespread knowledge as well) that Haas, Schmitter, Etzioni, Lindberg and others had analysed the link between the integration of *political functions* and the rise of contestation, at least in a theoretical fashion. While contestation is largely lacking from Haas' (1958/2004) masterpiece on the *Uniting of Europe*, it emerges as a consequence of political spillovers in his general theory of functional integration, summarized in *Beyond the Nation-State* (Haas 1964). Similarly, Schmitter (1970) clarifies that while the building-up of supranational institutions advances through cycles of crisis-led integration, the latter cycles ("transformation cycles", as opposed to the previous "initiation cycles" and "priming cycles") are characterized by the spillover of integration into "high politics", in turn producing politicization by contestation of the integration process. Contemporary integration scholars (such as Hooghe and Marks 2009; Genschel and Jachtenfuchs 2016) share this perspective, viewing the spilling over of integration into "core state powers" as a fundamental driver of negative politicization. In other words, modern (Neofunctionalist-inspired) integration theory does not exclude politicization as an outcome (as the original work from Haas did), but it relegates it to the latter stages of integration (the "transformative cycle") when crisis-led integration finally reaches the stage of core state powers.

Now, the idea that the shifting of political authority generates a pushback in the communities that lose such authority, manifested through the emergence of parties and social movements mobilized against the new centre, is no far-fetched theoretical puzzle for integration scholars. The fundamental idea embedded in early functionalist scholarship anticipates—albeit in a far less articulated way—at least some of the intuitions put forward in the famed Lipset and Rokkan (1967) work on societal cleavages and party formation. While generations of political science students have approached the Lipset–Rokkan model with a focus on the specific (historical) evolution of Western societies and party systems, anchoring its logic into party and perhaps nation-state formation history, in truth the analysis of the latter is used, in the original piece, as an empirical verification for a broader theory of cleavages.

The implicit proximity between the Lipset–Rokkan cleavage theory and Neofunctionalist thinking emerges strikingly in Sect. 2 of the *Introduction* to *Cleavage Structures, Party Systems and Voter Alignment*, where the full scope of the cleavage model is contained in a two-dimensional system composed of a *functional* and by a *territorial* dimension (Lipset and Rokkan 1967: 10). Furthermore, of particular relevance in understanding the vows of contemporary Europe is the sequencing and nature of the cleavages that Lipset and Rokkan identify. Not by chance, the original Lipset–Rokkan framework describes the centre–periphery divide as the first to appear in modern states. While the usual interpretation of the first cleavage often simplifies it into an urban–rural divide, such simplification is highly misleading; in fact, the rural–urban divide is nothing else than a manifestation of the conflict driven by the *l*-end[6] of the territorial axis in the two-dimensional space: a struggle between

[6]By *l*-end of the territorial axis, Lipset and Rokkan mean "regional and local oppositions" to the established national élites (ibid., 10).

"rationalising, centralising national élites" and local, regional communities (ibid., 10). *Mutatis mutandis*, it is not hard to see the mirroring in current phenomena: the decision concerning the allocation of powers between centre and periphery (between old regional and local centres and the new national authority in the times of nation-state formation; between the old nation states and the new European authority in time of European integration) is the first to emerge in a newborn political system. Indeed, it is not fortuitous that the first cleavage faced by newborn political authorities concerns the allocation of powers between the centre and the peripheries, for the agreement on such power balance concerns the very core of a political system's material constitution. Such centralization divide is not dissimilar from the one faced today by the EU. In this perspective, I argue that the nationalist–Europeanist divide would not constitute a brand new cleavage, but rather the transformation of the centralization cleavage in the light of the progressive emersion of a new centre, as well as the progressive "peripheralization" of the old ones.

In sum, Lipset–Rokkan and integration scholars expect a politicization process to emerge along with the transfer of political authority; a process characterized by opposition at first, followed by polarization, progressively determining the fault lines of the political spectrum until the *constitutional* question on the allocation of core state competences is not settled. Once such conflict is solved (with either outcome: disintegration, a weak centre, a strong centre), the salience of the centre–periphery cleavage is expected to decrease, as the "rules of the game" are set and the political agents can start once more to focus on redistributive, rather than constitutional conflicts (Fig. 3). In a way, such argument assumes that this "new cleavage" (which, as

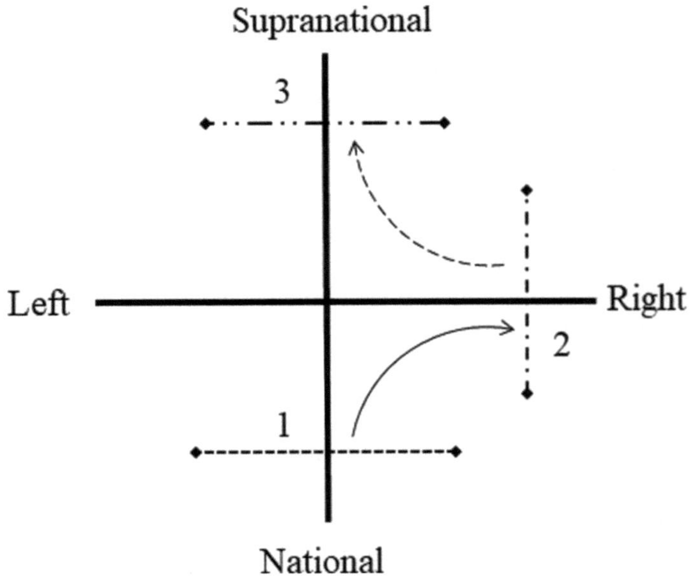

Fig. 3 Shifting cleavages

we have seen, is all but new in fact) is by construction "temporary", since it determines the conditions under which the latter conflicts—redistributive in nature—take place. Yet even if one moves beyond this eminently ordo-liberal perspective to the point of assuming that constitutional agreements, rather than setting rules for the redistribution game, constitute a redistributive decisional set *di per se*, the salience of a territorial/identitarian cleavage, rather than a simple redistributive one, cannot be overlooked. For one thing is political conflict over redistribution (typically characterising left/right cleavages), and another is an agreement on whom is part of the community committed to, and subject of, redistributive decisions. In other words, a purely ordo-liberal interpretation of the process leads to a simple problem of a constitutional distribution of powers; rather than substituting this interpretation of the conflict, a more socially oriented perspective builds on it and attaches an undistinguishable redistributive element to the constitutional one; either way, identities constitute the key element of the localist pushback against "the centralizing, standardizing, rationalizing machinery of the dominant (…) élites" (Lipset and Rokkan 1967: 10). In sum, some of the original features of the Lipset–Rokkan model are really best seen as a *cycle* model through which political systems go through in their formation, rather than a mere historical recounting of the evolution of European party systems, and the peculiar polarization witnessed in the European context marks the beginning of such cycle for the European Union. Such a transformative step (Schmitter 1970) may drive integration further or lead to permanent disintegration, depending on how the system reacts and evolves to integration-induced politicization. To investigate this further, the next section brings together the Lipset–Rokkan cycle model and the theory of functional legitimacy proposed earlier in this chapter.

6 Politicization in Times of Functional Legitimacy: Which Kind of (Dis)integration Feedback?

As discussed, the politicization counter-movement at domestic level is not simply domestic contestation, but rather—as recently postulated by Hooghe and Marks (2018)—a process of re-alignment of the party system over the (new) centre–periphery cleavage. Let us not forget that the drivers of politicization are to be found in the *spilling over* of integration (due to functional pressures) into "core state powers" (Bundesverfassungsgericht 2009: 242; Genschel and Jachtenfuchs 2016). According to the functional legitimacy theory proposed here, the transfer of high politics at international level creates a need for input legitimacy, hence for *within-system* mechanisms of democratic contestation and change. Nevertheless, since the newly integrated "core state powers" are held in non-majoritarian, non-contendable institutions, the opportunities for opposition *in the system* are greatly reduced, hence expanding the scope for opposition *to the system* rather than *in the system* (Mair 2007). Therefore, the reconfiguration of the political spectrum on the centre–periphery is, possibly, a temporary by-product of the lack of within-system mechanisms of policy contestability. If democratic contestability would be re-established on core powers, then the classical "left/right" dimension would return salient, as discussed in the next paragraphs. One may observe, at this point, that the construction of appropriate mechanisms of contendibility at supranational level is, again, represented by the institutional politicization counter-movement. The construction of appropriate supranational vehicles for representation not only creates the institutional (and legal, if the *Bundesverfassungsgericht* is to be taken seriously) conditions for pursuing integration of core state powers, but also will help defuse the domestic politicization challenge (which is, inherently, represented by a centre–periphery dynamic) by enabling the re-emersion of a supranational left–right dimension (Fig. 3).

The end state of the original Lipset–Rokkan configuration is captured by phase 1 of the diagram. Mirroring Vivien Schmidt's conceptualization, phase 1 could be named "*domestic politics with domestic policies*", where the main lines of political tensions are between left and right at national level. The expansion of powers of supranational, non-majoritarian institutions translates the equilibrium to phase 2 ("*European policies without politics, domestic politics without policies*"); in turn, this politicization gap—abundantly discussed in this chapter—leads to the two politicization counter-movements in sequence. First, domestic politicization aiming, primarily, at solving the domestic politicization gap by bringing "policies" back to the domestic level, would restructure the domestic party system over a supranational/national axis, rather than on a left/right axis. At this point, if the second political counter-movement is successful—i.e. if supranational élites successfully create spaces for contestability at supranational level maintaining integration along the central path discussed in Fig. 1—then the constitutional question between the centre and the periphery is addressed, starting a new Lipset–Rokkan cycle; the party system will thus go through a second transformation, recomposing itself over the left–right dimension, this time at supranational level.

7 Concluding Remarks

As discussed in this chapter, the era of "constraining dissensus" should not simply be seen as a threat for Europe, but also considered as a natural phase that the Union has to go through in order to fully evolve into a complete political system. There is no democratic state that has not experienced, at some point of its formation, a centre–periphery cleavage. For a very long time, the "eternal crisis" of European integration [or, perhaps, the crisis/integration dynamics discussed in Nicoli (2018b)] did not push integration into the highly politicized fields of "core state" competence. However, the Euro-migration crises have surely pushed the EU to cross the line. While historical experience appears as a good omen for the future of Europe, let us not forget that history often suffers from the largest of biases: if truth be told, little we can say of those proto-states that failed and were torn apart by their own centrifugal dynamics. Whether the EU will join the collection of successful (con)federations, or whether it will be remembered as an example not to be followed, ultimately depends on the capacity of the EU of turning the politicization counter-movements into a force of integration rather than disintegration. However, two main hurdles stand in the way. First, failing to produce widespread benefits for the majority has two important side effects: on the one hand, it prevents the progressive construction of a genuine European identity (since identities and allegiances are, for the large part, endogenous to the benefits, experiences and education of individuals), thus failing to defuse the risk associated with nationalist attitudes (which, we show in Fig. 2, can hardly be associated with European integration, no matter how democratic the Union becomes); on the other hand, shortcomings on the output side of legitimacy are deemed to raise the question of policy contestability, hence, *mutatis mutandis*, any level of democratic deficit becomes more salient—and more dangerous—when output legitimacy is low. Second, maintaining integration on a pattern that reproduces an elitist vision of legitimacy (again, as represented in Fig. 3) can very possibly be perceived as illegitimate not only by nationalist and populist parties, but also by the large silent majorities of our democracies. This shift from "constraining dissensus" to "constraining consensus" could very well bring the European integration project to its ends. However, if the EU successfully navigates around these rocks, adapting instead to the challenges that the two politicization counter-movements analysed in this chapter naturally generate, it may very well return to be a prime example of conciliating globalization and political action, paving the way for a global community that is able to couple the benefits of globalization with the benefits of democratic rule.

Bibliography

Braun, D., & Popa, S. A. (2018). This time it was different? The salience of the *Spitzenkandidaten* system among European parties. *West European Politics, 41*(5), 1125–1145.

Braun, D., & Schwarzbözl, T. (2019). Put in the spotlight or largely ignored? Emphasis on the *Spitzenkandidaten* by political parties in their online campaigns for European elections. *Journal of European Public Policy, 26*(3), 428–445.

Bundesverfassungsgericht, 2 Senat. (2009, June). *Bundesverfassungsgericht—Decisions—Act approving the Treaty of Lisbon compatible with the Basic Law*.

Christiansen, T. (1997). Tensions of European governance: Politicized bureaucracy and multiple accountability in the European Commission. *Journal of European Public Policy, 4*(1), 73–90.

Christiansen, T. (2001). Intra-institutional politics and inter-institutional relations in the EU: Towards coherent governance? *Journal of European Public Policy, 8*(5), 747–769.

Dahl, R. A. (1989). *Democracy and its critics*. Yale University Press.

Deckarm, R. (2017). Assessing the effect of the European elections' Spitzenkandidaten procedure on the constitution of the European Commission. *European Politics and Society, 18*(2), 199–217.

Dinan, D. (2015). Governance and institutions: The year of the *Spitzenkandidaten*. *Journal of Common Market Studies, 53*, 93–107.

European Political Strategy Centre. (2017, February). *Building on the Spitzenkandidaten model*, Brussels.

Fabbrini, S. (2015). *Which European Union?* Oxford: Oxford University Press.

Genschel, P., & Jachtenfuchs, M. (2016). More integration, less federation: The European integration of core state powers. *Journal of European Public Policy, 23*(1), 42–59.

Haas, E. B. (1964). *Beyond the nation-state: Functionalism and international organization*. Stanford University Press.
Haas, E. B. (2004). *The uniting of Europe: Political, social, and economic forces, 1950–1957*. Notre Dame, Ind: University of Notre Dame Press.
Hernández, E., & Kriesi, H. (2016). The electoral consequences of the financial and economic crisis in Europe. *European Journal of Political Research, 55*(2), 203–224.
Hix, S., & Høyland, B. (2013). Empowerment of the European Parliament. *Annual Review of Political Science, 16*(1), 171–189.
Hix, S., & Marsh, M. (2011). Second-order effects plus pan-European political swings: An analysis of European Parliament elections across time. *Electoral Studies, 30*(1), 4–15.
Hix, S., Noury, A. G., & Roland, G. (2007). *Democratic politics in the European Parliament*. Cambridge University Press.
Hobolt, S. B., & de Vries, C. E. (2016). Public support for European integration. *Annual Review of Political Science, 19*(1), 413–432.
Hooghe, L., & Marks, G. (2009). A postfunctionalist theory of European integration: From permissive consensus to constraining dissensus. *British Journal of Political Science, 39*(01), 1.
Hooghe, L., & Marks, G. (2018). Cleavage theory meets Europe's crises: Lipset, Rokkan, and the transnational cleavage. *Journal of European Public Policy, 25*(1), 109–135.
Hooghe, L., Marks, G., & Wilson, C. J. (2002). Does left/right structure party positions on European integration? *Comparative Political Studies, 35*(8), 965–989.
Hutter, S., Grande, E., & Kriesi, H. (Eds.). (2016). *Politicising Europe: Integration and mass politics*. Cambridge: Cambridge University Press.
Kriesi, H. (2012). The political consequences of the financial and economic crisis in Europe: Electoral punishment and popular protest. *Swiss Political Science Review, 18*(4), 518–522
Kriesi, H. (2016). The political consequences of the financial and economic crisis in Europe: Electoral punishment and popular protest. *Swiss Political Science Review, 18*(4), 518–522.
Kriesi, H., Grande, E., Lachat, R., Dolezal, M., Bornschier, S., & Frey, T. (2006). Globalization and the transformation of the national political space: Six European countries compared. *European Journal of Political Research, 45*(6), 921–956.
Kriesi, H., Grande, E., Lachat, R., Dolezal, M., Bornschier, S., & Frey, T. (2008). *West European politics in the age of globalization*. Cambridge University Press.
Lipset, S. M., & Rokkan, S. (1967). *Party systems and voter alignments: Cross-national perspectives*. Free Press.
Mair, P. (2007). Political opposition and the European Union. *Government and Opposition, 42*(1), 1–17.
Majone, G. (1999). From regulatory state to a democratic default. *Journal of Common Market Studies, 52*(6), 1216–1223.
Majone, G. (2014). From regulatory state to a democratic default. *Journal of Common Market Studies, 52*(6), 1216–1223.
Meissner, C., & Schoeller, M. (2018). *Politicization by stealth? The European Parliament between integration and disintegration*. Working Paper, University of Wien (forthcoming: *Journal of European Public Policy*).
Moravcsik, A. (2002). Reassessing legitimacy in the European Union. *Journal of Common Market Studies, 40*(4), 603–624.
Nicoli, F. (2017a). Democratic legitimacy in the era of fiscal integration. *Journal of European Integration, 39*(4), 389–404.
Nicoli, F. (2017b). Hard-line Euroscepticism and the Eurocrisis: Evidence from a panel study of 108 elections across Europe: Hard-line Euroscepticism and the crisis. *Journal of Common Market Studies, 55*(2), 312–331.
Nicoli, F. (2018a). Integration through crises? A quantitative assessment of the effect of the Eurocrisis on preferences for fiscal integration. *Comparative European Politics*, 1–29 (online preprint).

Nicoli, F. (2018b) *The five trilemmas of European integration: Crisis and path-dependency from the common market to the European fiscal union*. Working Paper, University of Amsterdam (forthcoming: *Comparative European Politics*).

Nicoli, F., & Merler, S. (2018). *Europeanisation of identities: Does the economy matter?* Working Paper, University of Amsterdam.

Nicoli, F., & Reinl, A. K. (2018). *A tale of two crises? A regional-level investigation of the joint effect of economic performance and migration on the Eurosceptic milieu*. Working Paper, University of Amsterdam-GESIS Cologne.

Nicoli, F., & Zeitlin, J. (2019). The European Union beyond the polycrisis? Integration and politicization in an age of shifting cleavages. *Journal of European Public Policy* (forthcoming).

Rodrik, D. (2012). *The globalization paradox: Democracy and the future of the world economy*. New York: W. W. Norton and Company.

Scharpf, F. W. (1997). Economic integration, democracy and the welfare state. *Journal of European Public Policy, 4*(1), 18–36.

Scharpf, F. W. (2009). Legitimacy in the multilevel European polity. *European Political Science Review, 1*(2), 173–204.

Schmidt, V. A. (2006). *Democracy in Europe: The EU and national polities*. Oxford, New York: Oxford University Press.

Schmidt, V. A. (2019). Politicization in the EU: Between national politics and EU political dynamics. *Journal of European Public Policy* (forthcoming).

Schmitter, P. (1969). Three neo-functional hypotheses about international integration. *International Organization, 23*(1), 161–166.

Schmitter, P. (1970). A revised theory of regional integration. *International Organization, 24*(4).

Serricchio, F., Tsakatika, M., & Quaglia, L. (2013). Euroscepticism and the global financial crisis. *Journal of Common Market Studies, 51*(1), 51–64.

van der Veer, R. A., & Haverland, M. (2018). Bread and butter or bread and circuses? Politicisation and the European Commission in the European semester. *European Union Politics, 19*(3), 524–545

Weber, M. (1919) *Politik asl Beruf*. Lecture Notes, Munich, January 28, 1919.

Wilde, P. D., & Zürn, M. (2012). Can the politicization of European integration be reversed? *Journal of Common Market Studies, 50*(s1), 137–153.

Zürn, M. (2019). Politicization compared: National, European, global levels. *Journal of European Public Policy* (forthcoming).

Zürn, M., & de Wilde, P. (2016). Debating globalization: Cosmopolitanism and communitarianism as political ideologies. *Journal of Political Ideologies, 21*(3), 280–301.

Euroscepticism in Times of Crisis: A Macro-Level Analysis of the Euro Crisis' Effects on Public Opinion and Party Competition on European Integration

Constantin Schäfer and Martin Gross

> It will be years before we know the full consequences of the ongoing economic crisis in Europe, but there is no doubt that it has brought European integration (back) to the top of the political and, now also public, agenda. (Mudde 2012: 200)

1 Introduction

The sovereign debt and economic crisis in Europe, commonly called the "Euro crisis", has been the most relevant factor in European politics for many years. Triggered by the global financial crisis, it turned into a crisis of the Eurozone when several member states were not able to repay their excessive government debts anymore. The response by the European Union (EU) institutions and many member states' governments was the demand for strict austerity measures to re-balance the public deficits. These measures did not only lead to severe economic recessions in several countries, but have also been perceived as having "disabled national democratic legitimacy" (Scharpf 2012: 26). It thus seems logical that the Euro crisis has provoked strong reactions among citizens and parties across Europe. It has resulted in a stark decline in political trust among citizens (van Erkel and van der Meer 2016), a high government instability (Hernández and Kriesi 2016a) and an increase in support for Eurosceptic parties across Europe (Hobolt and de Vries 2016a). Moreover, the crisis has politicized the issue of European integration (Hutter et al. 2016) and made this matter more relevant to people's electoral choices (Schäfer and Debus 2018). But to

C. Schäfer (✉)
University of Mannheim, Mannheim, Germany
e-mail: constantin.schaefer@uni-mannheim.de

M. Gross (✉)
Ludwig-Maximilians-University of Munich, Munich, Germany
e-mail: martin.gross@gsi.uni-muenchen.de

© Springer Nature Switzerland AG 2020

M. Baldassari et al. (eds.), *Anti-Europeanism*,
https://doi.org/10.1007/978-3-030-24428-6_3

what degree have the public and party systems in Europe become more Eurosceptic during the Euro crisis?

In this chapter, we ask to what extent the Euro crisis has led to a rise in citizen- and party-based Euroscepticism in the EU member states. In doing so, we discuss the concept(s) of Euroscepticism, particularly regarding the levels of analysis and the objects of interest. After that, we theorize about the relationship between the Euro crisis, public opinion and party competition on European integration, while accounting for contextual differences that have become evident during the crisis. Following our theoretical section, we present how Euroscepticism in public opinion and party systems can be empirically measured and, then, relate these measurements to macroeconomic indicators, which represent the degree to which a country has been affected by the crisis. Our empirical macro-level analysis highlights the ways in which economic conditions, public opinion and party competition on European integration are inter-connected, and additionally reveals interesting inter-temporal and cross-national patterns of this relationship. In the final section, we summarize our findings and discuss their meaning for the political legitimacy of the EU after the Euro crisis.

2 Theoretical Framework

2.1 Euroscepticism

The term Euroscepticism[1] commonly refers to negative and opposing preferences towards the EU and the European integration process, which can be qualified in several ways (see, e.g., Szczerbiak and Taggart 2018; Vasilopoulou 2018). First, they can be held by different subjects or actors. They either take the form of beliefs, opinions and attitudes of individual citizens, or exist as positions of collective political actors, such as political parties. Second, the orientations can relate to different political objects on the European level. Among them are the EU as a political regime itself and the political authorities of the EU polity, but they can also refer to specific EU policies or the European unification process more generally. Third, the preferences can vary in their intensity, i.e. the degree to which they oppose the different objects. The most famous distinction in this regard goes back to the work of Taggart and Szczerbiak (2002), in which they define "hard Euroscepticism" as "principled opposition to the EU and European integration", whereas "soft Euroscepticism" expresses a "qualified opposition" to the EU reflecting dissatisfaction with the outputs or general trajectory of the union (Taggart and Szczerbiak 2002: 4). However, Eurosceptic

[1]The term *Euroscepticism* itself is not without problems, as it is a rather vague, negative construction that implies a common "ideological core where none exists" and makes "absolutely no academic sense", partly due to its creation "by non-academics using academic jargon" (Leruth et al. 2018: 4). Yet, it has emerged as a subfield of European studies and "has given way to hundreds of publications in increasingly prominent journals" (Szczerbiak and Taggart 2018: 12).

orientations do not necessarily need to be conceptualized in categorical terms but can also be understood to be located on a continuum from very positive to very negative positions towards European integration. In the following, we briefly discuss the different subjects, objects and degrees of Euroscepticism.

2.1.1 Levels of Analysis: Citizens Versus Parties

Two main actors hold Eurosceptic preferences: citizens and political parties. However, these subjects are rarely analysed in a joint approach, but have rather been independently investigated within two different research areas. One field analyses *popular Euroscepticism* as an attitudinal phenomenon, mainly studied in research on public opinion and electoral behaviour.[2] The second research area focuses on *party-based Euroscepticism* and studies Euroscepticism as an ideological or strategic feature of party behaviour and competition. Since our goal in this chapter is a joint perspective on both levels of analysis, we lay out the main propositions and findings of these two research fields in this section.

Popular Euroscepticism

Popular Euroscepticism refers to "a subset of negative attitudes towards the EU and/or the European integration process" (Serricchio et al. 2013: 52). This definition hints both to the multidimensional nature of EU attitudes (Boomgaarden et al. 2011) and to the fact that those can, in principle, also be positive, i.e. supportive. From this perspective, orientations towards European integration are studied under the label of "public support for European integration" (Hobolt and de Vries 2016a), which mostly relies on the "political support" concept developed by Easton (1965, 1975). He defines political support as "an attitude by which a person orients himself to an object either favorably or unfavorably, positively or negatively" (Easton 1975: 436). Based on the research framework of political culture (Almond and Verba 1963), the Eastonian support concept postulates that a political system receives its legitimacy by predominantly favourable orientations of its citizens. Unfavourable attitudes, in contrast, potentially endanger the legitimacy and stability of the political system.

The emergence of a political system on the European level has consequently inspired researchers to study attitudes towards the EU and the European unification process. It has been found that the European public were rather supportive but also largely indifferent towards European integration during the early decades. European unification promised peace and economic welfare for its member states, but it did not interfere much in the daily life of citizens. However, the so-called permissive consensus (Lindberg and Scheingold 1970) started to turn into a "constraining dissensus"

[2] In this chapter, we concentrate, however, more on popular Euroscepticism as a public opinion phenomenon and less on "electoral Euroscepticism", i.e. the increasing success of Eurosceptic parties in national and European elections. Nevertheless, it has to be added that Eurosceptic attitudes have also played a big role in the electoral behaviour of citizens across Europe (see, e.g., Hernández and Kriesi 2016a, b; Nicoli 2017; Schäfer 2017).

(Hooghe and Marks 2009) by the beginning of the 1990s. After the Maastricht Treaty, public scepticism towards European integration rose across Europe, a development which has been labelled the "post-Maastricht blues" (Eichenberg and Dalton 2007). This sentiment eventually manifested in the political arena, when the French and the Dutch citizens voted against ratifying the European Constitution in 2005. Accordingly, the study of Euroscepticism in public opinion research really began to unfold in the beginning of the 2000s and, for the large part, aimed at understanding people's growing opposition to the EU.

Today, three main explanations for Eurosceptic attitudes seem widely accepted: "utilitarian, identity, and cue-taking and benchmarking approaches" (Hobolt and de Vries 2016b: 420). The utilitarian approach stresses the importance of costs and benefits that individuals perceive to have from European integration, both on a personal level and on a societal level.[3] However, when the Maastricht Treaty "dramatically altered the nature of the integration process" (Eichenberg and Dalton 2007: 132), utilitarian factors became less and less able to sufficiently explain EU attitudes. In fact, empirical research soon found that these attitudes are rather dependent on "soft factors" (de Vreese et al. 2008) that relate to people's cultural identity and sense of belonging.[4] Lastly, cue-taking approaches claim that people do not possess sufficient information about the EU and thus rely on proxies or cues to overcome these deficits.[5]

Party-Based Euroscepticism

The study of Euroscepticism in party research has sparked simultaneously to the one in the public opinion literature and is now a "well-established subfield in EU studies" (Brack and Startin 2015: 241). Research has so far been dominated by two "schools" that use different approaches and methods but rarely speak to each other (Mudde 2012). On the one side, the "Sussex School" has emerged around the works of Taggart and Szczerbiak (2002, 2008) and their key concept of soft and hard Euroscepticism. The authors of the Sussex School mainly conduct qualitative analyses of Eurosceptic parties using a wide range of data sources, but concentrate on the official party literature. On the other side, the "North Carolina School" around Ray (1999, 2003) and Hooghe and Marks (2007) has a broader focus, as the authors aim to measure positions on European integration for all parties. They conduct surveys once every four years, in which they ask country experts to locate parties on quantitative

[3]Researchers found evidence for this in macroeconomic factors (Eichenberg and Dalton 1993), personal economic situations (Gabel 1998) and economic perceptions of citizens (Anderson and Kaltenthaler 1996).

[4]Those factors comprise national identification (Carey 2002), perceived cultural threats (McLaren 2002), fear of immigration (de Vreese and Boomgaarden 2005) or ethnic conflict (Hooghe and Marks 2005).

[5]They are, for example, influenced by media (Azrout et al. 2012) as well as by their preferred political parties (de Vries and Edwards 2009), and they use evaluations of their national government as proxies to form opinions about the EU (Anderson 1998).

seven-point scales ranging from "strongly opposed" to "strongly in favour" of European integration.[6]

The question of what drives party-based Euroscepticism is often framed as "ideology versus strategy". The North Carolina School understands Eurosceptic positions to be mainly associated with a party's basic ideological profile (Hooghe et al. 2002) and, thus, as rooted in national cleavages (Marks and Wilson 2000). The Sussex School additionally integrates strategic factors of party competition, such as the conflict between government and opposition parties (Sitter 2001). More generally, scholars nowadays agree that party-based Euroscepticism has moved "from the margins to the mainstream" (Brack and Startin 2015: 242). It is no longer an exclusive feature of extreme and niche parties but has been adopted by mainstream parties. Newer accounts in party research therefore focus, more generally, on how parties use the issue of European integration to mobilize voters (De Sio et al. 2016; Hobolt and de Vries 2015) and how they respond to an increasingly Eurosceptic public opinion (Rohrschneider and Whitefield 2016; Williams and Spoon 2015).

2.1.2 Objects of Analysis: European Union Versus European Integration

Political preferences regarding European integration are not unidimensional (Boomgaarden et al. 2011), as they can relate to different objects. Two main objects are the actual political regime in its current form, the EU, and its underlying "regime principle" (Dalton 1999: 58), namely the continuing process of European unification. Hobolt and de Vries (2016a), therefore, differentiate between two forms of support for European integration, namely "regime support" and "policy support". The first form directly refers to the concept of Easton (1965, 1975) and applies it to the political system of the European Union (see also Boomgaarden et al. 2011; Weßels 2007). From this perspective, citizen support for the political regime, its regime authorities and the political community of the EU is of central importance for the EU's legitimacy and stability. Policy support, in contrast, concerns the content of collective decisions and actions taken by EU actors. Although it can relate to different EU policies such as the common currency, overall policy support can be operationalized by "citizens' preference for speeding up policy integration within the European Union" (Hobolt and de Vries 2016b: 417). Taken together, we define Eurosceptic orientations as a lack of political support for the EU, regarding both the regime itself and the European unification process.

As shown by Kopecký and Mudde (2002), Easton's concept of political support can also be applied to party-based Euroscepticism. Besides distinguishing between two different objects, they also connect them to two different modes of support. More specifically, they characterize support for the general idea of European unification as "diffuse support" for European integration. In contrast, they label support for "the

[6] Mudde (2012: 200) summarizes the different strengths and weaknesses of the two approaches and concludes by calling for a "more integrated approach".

EU as it is and as it is developing" (Kopecký and Mudde 2002: 300) as "specific support" for European integration. In this line of reasoning, a loss of legitimacy for the EU only occurs when people and parties do not support the general idea of European integration anymore. Taken together with the Euroscepticism concept of Taggart and Szczerbiak (2002), the approaches yield two different kinds of Euroscepticism. The first is the softer form, which expresses principled support for European integration but dissatisfaction with the EU's current development and form. It refers to a lack of specific support for the regime of the EU. The second kind of Euroscepticism is a harder version,[7] as it does not only express dissatisfaction with the EU, but also principled opposition to the European integration process. It consequently combines lacking regime support with lacking policy support and could thus also be characterized as a lack of diffuse support (see also Krouwel and Abts 2007).

These approaches imply that an analysis of Euroscepticism needs to reflect the different levels and the multidimensional nature of Eurosceptic orientations. This means, at least, to account for different preferences on the EU as a specific, current political regime and for the general idea and process of European integration. Both Hobolt and de Vries (2016b) and Leconte (2010) empirically show that people actually do separate between these two basic orientations. Moreover, they demonstrate that diffuse support for European unification has usually been higher than specific support for the EU or a country's membership in the EU, even before the Maastricht Treaty (Leconte 2010: 164). Still, the extent to which the different forms of support have developed since Maastricht—particularly during the Euro crisis—remains an open question.

2.2 *Euro Crisis Effects*

2.2.1 On Public Opinion

So far, economic crises have coincided with a withdrawal of political support for European integration (Loveless and Rohrschneider 2011), which seems not surprising given the purely economic character of the early integration process. During the global financial crisis (2007–09) and the Euro crisis (2010–2013),[8] citizens affected by economic hardship also withdrew political support, both for their national democracies (Armingeon and Guthmann 2014) and for the EU (Braun and Tausendpfund 2014; Serricchio et al. 2013) and its institutions (Dotti Sani and Magistro 2016; Ehrmann et al. 2013; Roth et al. 2014).[9] However, the increase in Eurosceptic attitudes cannot merely be explained by a comeback of utilitarian determinants. Rather,

---

[7]In fact, Kopecký and Mudde (2002) call this hard form of Euroscepticism "Europhobia".

[8]Schimmelfennig (2014: 323), for example, calls the period between the beginning of 2010 and mid-2013 "the acute Euro crisis".

[9]Yet, the data sets used by these studies date from the time before the Euro crisis and thus do not take into account the potential effects of the imposed austerity measures following the Euro crisis on citizens' political support for the EU. Braun and Tausendpfund (2014), for example, insist on the

the fall in support seems to be triggered by an activation of national identities (Runge 2014; Serricchio et al. 2013), by an increasing distrust in political institutions on all levels or even by a transfer of distrust from the national political system to the EU (Armingeon and Ceka 2014). In the following, we lay out why we expect that the two aforementioned forms of support were differently affected by the crisis.

Specific Regime Support for the EU

The Euro crisis should have exerted a particularly negative effect on specific regime support for the EU in countries most affected by the crisis. This is, first, because the utilitarian approach suggests that the economic crisis in Europe has changed the cost-benefit calculation that many citizens associate with European integration, making them adapt their attitudes accordingly. Experiencing economic adversity, unemployment and income decline should have led to short-term disappointment with the EU and its current economic governance. Second, as specific regime support is dependent on evaluations of institutional performance, the crisis management of the EU institutions should have further eroded political support. The deficient construction of the monetary union that did not come along with a necessary fiscal and economic integration has been a main cause for the macroeconomic imbalances in Europe, which led to the excessive indebtedness of several Eurozone member states. In dealing with the sovereign debt crisis, the creditor countries together with the EU institutions—especially the so-called troika—imposed strict austerity measures on the debtor countries. This did not only go along with harsh cuts of public investments and social spending, but also with a loss of national sovereignty and the partial suspension of democratic processes. In many countries, therefore, the performance of national and international institutions before and during the crisis has not been evaluated positively (Armingeon and Guthmann 2014; Kriesi 2018; Roth et al. 2014).

Taken together, it seems straightforward that utilitarian motivations and negative evaluations of political institutions have led to a decline in specific support for the European Union. This is because the Euro crisis represents an "output failure" of the European political system, which should have led to a withdrawal of specific, i.e. output-related, political support (Easton 1975). Therefore, the rise in regime-related Euroscepticism should have been particularly pronounced in the most severely affected EU member states, which experienced the worst economic conditions and the most harmful consequences of the EU crisis management.

Diffuse Policy Support for European Integration

The expected effects of the crisis on diffuse support for European integration do not follow the same reasoning as the ones on specific regime support. Leconte (2010: 165) observed that during the economic crisis in the 1970s, support for further European unification has been much less volatile than more specific support for EU membership. Since the causes of the Euro crisis have partly been attributed to national political institutions, further European integration might have been regarded as part of the

necessity to distinguish between the global financial crisis and the Euro crisis, particularly because the latter potentially has had much greater socio-economic and political consequences for the EU citizens.

solution, rather than part of the problem. In the most severely affected countries, the Euro crisis has led to a desire for more economic governance and international redistribution (Kuhn and Stoeckel 2014). This reasoning is in line with approaches that postulate an increase in support for European integration in cases where national governments perform badly (de Vries 2018; Sánchez-Cuenca 2000). We can thus assume that many people in crisis-ridden countries carried the hope that further European integration in fiscal and economic policy, such as in the form of so-called Eurobonds, would help to solve their problems rather than making them worse.

On the other side, many citizens in countries less affected by the crisis became similarly upset with European integration, because they needed to bail out member states that were not able to service their public debts anymore. Rather than directing their dissatisfaction towards the regime authorities of the EU, citizens in creditor countries often became reluctant towards further European integration, as it tied their own fate even closer to the debtor countries. The findings of Kuhn and Stoeckel (2014: 637) suggest that "people in economically healthy member states are afraid that European economic governance may harm their economy, while people in crisis-ridden countries welcome it", which is also corroborated by other studies (Bechtel et al. 2014; Daniele and Geys 2015). The mode of political support that suffered most in these countries might therefore rather be diffuse and directed to the regime principle of the EU, namely the idea of European unification.

Furthermore, support for European integration has also suffered from a renationalization of social identities in all member states, especially when it came to whom to blame for the crisis. The public discourses in national media that accompanied these processes have often been dominated by populist parties and nationalist actors who searched for external scapegoats, thereby activating negative out-group feelings and stronger feelings of national identification, which is not unusual in times of perceived group conflict (Runge 2014). Therefore, we expect that decreasing diffuse support for further European integration is a feature of the public opinion not only in the crisis countries, but across the whole Eurozone.

2.2.2 On Party Competition

Parties have an incentive to adapt to changing voter preferences (for an overview, see Adams 2012) and to find answers to external pressures, such as globalization or economic crises (see, e.g., Calca and Gross 2019; Ward et al. 2011). The Euro crisis altered party competition in European states by leading to the rise of "challenger parties" with Eurosceptic views (Hobolt and Tilley 2016). Moreover, existing parties with Eurosceptic views have become even more Eurosceptic (Rohrschneider and Whitefield 2016). If and to what extent challenger parties have been successful in forcing other parties to promptly react and adopt more critical positions on European integration issues is still open to debate (see, e.g., Meijers 2017; Rohrschneider and Whitefield 2016; Williams and Spoon 2015). We argue that the overall position of a country's party system on European integration issues shifted towards a more negative stance when the Euro crisis had a severe impact in the respective country.

Even though political parties are usually reluctant to change their policy positions considerably (Dalton 2016), the Euro crisis has been an extraordinary event that should have led to an increase in party-based Euroscepticism in several ways.

First, since parties aim to be responsive to voters, they had incentives to reconsider their policy stances on European integration in cases where the public opinion has become more Eurosceptic. Here, parties should have felt the need to adapt to these changes in order to not increase the policy distance between themselves and the median voter or their core supporters (Adams et al. 2011: 370, 2014: 968). Second, the crisis provided an opportunity structure that opposition parties might have strategically exploited to attract new voters. The reason is that opposition parties are usually more flexible in their positions towards European integration and not bound to be as supportive as government parties, which are involved in governance at the EU level. Third, even parties that already had Eurosceptic profiles before the crisis should have become more opposed to European integration, as they have been intrigued to blame the EU for the worsening economy. Following the reasoning of Hooghe and Marks (2009: 21), Eurosceptic parties of the far left were reassured on their anti-capitalist views, whereas Eurosceptic parties of the far right saw the austerity measures implemented by the EU institutions as a severe violation of national sovereignty. Fourth, the crisis has also set the stage for new Eurosceptic parties to emerge, which also should have shifted the overall party system position to a more Eurosceptic stance.

3 Empirical Analysis

3.1 Data and Measurements

In order to empirically test our theoretically expectations, we use different data sources. We make use of official economic statistics provided by Eurostat to approximate the degree to which a country has been affected by the Euro crisis. To measure changes in public opinion and party competition on European integration since the beginning of the 1990s, we exploit data from the European Election Studies (EES) that include data on citizens and parties.[10] We measure citizens' attitudes with the EES voter surveys that are conducted in all EU member states within three months after an EP election and comprise about 1000 respondents per country. Party positions are measured with the Euromanifesto data sets that consist of the election programmes of all political parties running in the EP elections. The variables are aggregated at the macro-level to represent the level of Euroscepticism in a country's public opinion and party system. For a pre-crisis versus post-crisis comparison, we

[10]More information about this data source can be found on the EES website: http://europeanelectionstudies.net.

also calculate the first differences between those aggregate values between 2009[11] and 2014[12] for our whole country panel that consists of all EU member states at the respective point in time.[13]

3.1.1 Citizen-Based Euroscepticism

In line with Hobolt and de Vries (2016a), we operationalize citizens' political support with two items from the EES voter surveys. Specific regime support for the EU is represented by a respondent's answer to the question whether her country's EU membership is "a good thing" (3), "neither good nor bad" (2) or "a bad thing" (1). Our measure for diffuse support for European integration addresses an individual's attitudes towards the process of further European unification. Most commonly, respondents were asked to place themselves on a ten-point scale ranging from "European unification has already gone too far" (1) to "European unification should be pushed further" (10).[14] Both variables are aggregated to the country level using the EES design weights to render the survey data more representatively.

In Fig. 1,[15] we see how EU regime support has developed since the Maastricht Treaty over different EU country groups.[16] While it has remained relatively stable in the Western European member states over the last years,[17] it has increased in Eastern Europe[18] since these countries have joined the EU. In the six countries that

---

[11]The outbreak of the Euro crisis is commonly dated to 20 October 2009, when the Greek government publicly revealed the tripling of the public deficit indicating that the figure of 3.6% of the GDP reported by the previous government was inaccurate. It was upgraded to 12.8% of the GDP (Featherstone 2011), after the pre-crisis EP elections of 2009.

[12]While the Euro crisis could not be regarded as being *over* in 2014, it had certainly surpassed its "acute phase" between 2010 and 2013 (Schimmelfennig 2014: 323).

[13]Our analyses do not comprise Croatia and Malta due to data restrictions and the fact that Croatia only joined the European Union in 2013. Tables 2 and 3 in the Appendix provide summary statistics of all variables under consideration here.

[14]The respective item in the EES has slightly changed over the years in its wording and the response options. Slightly deviating versions have used a 4-point scale (1994) or an 11-point scale (2014), but these items are re-scaled here to match the 10-point scale of the items between 1999 and 2009. Moreover, in 1994, the wording was different, asking whether citizens are "in favour" or "against" European unification.

[15]All figures are based on the *plotplain* scheme in Stata version 15.1 (Bischof 2017).

[16]Although the three country groups distinguished here seem to be only broad geographical categorizations, they follow our reasoning to expect unique effects for countries most affected by the economic crisis (*crisis countries*). Moreover, we differentiate between the old member states (*Western Europe*) that joined the EU before 2004 and those who have joined later (*Eastern Europe*), since these two groups often show very different patterns in public opinion and party competition (see, e.g., Marks et al. 2006; Whitefield and Rohrschneider 2015).

[17]Austria, Belgium, Denmark, Finland, France, Germany, Luxemburg, Netherlands, Sweden, United Kingdom.

[18]Bulgaria, Czech Republic, Estonia, Hungary, Latvia, Lithuania, Poland, Romania, Slovakia, Slovenia.

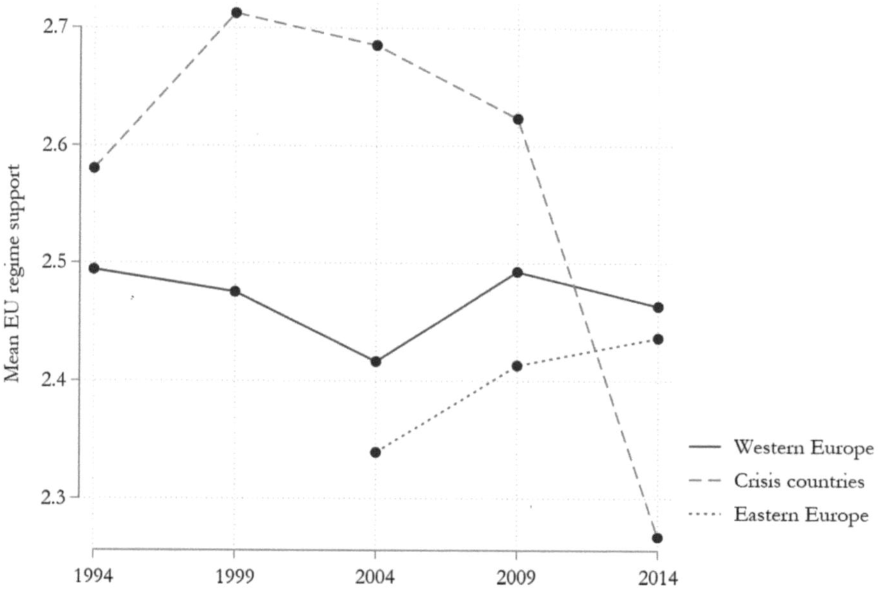

Fig. 1 Mean specific regime support for the EU over different country groups (1994–2014). *Source* European Election Studies (EES) voter surveys (1994, 1999, 2004, 2009, 2014). *Note* Values are unweighted country group means

have been most affected by the Euro crisis,[19] specific regime support for the EU had been much higher than in the other member states before the crisis. Yet, it has dramatically decreased after 2009, which is a first indication of a public opinion effect induced by the Euro crisis. Figure 2 displays a different pattern for the development of diffuse support for European integration by showing a slight downward trend over all three country groups under observation.[20] Although diffuse support for further European unification has decreased in the crisis countries during the Euro crisis, this development is neither exclusive for these member states nor does it diverge greatly from the negative trend that had already existed before.

3.1.2 Party-Based Euroscepticism

There is a vibrant scholarly debate on the appropriate way to measure parties' ideological preferences regarding European integration issues by either using expert judgments or manifesto content information (see, e.g., Marks et al. 2007; Ray 2007). This

[19] As such, we have defined the five countries that received financial assistance by the other Eurozone countries (Cyprus, Greece, Ireland, Portugal and Spain) and Italy, a country group sometimes called "PIIGS+C".

[20] The stark decline between 1994 and 1999 is likely to be caused by the changes in the question wording and the number of response options.

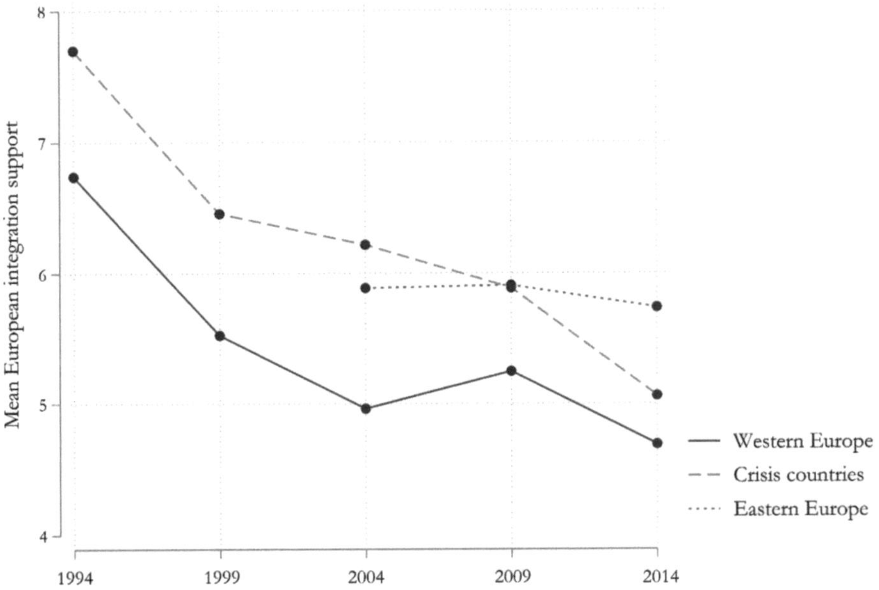

Fig. 2 Mean diffuse policy support for further European unification over different country groups (1994–2014). *Source* European Election Studies (EES) voter surveys (1994, 1999, 2004, 2009, 2014). *Note* Values are unweighted country group means

debate also exists within the research area of party-based Euroscepticism (Mudde 2012). For a number of reasons, we see the best way in answering our research question by using the Euromanifesto data set (Schmitt et al. 2018), which contains all election programmes that political parties have released for European Parliament elections. First, party manifestos are most likely to represent the collective expression of a party's policy preferences, as they are usually discussed and agreed upon by a party congress. The content of election manifestos therefore reflects the official party position on a specific issue ahead of the election and is thus communicated by party elites and activists during the election campaign.[21] Second, since we are interested in the overall position of national party systems towards European integration both in a longitudinal comparison and in a cross-national comparison, we need data on national party positions at the same point in time for all countries under study. Lastly, the EP elections of 2009 and 2014 were held at ideal points in time, since they allow for a pre- versus post-crisis comparison.

Although using manifesto data for measuring policy positions is not without controversy (see, e.g., Dinas and Gemenis 2010), they are widely used in research on party politics (for an overview, see Laver 2014), also when it comes to EP election manifestos (Spoon and Williams 2017). Their obvious advantages over other

[21] In contrast, expert surveys like the Chapel Hill Expert Survey (CHES) are sometimes criticized for their lack of validity, because, as Mudde (2012: 198) describes it, "rather than an expert study, this is really a peer survey".

measurements are their objectivity and the clear possibility of separating a party's political preferences from their actual behaviour. The implicit assumption of quantitatively analysing electoral manifestos is that "parties compete by emphasizing policy areas they believe give them electoral advantage and by glossing over or ignoring those areas that they deem to help their rivals" (McDonald and Mendes 2001: 91). To analyse their content, the Euromanifestos are broken down to "quasi-sentences", defined as political arguments that represent the coding units. Every single unit is then assigned to a content category—in terms of issues and policy areas—and to an evaluation of its connotation—positive or negative.[22] The variables that emerge from this coding procedure are quantitative measures of relative importance, namely the number of quasi-sentences per category. Since these absolute numbers are not very useful, as they strongly vary with the overall size of the manifesto, we divide the raw number by the total number of quasi-sentences.

The data set of our analysis contains all election manifestos released for the EP elections from 1994 to 2014 from all countries that have been EU members at the respective point in time ($n = 775$).[23] To measure a party system's overall position towards European integration, we first create an indicator measuring a party's position towards European integration that ranges from "totally in favour" to "totally against European integration". Hence, we include all arguments in favour and against the EU in general, the competences of its institutions, the transfer of powers to the European level, further EU enlargement, an EU constitution and the common currency. Moreover, we account for negative statements regarding the complexity of the EU's political system and those regarding national contributions to the financing of the EU or its policies. We use Lowe et al.'s (2011) logit scaling technique that "combines the advantages of both additive and ratio scaling methods for manifesto data, whilst avoiding the problem of polarization found in ratio scales, with the additional benefit of a diminishing impact of repeated emphasis, mirroring natural language" (Prosser 2016: 739). Positive values represent pro-EU positions, while negative values represent anti-EU positions. In a last step, we average overall parties in a country at a given point in time to get the overall party system position towards European integration.[24]

In Fig. 3, the development of the party systems' positions since Maastricht is displayed for the three country groups described before. Interestingly, we see again that the position in the ten Western European EU member states has remained relatively stable over the last twenty years. In stark contrast, the party systems of the

[22]In the original coding, every quasi-sentence is assigned a political level that it relates to—European, national or unspecified. However, this distinction is not sustained here, as it does not seem adequate for our purposes.

[23]Each political party is coded from the first time it was represented in the EP onwards. The coding of political parties which have not been represented in the EP for two consecutive legislative periods, however, is discontinued.

[24]We decided not to weigh the individual party positions by the relative sizes of the parties, i.e. the vote share or seat share that the party has received in the last national or European elections. The main reason is that we do not want to confound the programmatic decisions of political parties with the electoral behaviour of citizens.

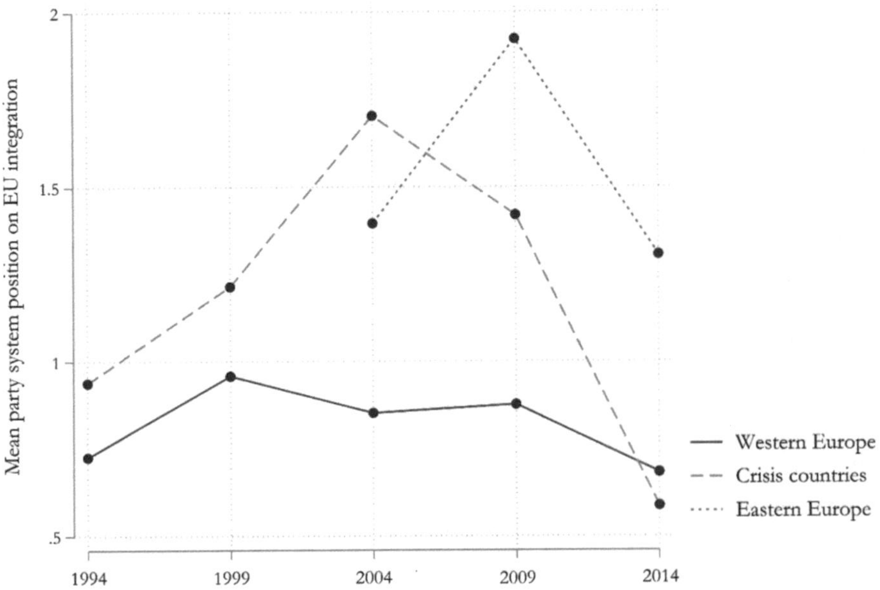

Fig. 3 Party system positions on European integration over different country groups (1994–2014). *Source* Euromanifesto data set (Schmitt et al. 2018). *Note* Own indicator using several categories related to European integration and computing an overall scale based on Lowe et al.'s (2011) logit scaling technique

six countries most affected by the Euro crisis have become supportive of European integration during the 2000s. However, especially during the Euro crisis, party systems in these countries have shown a rise in party-based Euroscepticism that resulted in the least pro-EU position among all three country groups. This observation indicates that the Euro crisis has not only affected public opinion but also party competition in the EU member states.

3.1.3 The Euro Crisis

The degree to which a country has been affected by the Euro crisis is measured by its unemployment rate.[25] The change of a country's stock of unemployed citizens is probably the most noticeable form of economic hardship in a society because many people either lose their own jobs or know other people who have lost theirs. Therefore, the change in the unemployment rate should be an adequate indicator of the socio-economic implications of the Euro crisis.

[25] To check the robustness of our findings, we have also conducted the analyses with other macroeconomic indicators, such as the GDP growth per capita and the interest rates on government bonds. We received similar results. The reason for this is that all three macroeconomic indicators are highly correlated with each other.

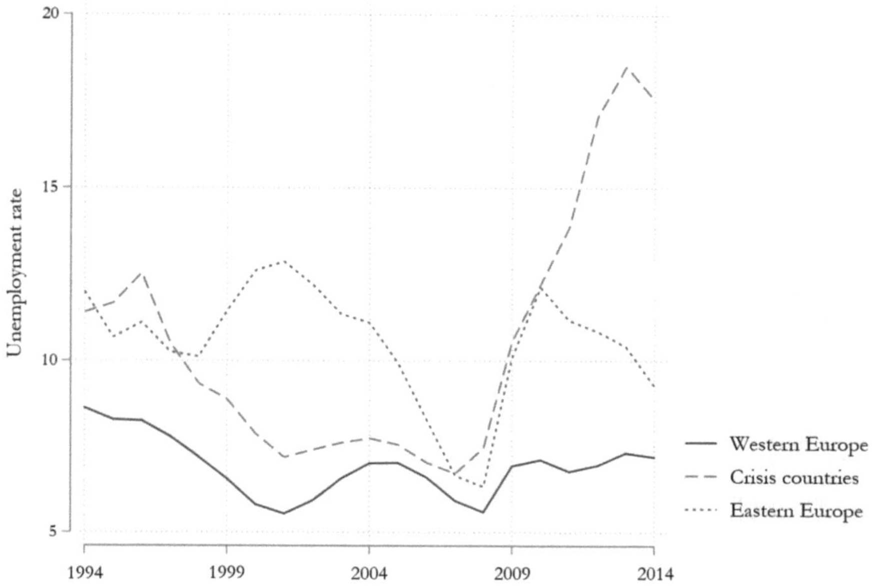

Fig. 4 Unemployment rates over different country groups (1994–2014). *Source* Eurostat. *Note* The values are the unweighted country group means

As we can see in Fig. 4, the unemployment rates in all country groups increased after the year 2008, but they only continued to rise in the countries most affected by the Euro crisis. Between 2010 and 2013, unemployment increased on average from 12 to 18% in the PIIGS+C countries, whereas it decreased to single digits in the rest of the EU. The first signs of recovery in the crisis countries only started to become visible after the year 2013. Because of this empirical confirmation of the theoretical argument made before, we take the change in unemployment rate per country between 2010 and 2013 as an indicator for the degree to which a country has been affected by the crisis.

3.2 *Bivariate Relationships*

In this section, we discuss the relationship between the Euro crisis and the changes in public opinion and in party competition on European integration to identify whether the crisis has led to increases in citizen- and party-based Euroscepticism. The first step is to look at the pairwise correlations between the four macro-level variables, namely the changes in the unemployment rate, specific regime support for the EU, diffuse policy support for European unification and overall party system position on European integration (see Table 1). It seems obvious that the strongest correlation with the Euro crisis indicator is the change in specific regime support. Evidently,

Table 1 Pairwise correlations of the four macro-level variables

	Δ Unemployment rate	Δ Regime support	Δ Diffuse support	Δ Party system position
Δ Unemployment rate (2010–13)	1			
Δ Specific regime support for the EU (2009–14)	−0.77*	1		
Δ Diffuse support for European unification (2009–14)	−0.36*	0.51*	1	
Δ Party system position on EU integration (2009–14)	−0.18	0.20	0.11	1

Sources Own calculations based on data from Eurostat and the European Elections Studies (EES)
Note The values are Pearson correlation coefficients; $N = 26$; *indicates statistical significance: $p < 0.1$

increases in the unemployment rate of a country are strongly connected to increases in the soft form of popular Euroscepticism that concerns the current performance of the European Union. Much weaker, but still statistically significant, is the correlation between the rise in unemployment and diffuse support for European unification. We can thus also infer that the degree to which a country has been affected by the Euro crisis has influenced the rise in the hard version of Euroscepticism that relates to the general idea of European integration.

When plotting these two relationships (see Fig. 5), we see that the strong correlation between the Euro crisis and EU regime support is particularly driven by the five Southern European member states that have been most severely affected during the Euro crisis. Moreover, it is also caused by the cases of the Baltic countries that have experienced more favourable macroeconomic conditions in the same period.[26] The comparatively weak relationship between the rise in unemployment and the change in diffuse policy support, on the other hand, is hampered by four countries—Ireland, Denmark, Slovakia and the Czech Republic—that have had experienced average economic conditions but a strong decline in support for European unification. On the contrary, Bulgaria shows a strong increase in integration support between 2009 and

[26] We have to add, however, that the Baltic countries had experienced very severe economic conditions during the global financial and economic crisis in 2007/08 (see Calca and Gross 2019). The positive development in unemployment rates between 2010 and 2013 therefore mainly represents their economic recovery after the global crisis. Still, it is interesting that this development has been accompanied by such large increases in EU regime support.

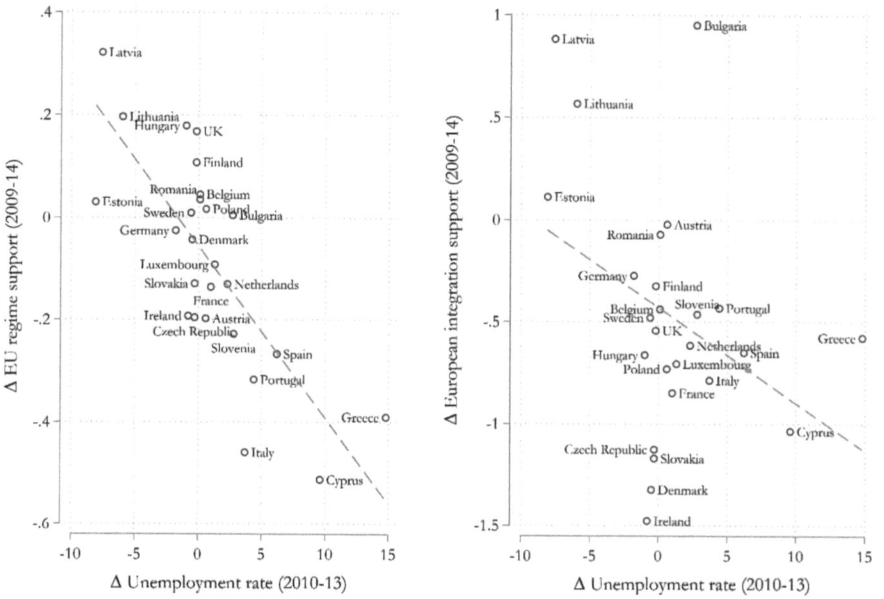

Fig. 5 Relationship between the Euro crisis and the public opinion on European integration. *Source* Own calculation based on EES voter surveys and Eurostat unemployment data. *Note* The dashed line is a fitted, bivariate regression line

2014, despite having simultaneously gone through a period of rising unemployment. Overall, it can be clearly stated that political support for the EU regime as well as for further European unification has declined in most countries over the course of the Euro crisis.

The same is true for the changes in party system positions on European integration during the Euro crisis (see Fig. 6). Most party systems have become more Eurosceptic, but this change has not been solely dependent on the degree to which a country has been affected by the Euro crisis. However, there is still a slightly negative relationship, which is strongly driven by the case of Spain, where party competition became much more Eurosceptic than in other countries during the Euro crisis.

In a similar fashion, party system changes relate to changes in public opinion (see Fig. 7). The graphs show that the strongest correlation, in fact, exists between the rise in party-based Euroscepticism and the type of popular output-orientated Euroscepticism that relates to the regime of the EU (see also Table 1). This finding provides evidence for our theoretical expectation that parties have taken up citizens' current grievances and their dissatisfaction with the EU by adapting their positions on European integration accordingly. However, the change in party system positions barely relates to people's change in diffuse support for further European unification. Again, Spain has a strong influence on this bivariate relationship, and so does Cyprus, by combining a drop in EU regime support with a strong Eurosceptic shift of its party system. Furthermore, the fact

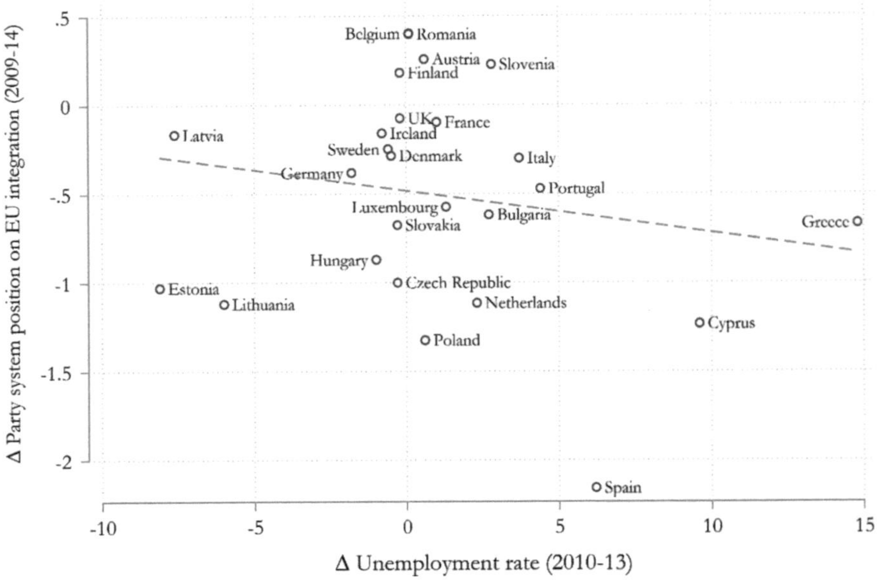

Fig. 6 Relationship between the Euro crisis and the party competition on European integration. *Source* Own calculation based on EES voter surveys and Eurostat unemployment data. *Note* The dashed line is a fitted, bivariate regression line

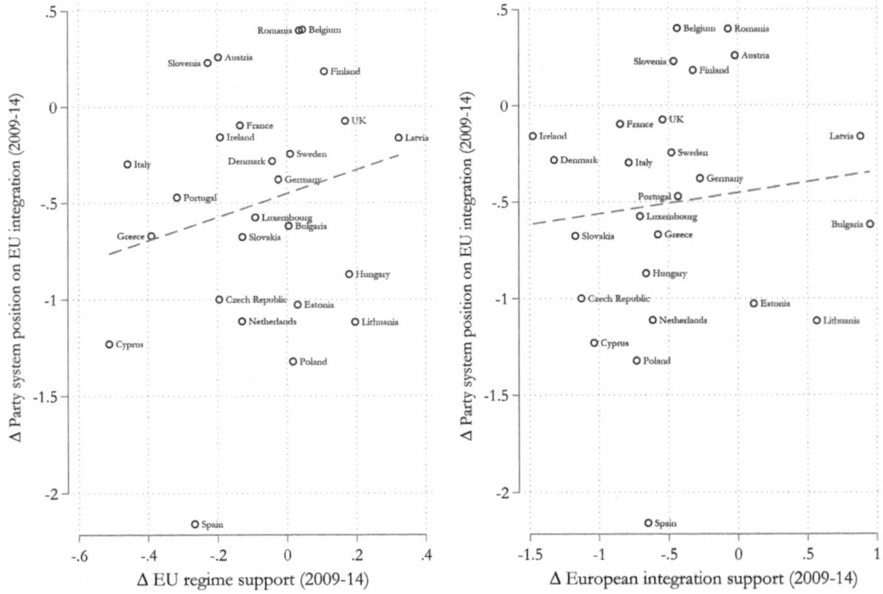

Fig. 7 Relationship between public opinion and party competition on European integration. *Source* Own calculation based on EES voter surveys and Eurostat unemployment data. *Note* The dashed line is a fitted, bivariate regression line

that party systems in Estonia and Lithuania have experienced strong increases in Euroscepticism despite an increasingly EU-friendly public opinion seems surprising. However, this might even be a late reaction to the severe economic downturns that the Baltic countries have faced just a few years earlier.

4 Conclusion

In this chapter, we adopted a combined macro-level perspective to shed light on the effects of the Euro crisis on public opinion and party competition regarding the issue of European integration. By distinguishing between popular Euroscepticism and party-based Euroscepticism, as well as disentangling specific regime support for the EU from diffuse support for European unification, we have detected several interesting findings in our country-level analysis.

First, in line with our expectations, citizens reacted to the economic hardship brought about by the Euro crisis with the withdrawal of specific regime support for the EU. In other words, public opinion on European integration has become more Eurosceptic because of their dissatisfaction with the political and economic outputs that the EU delivered, especially in the member states most affected. This finding is in line with the utilitarian approach of explaining attitudes towards European integration and the concept of political support, more generally (Easton 1965, 1975). It implies that the crisis has been perceived, at least partly, as an output failure of the political system of the EU.

Second, this is much less the case for the level of diffuse policy support for the general process of European integration. Although the idea of further European integration has also suffered during the period of the Euro crisis, it has not only been affected by the extent to which a country was hit by socio-economic turbulences. Moreover, the development that we have seen during the Euro crisis seems to be a continuing trend in most EU member states since the Maastricht Treaty, namely that the general project of European integration is increasingly under pressure. The Euro crisis has visibly reinforced this development, but it is not the root cause of this harder type of Euroscepticism, which generally opposes the idea of further European unification.

Third, party competition on European integration in EU member states has been affected by the Euro crisis, but the mean party system position on this issue has only slightly changed to a more Eurosceptic stance. As we have seen, this development is strongly driven by the case of Spain, whose parties have evidently shifted strongly towards more anti-EU positions over the course of the crisis. This is similar to the relationship between the changes in party competition and the changes in specific regime support, which indicates that in many member states parties have adapted to an increasingly dissatisfied and Eurosceptic public opinion.

However, we cannot make any causal claims based on our empirical findings, as we have merely related different developments in the economic conditions, public opinion and party competition over the same period. Moreover, our analysis has remained on the macro-level, i.e. the country level. In order to more clearly identify the effects of economic conditions on citizens' and parties' support for European integration, empirical research needs to analyse the Euro crisis effects on the micro-level, i.e. on the level of individual citizens (see, e.g., Hobolt and de Vries 2016a) and political parties (see, e.g., Rohrschneider and Whitefield 2016; Spoon and Williams 2017).

Nevertheless, our findings on the relationships between macroeconomic conditions and macro-political outcomes during times of crisis in a combined approach are a valuable piece of the puzzle that has shed light on the question to what degree the public and the party systems in Europe have become more Eurosceptic in response to the Euro crisis. Although we have detected a rise in citizen and party system Euroscepticism across Europe, particularly in the most affected countries, our results suggest that the Euro crisis has not fundamentally shattered the EU's political legitimacy. Rather, our results indicate that positive economic outcomes in future could increase the level of specific regime support again. Yet, the question whether this would also stop the long-term trend of decreasing diffuse support for European unification remains to be answered by further empirical research.

Appendix

See Tables 2 and 3.

Table 2 Summary statistics of the four macro-level variables

Variable	*N*	Mean	SD	Min	Max
Δ Unemployment rate (2010–13)	26	0.88	4.70	−8.10	14.80
Δ Specific regime support for the EU (2009–14)	26	−0.08	0.21	−0.51	0.32
Δ Diffuse support for European unification (2009–14)	26	−0.47	0.60	−1.48	0.95
Δ Party system position on EU integration (2009–14)	26	−0.51	0.61	−2.16	0.40

Table 3 Macro-level variables per country

Country	Δ Unemployment rate (10–13)	Δ Specific regime support (09–14)	Δ Diffuse policy support (09–14)	Δ Party system position (09–14)
Austria	0.60	−0.20	−0.02	0.26
Belgium	0.10	0.05	−0.44	0.40
Bulgaria	2.70	0.01	0.95	−0.62
Cyprus	9.60	−0.51	−1.04	−1.23
Czech Republic	−0.30	−0.20	−1.13	−1.00
Denmark	−0.50	−0.04	−1.32	−0.29
Estonia	−8.10	0.03	0.11	−1.03
Finland	−0.20	0.11	−0.32	0.18
France	1.00	−0.14	−0.85	−0.10
Germany	−1.80	−0.02	−0.27	−0.38
Greece	14.80	−0.39	−0.58	−0.67
Hungary	−1.00	0.18	−0.66	−0.87
Ireland	−0.80	−0.19	−1.48	−0.16
Italy	3.70	−0.46	−0.79	−0.30
Latvia	−7.60	0.32	0.88	−0.17
Lithuania	−6.00	0.20	0.57	−1.12
Luxembourg	1.30	−0.09	−0.71	−0.58
Netherlands	2.30	−0.13	−0.62	−1.11
Poland	0.60	0.02	−0.73	−1.32
Portugal	4.40	−0.32	−0.43	−0.47
Romania	0.10	0.04	−0.07	0.40
Slovakia	−0.30	−0.13	−1.17	−0.68
Slovenia	2.80	−0.23	−0.46	0.23
Spain	6.20	−0.27	−0.65	−2.16
Sweden	−0.60	0.01	−0.48	−0.25
UK	−0.20	0.17	−0.54	−0.08
Mean (EU)	0.88	−0.08	−0.47	−0.50

References

Adams, J. (2012). Causes and electoral consequences of party policy shifts in multiparty elections: Theoretical results and empirical evidence. *Annual Review of Political Science, 15*, 401–419.

Adams, J., Ezrow, L., & Somer-Topcu, Z. (2011). Is anybody listening? Evidence that voters do not respond to European parties' policy statements during elections. *American Journal of Political Science, 55*(2), 370–382.

Adams, J., Ezrow, L., & Somer-Topcu, Z. (2014). Do voters respond to party manifestos or to a wider information environment? An analysis of mass-elite linkages on European integration. *American Journal of Political Science, 58*(4), 967–978.

Almond, G. A., & Verba, S. (1963). *The civic culture. Political attitudes and democracy in five nations*. Princeton: Princeton University Press.
Anderson, C. J. (1998). When in doubt, use proxies: Attitudes toward domestic politics and support for European integration. *Comparative Political Studies, 31*(5), 569–601.
Anderson, C. J., & Kaltenthaler, K. C. (1996). The dynamics of public opinion toward European integration, 1973–93. *European Journal of International Relations, 2*(2), 175–199.
Armingeon, K., & Ceka, B. (2014). The loss of trust in the European Union during the great recession since 2007: The role of heuristics from the national political system. *European Union Politics, 15*(1), 82–107.
Armingeon, K., & Guthmann, K. (2014). Democracy in crisis? The declining support for national democracy in European countries, 2007–2011. *European Journal of Political Research, 53*(3), 423–442.
Azrout, R., van Spanje, J., & de Vreese C. H. (2012). When news matters: Media effects on public support for European Union enlargement in 21 countries. *JCMS: Journal of Common Market Studies, 50*(5), 691–708.
Bechtel, M. M., Hainmueller, J., & Margalit, Y. (2014). Preferences for international redistribution: The divide over the Eurozone bailouts. *American Journal of Political Science, 58*(4), 835–856.
Bischof, D. (2017). New graphic schemes for Stata: Plotplain and plotting. *The Stata Journal, 17*(3), 748–759.
Boomgaarden, H. G., Schuck, A. R. T., Elenbaas, M., & de Vreese, C. H. (2011). Mapping EU attitudes: Conceptual and empirical dimensions of Euroscepticism and EU support. *European Union Politics, 12*(2), 241–266.
Brack, N., & Startin, N. (2015). Introduction: Euroscepticism, from the margins to the mainstream. *International Political Science Review, 36*(3), 239–249.
Braun, D., & Tausendpfund, M. (2014). The impact of the Euro crisis on citizens' support for the European Union. *Journal of European Integration, 36*(3), 231–245.
Calca, P., & Gross, M. (2019). To adapt or to disregard? Parties' reactions to external shocks. *West European Politics, 42*(3), 545–572.
Carey, S. (2002). Undivided loyalties. Is national identity an obstacle to European integration? *European Union Politics, 3*(4), 387–413.
Dalton, R. J. (1999). Political support in advanced industrial democracies. In P. Norris (Ed.), *Critical citizens: Global support for democratic government* (pp. 57–77). Oxford: Oxford University Press.
Dalton, R. J. (2016). Stability and change in party issue positions: The 2009 and 2014 European elections. *Electoral Studies, 44*, 525–534.
Dalton, R. J., & McAllister, I. (2015). Random walk or planned excursion? Continuity and change in the left-right positions of political parties. *Comparative Political Studies, 48*(6), 759–787.
Daniele, G., & Geys, B. (2015). Interpersonal trust and welfare state support. *European Journal of Political Economy, 39*, 1–12.
De Sio, L., Franklin, M. N., & Weber, T. (2016). The risks and opportunities of Europe: How issue yield explains (non-)reactions to the financial crisis. *Electoral Studies, 44*, 483–491.
de Vreese, C. H., & Boomgaarden, H. G. (2005). Projecting EU referendums. Fear of immigration and support for European integration. *European Union Politics, 6*(1), 59–82.
de Vreese, C. H., Boomgaarden, H. G., & Semetko, H. A. (2008). Hard and soft: Public support for Turkish membership in the EU. *European Union Politics, 9*(4), 511–530.
de Vries, C. E. (2018). *Euroscepticism and the future of European integration*. Oxford: Oxford University Press.
de Vries, C. E., & Edwards, E. E. (2009). Taking Europe to its extremes. Extremist parties and public Euroscepticism. *Party Politics, 15*(1), 5–28.
Dinas, E., & Gemenis, K. (2010). Measuring parties' ideological positions with manifesto data: A critical evaluation of the competing methods. *Party Politics, 16*(4), 427–450.

Dotti Sani, G. M., & Magistro, B. (2016). Increasingly unequal? The economic crisis, social inequalities and trust in the European Parliament in 20 European countries. *European Journal of Political Research, 55*(2), 246–264.
Easton, D. (1965). *A framework of political analysis*. Englewood Cliffs, NJ: Prentice Hall.
Easton, D. (1975). A re-assessment of the concept of political support. *British Journal of Political Science, 5*(4), 435–457.
Ehrmann, M., Soudan, M., & Stracca, L. (2013). Explaining European Union citizens' trust in the European Central Bank in normal and crisis times. *The Scandinavian Journal of Economics, 115*(3), 781–807.
Eichenberg, R. C., & Dalton, R. J. (1993). Europeans and the European community: The dynamics of public support for European integration. *International Organization, 47*(4), 507–534.
Eichenberg, R. C., & Dalton, R. J. (2007). Post-Maastricht Blues: The transformation of citizen support for European integration, 1973–2004. *Acta Politica, 42*(2), 128–152.
Featherstone, K. (2011). The JCMS annual lecture: The Greek sovereign debt crisis and EMU: A failing state in a skewed regime. *JCMS: Journal of Common Market Studies, 49*(2), 193–217.
Gabel, M. (1998). Public support for European integration: An empirical test of five theories. *The Journal of Politics, 60*(2), 333–354.
Hernández, E., & Kriesi, H. (2016a). The electoral consequences of the financial and economic crisis in Europe. *European Journal of Political Research, 55*(2), 203–224.
Hernández, E., & Kriesi, H. (2016b). Turning your back on the EU. The role of Eurosceptic parties in the 2014 European Parliament elections. *Electoral Studies, 44,* 515–524.
Hobolt, S. B., & de Vries, C. E. (2015). Issue entrepreneurship and multiparty competition. *Comparative Political Studies, 48*(9), 1159–1185.
Hobolt, S. B., & de Vries, C. E. (2016a). Turning against the union? The impact of the crisis on the Eurosceptic vote in the 2014 European Parliament elections. *Electoral Studies, 44,* 504–514.
Hobolt, S. B., & de Vries, C. E. (2016b). Public support for European integration. *Annual Review of Political Science, 19,* 413–432.
Hobolt, S. B., & Tilley, J. (2016). Fleeing the centre: The rise of challenger parties in the aftermath of the Euro crisis. *West European Politics, 39*(5), 971–991.
Hooghe, L., & Marks, G. (2005). Calculation, community and cues. Public opinion on European integration. *European Union Politics, 6*(4), 419–443.
Hooghe, L., & Marks, G. (2007). Sources of Euroscepticism. *Acta Politica, 42*(2–3), 329–351.
Hooghe, L., & Marks, G. (2009). A postfunctionalist theory of European integration: From permissive consensus to constraining dissensus. *British Journal of Political Science, 39*(1), 1–23.
Hooghe, L., Marks, L., & Wilson, C. J. (2002). Does left/right structure party positions on European integration? *Comparative Political Studies, 35*(8), 965–989.
Hutter, S., Grande, E., & Kriesi, H. (2016). *Politicising Europe. Integration and mass politics*. Cambridge: Cambridge University Press.
Kopecký, P., & Mudde, C. (2002). The two sides of Euroscepticism. Party positions on European integration in East Central Europe. *European Union Politics, 3*(3), 297–326.
Kriesi, H. (2018). The 2017 French and German Elections. *JCMS: Journal of Common Market Studies, 56*(51), 51–62.
Krouwel, A., & Abts, K. (2007). Varieties of Euroscepticism and populist mobilization: Transforming attitudes from mild Euroscepticism to harsh Eurocynicism. *Acta Politica, 42*(2), 252–270.
Kuhn, T., & Stoeckel, F. (2014). When European integration becomes costly: The Euro crisis and public support for European economic governance. *Journal of European Public Policy, 21*(4), 624–641.
Laver, M. (2014). Measuring policy positions in political space. *Annual Review of Political Science, 17,* 207–223.
Leconte, C. (2010). *Understanding Euroscepticism*. Houndmills, Basingstoke: Palgrave Macmillan.
Leruth, B., Startin, N., & Usherwood, S. (2018). Defining Euroscepticism: From a broad concept to a field of study. In B. Leruth, N. Startin, & S. Usherwood (Eds.), *The Rutledge handbook of Euroscepticism* (pp. 3–10). Milton Park: Routledge.

Lindberg, L. N., & Scheingold, S. A. (1970). *Europe's would-be polity*. Englewood Cliffs, NJ: Prentice Hall.

Loveless, M., & Rohrschneider, R. (2011). Public perceptions of the EU as a system of governance. *Living Reviews in European Governance, 6*(2).

Lowe, W., Benoit, K., Mikhaylov, S., & Laver, M. (2011). Scaling policy preferences from coded political texts. *Legislative Studies Quarterly, 36*(1), 123–155.

Marks, G., Hooghe, L., Nelson, M., & Edwards, E. (2006). Party competition and European integration in the East and West. *Comparative Political Studies, 39*(2), 155–175.

Marks, G., Hooghe, L., Steenbergen, M. R., & Bakker, R. (2007). Crossvalidating data on party positioning on European integration. *Electoral Studies, 26*(1), 23–38.

Marks, G., & Wilson, C. J. (2000). The past in the present: A cleavage theory of party response to European integration. *British Journal of Political Science, 30*(3), 433–459.

McDonald, M. D., & Mendes, S. M. (2001). The policy space of party manifestos. In M. Laver (Ed.), *Estimating policy positions of political actors* (pp. 90–114). London and New York: Routledge.

McLaren, L. M. (2002). Public support for the European Union: Cost/benefit analysis or perceived cultural threat? *The Journal of Politics, 64*(2), 551–566.

Meijers, M. J. (2017). Contagious Euroscepticism: The impact of Eurosceptic support on mainstream party positions on European integration. *Party Politics, 23*(4), 413–423.

Mudde, C. (2012). The comparative study of party-based Euroscepticism: The Sussex versus the North Carolina school. *East European Politics, 28*(2), 193–202.

Nicoli, F. (2017). Hard-line Euroscepticism and the Eurocrisis: Evidence from a panel study of 108 elections across Europe. *JCMS: Journal of Common Market Studies, 55*(2), 312–331.

Prosser, C. (2016). Dimensionality, ideology and party positions towards European integration. *West European Politics, 39*(4), 731–754.

Ray, L. (1999). Measuring party orientations towards European integration: Results from an expert survey. *European Journal of Political Research, 36*(2), 283–306.

Ray, L. (2003). When parties matter: The conditional influence of party positions on voter opinions about European integration. *The Journal of Politics, 65*(4), 978–994.

Ray, L. (2007). Validity of measured party positions on European integration: Assumptions, approaches, and a comparison of alternative measures. *Electoral Studies, 26*(1), 11–22.

Rohrschneider, R., & Whitefield, S. (2016). Responding to growing European Union-skepticism? The stances of political parties toward European integration in Western and Eastern Europe following the financial crisis. *European Union Politics, 17*(1), 138–161.

Roth, F., Gros, D., & Nowak-Lehmann, F. D. (2014). Crisis and citizens' trust in the European Central Bank—Panel data evidence for the Euro area, 1999–2012. *Journal of European Integration, 36*(3), 303–320.

Runge, P. (2014). Nationale und europäische Identitäten und politische Unterstützung der Europäischen Union im Kontext der Wirtschafts- und Finanzkrise. *Zeitschrift für Vergleichende Politikwissenschaft, 8*(2), 55–78.

Sánchez-Cuenca, I. (2000). The political basis of support for European integration. *European Union Politics, 1*(2), 147–171.

Schäfer, C. (2017). Euroskeptizismus und Wahlenthaltung. Motivationen unterschiedlicher Nichtwählertypen bei der Europawahl 2014. *Zeitschrift für Vergleichende Politikwissenschaft, 11*(1), 50–80.

Schäfer, C., & Debus, M. (2018). No participation without representation. Policy distances and abstention in European Parliament elections. *Journal of European Public Policy, 25*(12), 1835–1854.

Scharpf, F. W. (2012). Legitimacy intermediation in the multilevel European polity and its collapse in the Euro crisis. *MPiFG Discussion Paper, 12*(6).

Schimmelfennig, F. (2014). European integration in the Euro crisis: The limits of postfunctionalism. *Journal of European Integration, 36*(3), 321–337.

Schmitt, H., Braun, D., Popa, S. A., Mikhaylov, S., & Dwinger, F. (2018). *European Parliament election study 2014, Euromanifesto study*. GESIS Data archive, Cologne. ZA5162 Data File Version 1.0.0.

Serricchio, F., Tsakatika, M., & Quaglia, L. (2013). Euroscepticism and the global financial crisis. *JCMS: Journal of Common Market Studies, 51*(1), 51–64.

Sitter, N. (2001). The politics of opposition and European integration in Scandinavia: Is Euroscepticism a government-opposition dynamic? *West European Politics, 24*(4), 22–39.

Spoon, J., & Williams, C. (2017). It takes two: How Eurosceptic public opinion and party divisions influence party positions. *West European Politics, 40*(4), 741–762.

Szczerbiak, A., & Taggart, P. (Eds.). (2008). *Opposing Europe? The comparative party politics of Euroscepticism. Volume 2: Comparative and theoretical perspectives*. Oxford: Oxford University Press.

Szczerbiak, A., & Taggart, P. (2018). Contemporary research on Euroscepticism: The state of the art. In B. Leruth, N. Startin, & U. Simon (Eds.), *The Routledge handbook of Euroscepticism* (pp. 11–21). Milton Park: Routledge.

Taggart, P., & Szczerbiak, A. (2002). *The party politics of Euroscepticism in EU member and candidate states*. Working Paper, Sussex European Institute, University of Sussex.

Taggart, P., & Szczerbiak, A. (Eds.). (2008). *Opposing Europe? The comparative party politics of Euroscepticism. Volume 1: Case studies and country surveys*. Oxford: Oxford University Press.

van Erkel, P. F. A., & van der Meer, T. W. G. (2016). Macroeconomic performance, political trust and the great recession: A multilevel analysis of the effects of within-country fluctuations in macroeconomic performance on political trust in 15 EU countries, 1999–2011. *European Journal of Political Research, 55*(1), 177–197.

Vasilopoulou, S. (2018). Theory, concepts and research design in the study of Euroscepticism. In B. Leruth, N. Startin, & S. Usherwood (Eds.), *The Routledge handbook of Euroscepticism* (pp. 22–35). Milton Park: Routledge.

Ward, H., Ezrow, L., & Dorussen H. (2011). Globalization, party positions, and the median voter. *World Politics, 63*(3), 509–547.

Weßels, B. (2007). Discontent and European identity: Three types of Euroscepticism. *Acta Politica, 42*(2–3), 287–306.

Whitefield, S., & Rohrschneider, R. (2015). The salience of European integration to party competition. Western and Eastern Europe compared. *East European Politics and Societies: And Cultures, 29*(1), 12–39.

Williams, C., & Spoon, J. (2015). Differentiated party response: The effect of Euroskeptic public opinion on party positions. *European Union Politics, 16*(2), 176–193.

Redefining Democracy and Political Assertiveness: A Constructivist Exposition of European Populism

Najimdeen Bakare

1 Introduction

The end of the Cold War and the race towards a liberal democracy led political observers to the assertion of the end of history and the dawn of a new political reality (Fukuyama 2006). The political reforms and transformations in the former communist countries and the readiness to imbibe the democratic values of Western Europe strengthened the unveiling political reality. Conversely, there was no political forethought that after two decades, Europe would be revisited by political agency (political parties) characterised as radical/extremist, populist, and nationalist, capable enough to threaten the established political system and parties.

Political populism has become a conventional political enterprise across the globe, challenging the old political narratives by either supplanting them or presenting an alternative political lens. In the European context, populism has proven to be a reckonable force as every country in Europe is grappling with this socially constructed political reality that employs sociopolitical narratives to challenge political establishments (Hameleers 2018: 2171; Viviani 2017; Şandru 2013: 65; Van Leeuwen 2006; Brodeur 2005).

The populist far-right political parties are increasingly seizing political geographies all over the continent, with no exemption for the more mature democratic states. To derogate the political achievements of the 'family of populist parties' (far-right and left) belies their accomplishments in recent elections across Europe (Tharoor 2018; Stone 2017), though political observers still consider them as parties on the periphery and ideologically distinctive, nonetheless rhetorically similar (Golder 2016; Mudde 1996).

It is not the subject of this chapter to dive into the oceanic discourse of populism; countless research has done justice to that. Despite the numerous works on the subject,

N. Bakare (✉)
Centre for International Peace and Stability, National University of Sciences and Technology, Islamabad, Pakistan
e-mail: drnajimdeen.pcs@nipcons.nust.edu.pk

© Springer Nature Switzerland AG 2020

M. Baldassari et al. (eds.), *Anti-Europeanism*,
https://doi.org/10.1007/978-3-030-24428-6_4

it remains debatable whether or not populism is an ideology, partially because 'ideology is the most elusive concept on the whole of social science' (McLellan 1995: 1). Nevertheless, upon considering the different debates surrounding populism, Mudde and Kaltwasser (2017) present populism as a '*thin-centred ideology* that considers society to be ultimately separated into two homogeneous and antagonistic camps, "the pure people" versus "the corrupt elite"... politics should be an expression of the people'. But the question is, does contemporary European populism qualify as an ideology? Populism today acts like an ideology because it influences people consciously and otherwise, regardless of whether or not people are aware of it, aiding the processing of information, and how people deal and contend with their immediate sociopolitical environment. Similar to the way ideology works, populism is an 'acceptable truth' by a group of people, who socially construct a world in their own acuity, how it should be, its organisation, and why the 'acceptable value' should be strictly followed. Populism has always navigated between being an ideology, a perceived way of life, or an instrument of change (Mudde and Kaltwasser 2017; Sargent 2009).

The chapter uses the framework of constructivism to describe the phenomenon of European populism and, in addition, employs the conceptual lenses of 'socialisation breakdown' and market theory for a deeper understanding of populism and how narratives are socially constructed within the European political theatre. Lastly, the chapter contextually identifies the different manifestations of populism in different European states and explores the consequences of populism in contemporary Europe.

2 Constructivism

Bur (2015) did not only present a comprehensive understanding of constructivism, but wrote that this epistemological lens 'cautions us to be ever suspicious of our assumptions about how the world appears to be'. Constructivism interrogates social reality and advocates the reconstruction of reality as we deemed it. The ontological position of constructivism asserts that social phenomena and their meanings are not independent of social actors, who through social interaction generate meanings from symbols, norms, and shared thought. Constructivism further explains the constant state of revision of social reality (Bryman 2012: 33) and underpins the importance of culture, symbols, normative discourses, social communities as collective and embracing tools for reconstructing new narratives and social reality and as a source of knowledge and interaction (Berger and Thomas 2011; Reus-Smit 2005; Fosnot 2005).

European populist parties have demonstrated the ability to skilfully craft and reconstruct social narratives that reawaken the notion of cherished historical and shared identity, past, beliefs, and values (Ruzza 2017; Bergmann 2016; Reus-Smit 2005: 196). Populism resonates with social narratives that exploit cultural sentiment and normative structures, reinforces the 'self' over the 'other', and reasserts cognitive and cultural identity. Through a constructivist prism, European populism is steadily putting together the narrative of 'the pure people' versus the 'corrupt elite', 'truly European' versus 'European of migrant origin', 'European values and norms' versus 'non-European values and norms' (Mudde and Kaltwasser 2017; Reus-Smit 2005).

Populism is reviving and animating both historical and contemporary grievances to position itself within the mainstream. Through the constructivist mantra, populism legitimises itself on two fronts—the public (people) and political ones. The former generates people's blessings—a requirement for every political ideology—and the latter crowns it by offering a political authority that legitimises political views that were once considered democratically offensive and incorrect. The amalgam of the two (public and political) enables the institutionalisation of radical political views and actions. Rather than criminalising what was considered an unhealthy past, populism rather espouses its celebration and glorification. Certain cases (mentioned later in the chapter) strongly advocate against defaming, but promote a benign narrative of Nazism (Taub and Fisher 2017; Anoosh 2017; Dunai 2016). Not too long ago, public celebration of Nazism or outright anti-Semitism was considerably unacceptable, but the wind of populism and its exploitation of constructivist languages has triumphantly undone that. The spirit of populism challenges the established grand narratives, breaks down old notions, and promotes radical ideation, which might necessarily be receptive only to few people.

Constructivism by itself would not score the imagined and intended goal; it has to be complemented by a more graphic representation of how notions and ideas are socially constructed. The construction of any narrative does not take place outside the realm of socialisation, where the different arenas and agents of socialisation are active participants (Frones 2016). This is also true for the deconstruction of any idea or narrative, as it must involve the rejection or breaking down of one socialisation structure in order to create a niche for another (Katsas 2012).

2.1 Socialisation Breakdown

Societies have historically regulated, monitored, and maintained social order through a socialisation process. While the latter rationalises and legitimises norms and values habitually considered dominant, the keepers of the dominant culture ensure that the socialisation process is unperturbed for the safety of the system and order. But history indelibly records that socialisation breakdown is never implausible. Among other reasons, it breaks down upon a radical confrontation or opposition against the established rationality and status quo.

Socialisation breakdown is the political rupture that paves the way for oppositional values based on radical ideology, with the intent to cause radical replacement of the dominant ideology (Taylor and Flint 2000). It is always a gradual manifestation; it is never an overnight development nor is it spontaneously ignited by populism, though the latter adds to its acceleration. This breakdown mirrors public sentiment (at a given point) and a longing for change. Theoretically, socialisation breakdown is induced by a host of (internal and external) factors: the growing economic gap between the rural and urban settlement, the disconnection between the old and the young, increasingly elitist politics, harsh reality of the financial crisis, tussles between the globalist–cosmopolitans and the nationalists (Bakare 2017).

European populism does not only represent the breakdown of socialisation, it equally exploits and further accelerates its erosion. It is increasingly becoming a significant and alternative political agency across Europe (Davies and Jackson 2008), employing socially constructed rhetoric to contest and redesign political and electoral geographies that are historically dominated by established, traditional political parties. Besides, populism confidently sees itself as the future of Europe amidst mounting challenges facing the continent and claims that current European leadership has no stomach for the problems.

European populism should be considered an evolving political socialisation geared at breaking down and replacing the existing status quo. It exploits the long-harboured resentment of segments of the society against the established system. Contemporary European populism underscores the fact that crude philosophy was not imported, forced, and invented, but it is a socially constructed political calculus that takes advantage of enduring discontentment lingering within the public (Bakare 2017). Over the years, populist parties have enjoyed considerable public support through emotional galvanisation, cultural sensitivity, and exposure of social difference. The populist parties have delightedly crafted a Marxist-like narrative and have presented themselves as the political agency of the voiceless, dissatisfied, discontented, and aggrieved citizens, who lack political stamina to express their discomfort and disdain for being left behind by the corporate globalists supported by the political establishment (Galstan 2018; Viviani 2017; Martinelli 2016; Selby 2014; Kallis et al. 2013). Over the years, the public resentment against the establishment did not just precipitate the breakdown of grand socialisation; it represented 'hibernated germs' that needed time and agencies (populist parties) to de-hibernate. What this suggests is that populism intersects with the people; the alliance between the two grants legitimacy and political assertiveness to the populist elites. Hence, Schopflin (2015) argues that by demonising populist politicians, European democracy is directly criticising and demonising the people, who are the representatives of democratic sovereignty.

The populists' use of socially constructed rhetoric exposes the vulnerability of established political norms as un-insulated from socialisation breakdown (Taylor and Flint 2000: 302). Hence, with a political agenda and public legitimacy, populism is increasingly opposing and dismantling the sociopolitical norms and thus leaves room for 'oppositional values based on radical ideology that is designed to counter and replace the dominant ideology' (Taylor and Flint 2000: 304). Despite the degree of differences amongst them, the populist parties share common disdain. In their view, the established political system is not representative enough (particularly for the ordinary citizens), and hence the cogent reason why there must be a change that must include, but is not limited to, breaking down the existing political system and socialisation (Crenshaw and Pimlott 1997: 206; Akkerman et al. 2016: 56; Tillerson 2017). Mudde (2000) argues that extreme ideologies often advocate the replacement of a political system and its supporters (politicians), ultimately culminating in a revolutionary change of the entire system.

Prior to the ongoing wave of populism in Europe, the continent has, for some time, developed a dynamic neighbourhood effect with 'the experiences of individuals within their specific localities that provide the context and raw material for socialisation' (Taylor and Flint 2000). In the same context, most European electorates offer loyalty to the established political parties. Incidentally, the wave of populism is eroding and fragmenting that loyalty and thus generating a new form of socialisation and, by extension, a crop of new electable and electorates (youth), who see the old ones as incapable to address their concerns. Given the breakdown of the old socialisation, populism is rapidly becoming the platform for the political radicalisation of European youth (Vorlander 2016; Sakellartou 2015). The latter considers populism as a 'change' and emancipation from the old regime.

The populist political rhetoric exposes the nexus of constructivism and socialisation breakdown (Ruzza 2017). The socially constructed narrative intersects with socialisation breakdown and re-socialisation process manifolds. At the same time, populist politicians are progressively assertive and redefining democratic practices through the utility of socially manufactured discourse. Invariably, the latter precipitates the breakdown of established political socialisation and the emergence of a new political rationality. Populist expression finds a breathing space in the breakdown of socialisation, a leverage to redefine democracy the way it best perceives it and the propensity to sway heavily on an 'identified political target' using ethno-racial, nationalist, religio-cultural, and identity expressions (Bakare 2017). With the growing public acceptance of these expressions, the European political landscape is witnessing fundamental restructuring. The institutionalisation of populism causes discomfort to the traditional dichotomy of left and right politics—populism challenges left and right politics (Galstan 2018). Asides from being alarmed by public acceptance and assertiveness of the radical forces, the traditional political parties are equally infected by the contagious mantra of populism. In order to remain relevant, the traditional parties are employing similar radical narratives, which they would otherwise dub politically incorrect (Bakare 2017; Boztas et al. 2017). In doing so, radical views tend to become mainstream (Odmalm and Hepburn 2017). Populist narratives nourish political discourse, engendering 'a new normal' and the mainstreaming of hitherto politically incorrect rhetoric.

Across the EU states, there is growing disorientation and attitudinal change towards the EU. Szczerbiak and Taggart (2008) refer to this attitude as Euro-criticism or Euro-contestation. The socialisation that has been promoting the union of people bound together by common values, identity, and history is now being threatened by the new wave of populism. Contemporary European populism is engineering its own form of socialisation that will rupture and breakdown the existing socialisation with the intent of supplanting it with a more radical replacement (Taylor and Flint 2000).

Unsurprisingly, the impact of socialisation breakdown transcends domestic European politics and is growingly reflective on the EU supranational arrangement. The tidal wave of anti-EU populist parties is disturbing and threatening the constructivist notion of cognitive regionalism, a form of regionalism in which EU member states get socialised, integrate into a 'European' value system, and work together towards cognitive regionalism and interdependence (Dent and Huang 2002; Adler

1997, Smith 1992; Wallace 1990). Arguably, the ongoing socialisation breakdown creates a favourable climate for populist parties to boldly describe as moribund the neo-functionalism's rationale for the creation of the European Community/European Union, where 'high and rising levels of interdependence would set in motion an ongoing process of cooperation that would lead eventually to political integration' (Hurrell 1995). Equipped with nationalist narratives, populism is riding on ruptured socialisation to weaken the long-endured process of 'socialisation through regionalism and institutionalism' that characterises the functioning of the EU. The growing number of EU-sceptic populist parties and their radical policies underscores this assertion; they are bent on (re)negotiating change and reform from within the EU institutional structures in order to promote suitable national interest, guided by a populist agenda (Vasilopoulou 2011: 223–244). In addition to depicting the vulnerability of 'socialisation through regionalism', populism allows minority voices (Central and Eastern European states) to release their long guided reluctance to appear anti-European. Across Europe, populism explicitly presents itself as the platform and mouthpiece for individual and groups estranged from the EU project.

As demonstrated by recent radical, anti-EU, and political jingoism in Italy, Austria, France, Germany, The Netherlands, Poland, and Hungary (to mention a few), populism is greasing the breakdown of socialisation within the EU; it does so by threatening the collective spirit of regional cooperation and integration, enabling the resuscitation and reawakening of 'selfish and state-centric nationalism' and endangering the long laboured and cultivated supra-nationalism (Vossen 2017; Markovi 2017; Sakellartou 2015; Topaloff 2012; Kelstrup 2012). It is not unconceivable, therefore, that amidst a growing misgiving about the EU (Kallis et al. 2013; Stratfor 2013) and with the aid of a socially constructed nationalist language, populism has managed to exacerbate doubt about the EU, either as an institution that has outlived its usefulness or as having no propensity to match the imagined 'future' envisaged by the populist politicians. Allaying the fear and apprehension among their supporters about the 'eventual collapse of the EU project', populist politicians borrow from the language of constructivism, stressing that all regions (and notion of regionalism) are socially constructed and hence politically contested. Hence, the call for dismantling of the EU project, as in the case of Brexit and similar threats of EU exit (in Sweden and The Netherlands), should hardly be a surprise (Khan 2018; Forster 2016).

As demonstrated above, the intersection of populism and people and public acceptance of populist rhetoric is revealing of the fact that there is a demand for populist narrative. Otherwise, as a political product, it will be less captivating to the people. Glaringly, it is hard to refute that populism is a competitive political product, challenging the established political structure. Like every form of idea, populism has demonstrated it can represent a niche in the market place of ideas.

2.2 Market Theory Perspective

Classical economists define the market as any arrangement that enables buyers and sellers to contract, interact, and do business with each other. In addition to being a competitive arena, market theory characterises markets as liberal because of the free entry and exit operations and considers buyers as rational consumers (Baumol and Blinder 2008). Competition is an important market component, well-defined by comparative, competitive, and differential advantages. Whether or not a market is perfect depends on these competitive values, though an imperfect market is characterised by the domination of single, dual, and oligarchic market forces (Baumol and Blinder 2008; Mentzer 2001: 71–72). An imperfect market leads to frustration, as frustrated sellers who feel marginalised and estranged from the market forces will often seek a way to break the encumbrance of frustration and find their niche, though that is often achieved through an alliance with frustrated buyers, who similarly consider themselves marginalised and estranged from the market forces and therefore agitate and demand for a change from within (Hahnel 2002; Hirschman 1970).

Democracy, like the market, is a platform where electorate and elected meet to interact, dialogue, and do political business with each other. It equally carries the free entry and exit feature of markets, hence democracy, aside from allowing alternative political products in the market of narratives, also ensures the liberal principle of free entry and exit of political parties.

Meanwhile, from an imperfect prism, the European political theatre shares some semblance of the market scenario, wherein certain parties and electorates believe the political establishment marginalises their sentiments and concerns. This sense of marginalisation cements an alliance (between the people and populist parties) and further contributes to the socialisation breakdown. Over the years, the cooperation of the two (populist party and frustrated electorates) brings to bear five important points.

One: like market oligopoly, electoral oligopoly has its own vulnerability, and it can be threatened and challenged by formidable and competitive narratives. Two: the acceptance of a populist narrative shows the consumerist tendency of voters—whose concerns and longings have been inadequately satiated by the traditional–established parties—and hence the need for an alternative, but politically consumable product. Three: populism promotes political ideology as a commodity and the electorates as rational actors (consumers), capable and at liberty to make rational choices on what sort of political commodity best suits their interest. Four: in the light of market analysis, change in price, taste, and state of economy can cause rational consumers to desire alternative products other than those they are familiar with. This is equally true in a political sense. The propensity of the electorates to switch loyalty from one (political ideology or commodity) to another further underscores the socialisation breakdown and the level of dissatisfaction for the established parties. Five: by dwelling on social construction, populist elites have demonstrated that they are not just willing, but that they have a competitive political product/narrative worthy of consumers/electorates' taste and readily available to the sympathisers of their view.

3 Populism and Democracy

Over the last couple of years, populism has demonstrated the propensity to cause political re-engineering through socially constructed normative discourses. Employing sociocultural symbols and a language that echoes with sections of society, populism is not only changing the complexion of democracy, but it is crafting a radical political message that has no bearing with the prevailing democratic norms. As an ideology that strongly believes in parallel social reality, the homogenous politics of populism threatens the pluralism, inclusiveness, and tolerance that characterise liberal democracy (Sargent 2009). It might be instructive to investigate the extent to which populist social construction and breakdown of socialisation disturb the democratic landscape in Europe.

The recent rise and political achievements of populism across Europe (Stone 2017; Shuster 2017; Rettman 2015) have dramatically influenced political language and what is politically correct and acceptable. The breakdown of socialisation and the consequent neighbourhood effect has brought forth a new political experience. Far-right political parties are now inclined to act or pitch speeches that may once have been considered politically incorrect. The breakdown climate is challenging the established political narrative, though such possibility would have been implausible without a certain degree of political support from the public, whose legitimation strengthens the populist position. For instance, the far-right political lens is increasingly gaining footing and becoming part of public and political discourse, while the concern of public ire against political incorrectness is losing importance. For a long time, the far-right parties could not afford to have public assemblies, wary of public resentment; but as the over-layer against them gets lifted due to the breakdown of political socialisation, the likes of the Koblenz Summit are not just a reality, but underpin the public acceptability of their political prism. It is safe to assert that populism is creating a 'new normal' (Beyme 2018: 42; Muller 2016). Traditional and established political parties are not immune from the 'new normal', though the established parties have moderately traded and gambled with the 'new normal' political discourse. In a similar vein, leftist parties are taking harder measures, showing that they are deeply nationalistic, and as security conscious and people oriented as much as the far-right (Bakare 2017).

Second, amidst the growing wave and acceptance of populism, established political parties are forced to rethink on the best way to remain relevant. Like every form of change, European populism has generated three important Rs: *readjustment, realignment, and reconstruction*. For the sake of remaining relevant, most political parties are increasingly readjusting their parties along the constructivist and nationalistic narratives generated by the populist parties. Populism is challenging the grand political narratives and socialisation and, consequently, the cogent factor why parties are seemingly reconstructing their political language. One of the key challenges brought forth by the wave of populism is the blurring of traditional left and right political characterisation (Galstan 2018). It causes the left to go farther left and the right farther right, mirroring the image of the extremist and closed politics of nativism, protectionism, and isolationism rather than an open politics that embraces all and sundry. Such a closed democratic dispensation is uncharacteristic of democratic norms (Bergmann 2016; Martinelli 2016; O' Brien 2016); it engenders authoritarian and non-inclusive politics (Sandford 2017; Pirro 2015), and hence the intolerance and aversion for the 'other', be it the native 'other' or hybrid/foreign 'other'. This would not stand a chance of success without the breakdown of socialisation and public acceptance of populist mantra.

Democracy is hailed as one of the finest systems that promotes multiculturalism, but ridding on social narratives, exploiting cultural sentiment and normative structures that promote and reassert parochial identity. Populism, conversely, reinforces the 'self' over the 'other' and exacerbates the debate of multiculturalism. By its nature of anti-pluralism, populism makes scholars grapple on its real perilousness to democracy (Mudde and Kaltwasser 2017; Martinelli 2016; Liang 2007: 265 and Dix 1985). While multiculturalism has been a protracted and contentious public discourse, the rise of populism exploited it for political polarisation, thus significantly worsening the conversation (Grabow 2016). From Western to Southern Europe, up to Scandinavia and the VISEGRAD region, anti-multiculturalism is now an integral part of populist discourse rooted in social construction.

4 Populism and Domestic Politics

Contemporary European populism has fairly caused a socialisation breakdown and its replacement with a populist worldview. Conversely, traditional political parties are striving to mellow down the wave of populism through an electoral defeat. However, this does not discount the infectious and indelible imprint of populist narrative on both the collective and individual mind. The swaying influence of populist narrative is increasingly glaring as established political parties are employing few conservative and hard policies from the far-right, particularly on the current debate of immigration and the Muslim community in Europe. For instance, months into the Dutch elections, the Dutch Prime Minister Mark Rutte became demanding and rhetorical, asking the immigrants to 'be normal or be gone … reject our values' or leave the Netherlands (Ruzza 2017; Boztas et al. 2017). Such borrowing not only did not undercut the rising tides of far-right spiteful rhetoric, but it also exposed a strong vulnerability and provided the established political parties with a strong case for the debate of multiculturalism. While discussing the ban on veils in Germany, the Interior Minister Thomas de Maizière said 'Integration also means that we should make clear and impart our values and where the boundaries of our tolerance toward other cultures lie … the draft law we have agreed on makes an important contribution to that' (Reuters 2017; Smale 2016). This is equally true for how the government of Angela Merkel reversed Germany's open-door refugee policy (Copley 2016). Employing the 'new normal', the established political parties sealed electoral victories in France, Netherland, Austria, and in the local elections in Germany.

Democracy enunciates the protection of minority's rights, but the question is whether populism will keep that democratic promise. In countries where the far-right political parties are significantly salient, minority communities are increasingly nurturing fear of uncertainty, anticipating a rise in harsh government policies, xenophobic, anti-immigrant, anti-Muslim sentiments against the backdrop of already volatile climate, clouded by the incidents of Muslim extremism (Taub and Fisher 2017; Carassava 2017; Vossen 2017; Markovi 2017; Vorlander et al. 2016; Sakellartou 2015; Lidegaard 2015; Alderman 2012; Burke 2004). Arguably, a parochial sentiment as opposed to tolerant democratic norms is increasingly making a foothold. What energises this is the social construction that boldly re-emphasises 'pure people' versus the 'impure other' (Mudde and Kaltwasser 2017; Reus-Smit 2005). This binary worldview might offer an explanation for the exacerbation of hate crimes in the EU (Engel 2018; European Union Agency for Fundamental Rights 2006; Chakraborti and Garland 2009: 124). Though several European governments have laws meant to proscribe and mitigate such crimes, the intriguing report on the rise of racial crimes either committed by people who are ideologically and politically associated with the far-right, or motivated by the charged political climate, further underlines the anxiety of the minority community. But more worrying is the oversight and lack of neutrality of security personnel towards such crimes (European Union Agency for Fundamental Rights 2018; Ojeaku 2014) even though the European Union Agency for Fundamental Rights (2012) says 'overlooking the bias motivation behind a crime amounts to a violation of Article 14 of the European Convention of Human Rights (ECHR)'. Though it is irrefutable that hate crime is a phenomenon prior to the salient manifestation of contemporary populism, given the plethora of reports on hate crime, the question that comes to mind is whether hate crime is now an integral part of the new normal.

Despite having a Muslim (Ahmed Aboutaleb) as the speaker of the Dutch Parliament, the Muslim community in The Netherlands does not underestimate Geert Wilders's Party. Wilders's political rhetoric debases migrant communities, and his generalisation of immigrant community as the breeding ground for terrorists is extremely disturbing. A civil organisation working in The Netherlands reported an estimate of 174 hate crimes against Muslims, tripling the number recorded by the government (Rubin 2017a, b, c, d, e). Aggressive policy towards the minority and Muslim community is plausible in a political environment ruled by a populist leader like Wilders, whose reference to Moroccans as 'scum' and incitement of racial discrimination got him indicted and found guilty by a Dutch court. The verdict says, 'It doesn't matter that Wilders gave another message afterwards [saying he was referring only to criminal Moroccans and benefits claimants],' … 'The message that evening from the podium, via the media, was loud and proud and did its work … The group was collectively dismissed as inferior to other Dutch people' (Boztas 2016). As a rejoinder to the court's verdict, Wilders wrote 'Three PVV hating judges declare that Moroccans are a race and convict me and half of The Netherlands … madness'. He further opined 'I still cannot believe it, but I have been convicted because I asked a question about Moroccans. The Netherlands has become a sick country. The judge who convicted me [has] restricted the freedom of speech for millions of Dutch. I will never be silent. I am not a racist and neither are my voters.' (Ibid). In addition, he was reported to have said 'when I become the Prime Minister of The Netherlands, I will clear the decks' (Janssen 2017).

The ruling of the European Court of Human Rights (ECHR) that disregards and disallows wearing of headscarves in workplaces, provided legal support and further strengthened the position of the Belgian government over the ban on the public wearing of the full-face veil (Bilefsky 2017, Crisp 2017). Unsurprisingly, the affected Muslim women considered the ruling as a viable legal tool that could be weaponised by anti-Muslim 'entities', to further undermine their religious freedom, human rights, and resultantly, that would further make their integration more challenging. Indeed, the ruling generated a feeling of euphoria amongst the far-right parties, as for them, it was an endorsement of populist proselytization (Rankin and Oltermann 2017). The court ruling did not just present the European far-right an incentive to further chart their cause and raise slogans against supposedly un-European actions and norms, but it became a weapon for any instrumentalist to undermine the human rights of the minority community. It remains debatable whether or not the court was swayed by the political climate or was fundamentally legalistic in its decision.

5 Conclusion

It is not that the existing democratic system on the continent has turned out to be a complete failure and has consequently led to populism—it is the populist parties that have identified the crack in the political system. They have exploited and used it to propel themselves into the national spotlight. European populism should be ceased to be seen as an imposition, and it is rather a socially constructed political calculus and process that feeds on sociopolitical discontentment.

Populist politics are incontrovertibly succeeding across democracies in Europe and ascending to legitimate electoral power. They are presented by a confluence of ideologies and narratives geared at eroding the established political norms. The radical propensity of populism belies the democratic norms of tolerance and accommodation of the 'other'. The anti-immigration, Islamophobic, anti-multiculturalism, and anti-globalisation outlook of populism is clearly at odds with liberal democratic values and principles. Despite all attempts to tame populism across the continent, populist leaders have proven to be reckonable forces and introduced contagious narratives. As much as socialisation breakdown continues, populism will remain virile.

The beauty of democracy is the propensity for heterogeneity, dialogue, inclusiveness, and pluralism. These elements are indeed the opportunity structures provided by democracy to an extent that populism is thriving on these structures. Democratic norm does not simply allow voting for another party (Schopflin 2015: 12), but promotes engaging people across the political spectrum. This norm should not only be respected by the populist elites, but should ensure that their views do not infringe the fundamental rights of others.

References

Adler, E. (1997). Imagined (Security) communities: Cognitive regions in international relations. *Journal for International Studies, 26*(2), 249–277.

Akkerman, T., Lange, S., & Rooduijn, M. (2016). *Radical right-wing populist parties in Western Europe: Into the mainstream?*. New York: Routledge.

Alderman, L. (2012, July). Greek far right hangs a target on immigrants. *New York Times*. http://www.nytimes.com/2012/07/11/world/europe/as-golden-dawn-rises-in-greece-anti-immigrant-violence-follows.html. Accessed June 12, 2016.

Anoosh, C. (2017, March 8). *Rise of the nationalists: A guide to Europe's far-right parties*. New Statesman. http://www.newstatesman.com/world/europe/2017/03/risenationalists-guide-europe-s-far-right-parties.

Austria far right: Freedom Party wins key posts in new government. (2017, December). *BBC*. Retrieved from http://www.bbc.com/news/world-europe-42379985.

Bakare, N. (2015). Europe and the Muslim World some issues and approaches. *Policy Perspectives, Institute of Policy Studies, 12*(1), 51–80.

Bakare, N. (2016). Europeans' three dimensional approaches towards Middle East refugee crisis. *Policy Perspectives, Institute of Policy Studies, 13*(2), 63–91.

Bakare, N. (2017). The breakdown of socialization and political re-assertiveness of European far-right. *Policy Perspective, 14*(2), 55–82.

Baumol, W., & Blinder, A. (2008). *Economics: Principles and policy*. Singapore: Cengage Learning.

Berger, P. L., & Thomas, L. (2011). *The social construction of reality: A treatise in the sociology of knowledge*. New York: Open Road Media.

Bergmann, E. (2016). *Nordic Nationalism and Right-Wing populist politics: Imperial relationships and national sentiments*. London: Palgrave Macmillan.

Berman, S. (2016, Nov/Dec). Populism is Not Fascism. *Foreign Affairs, 95*(6), 39–44.

Beyme, K. (2018). *From post-democracy to neo-democracy*. Cham: Springer.

Bilefsky, D. (2017, March). Ban on head scarves at work is legal, E.U. Court Rules. *New York Times*. https://www.nytimes.com/2017/03/14/world/europe/headscarves-ban-european-court.html. Accessed March 15, 2017.

Boztas, S. (2016, December). Anti-Islam Dutch MP Geert Wilders found guilty of inciting racial discrimination. *Telegraph*. http://www.telegraph.co.uk/news/2016/12/09/anti-islam-dutch-mp-geert-wilders-found-guilty-discrimination/. Accessed March 15, 2017.

Boztas, S., Chazan, D., & Foster, P. (2017, January). Dutch prime minister warns migrants to 'be normal or be gone', as he fends off populist Geert Wilders in bitter election fight. *Telegraph*. http://www.telegraph.co.uk/news/2017/01/23/dutch-prime-minister-warns-migrants-normal-gone-fends-populist/. Accessed March 15, 2017.

Brodeur, S. (2005). *Why support the radical right? A theory for the social construction of radical right populist identities*. Lund: Lund University Press.

Bryman, A. (2012). *Social research methods*. Oxford: Oxford University Press.

Bur, V. (2015). *An introduction to social constructionism*. London: Routledge.

Burke, J. (2004, November). The murder that shattered Holland's liberal dream. *The Guardian*. Retrieved from https://www.theguardian.com/world/2004/nov/07/terrorism.religion.

Carassava, A. (2017, January). How the rise of Donald Trump has Re-Energised Greece's neo-Nazis. *Independent*. http://www.independent.co.uk/news/world/europe/donald-trump-muslim-ban-greece-neo-nazi-golden-dawn-athens-march-protest-a7555706.html. Accessed February 2, 2017.

Chakelian, A. (2017, March). Rise of the nationalists: A guide to Europe's far-right parties. *New Statesman*. http://www.newstatesman.com/world/europe/2017/03/rise-nationalists-guide-europe-s-far-right-parties. Accessed March 9, 2017.

Chakraborti, N., & Garland, J. (2009). *Hate crime: Impact, causes and responses*. London: Sage Publications.

Connolly, K. (2017, January). After the US, far right says 2017 will be the year Europe wakes up. *The Guardian*. https://www.theguardian.com/world/2017/jan/21/koblenz-far-right-european-political-leaders-meeting-brexit-donald-trump. Accessed February 2, 2017.

Copley, C. (2016, February). Refugee crisis: Germany agrees new measures aimed at reducing arrivals. *Independent*. http://www.independent.co.uk/news/world/europe/refugee-crisis-germany-agrees-new-measures-aimed-at-reducing-arrivals-a6851591.html. Accessed February 3, 2017.

Crenshaw, M., & Pimlott, J. (1997). *International encyclopedia of terrorism*. London: Fitzroy Dearborn Publishers.

Crisp, J. (2017, July). Belgian ban on Muslim full-face veil is legal, European Court of Human Rights Rules. *Telegraph*. http://www.telegraph.co.uk/news/2017/07/11/belgian-ban-full-face-veil-legal-european-court-human-rights/. Accessed July 11, 2017.

Cumming-Bruce, N. (2017, February). Switzerland votes to ease citizenship for third-generation immigrants. *New York Times*. https://www.nytimes.com/2017/02/12/world/europe/switzerland-citizenship-3rd-generation-referendum.html. Accessed February 12, 2017.

Davies, P., & Jackson, P. (2008). *The far right in Europe: An encyclopedia. Westport*. Connecticut: Greenwood World Press.

Dent, M. C., & Huang W. F. D. (2002). *Northeast Asian regionalism: Lessons from the European experience*. London: Routledge.

Dix, R. H. (1985). Populism: Authoritarian and democratic. *Latin American Research Review, 20*(2), 29–52.

Dunai, M. (2016, October). Hungary's Orban rejects 'Sovietization' by Brussels, defends nation state. *Reuters*. http://www.reuters.com/article/us-hungary-orban-idUSKCN12N0PJ. Accessed February 2, 2017.

Dutch MPs oppose headscarf proposal for Amsterdam police. (2017, May). *The express tribune*. https://tribune.com.pk/story/1414159/dutch-mps-oppose-headscarf-proposal-amsterdam-police/. Accessed May 20, 2017.

Dzankic, J., & Soeren, K. (2017). State-sponsored populism and the rise of populist governance: The Case of Montenegro. *Journal of Balkan and Near Eastern Studies, 19*(4), 403–418.

Engel, V. (2018). *Xenophobia, radicalism, and hate crime in Europe*. Moscow: Editus.

Erlanger, S. (2017a, June). For Britain, political stability is a Quaint Relic. *New York Times*. https://www.nytimes.com/2017/06/11/world/europe/britain-politics-theresa-may.html. Accessed June 12, 2017.

Erlanger, S. (2017b, March). E.U. is turning 60 and searching for something to celebrate. *The New York Times*. https://www.nytimes.com/2017/03/24/world/europe/eu-is-turning-60-and-searching-for-something-to-celebrate.html. Accessed June 12, 2017.

Europe's Rising Far Right: A Guide to the Most Prominent Parties. (2016, December). *The New York Times*. https://www.nytimes.com/interactive/2016/world/europe/europe-far-right-political-parties-listy.html. Accessed February 2, 2017.

European Union Agency for Fundamental Rights. (2018, June). Hate crime recording and data collection practice across the EU.

European Union Agency for Fundamental Rights. (2012, November). Hate crime in the European Union.

European Union Agency for Fundamental Rights. (2006, November). Current migration situation in the EU: Hate Crime.

Eurozone confident on Cyprus bailout. (2013, March). *BBC News business*. http://www.bbc.com/news/business-21655475. Accessed February 2, 2017.

Forster, K. (2016, November). Europe's new fascism? The far-right leaders hoping to take power in 2017. *Independent*. http://www.independent.co.uk/news/world/europe/marine-le-pen-geert-wilders-norbert-hofer-rise-of-fascism-europe-far-right-leaders-donald-trump-a7417276.html. Accessed August 2, 2017.

Fosnot, C. T. (2005). *Constructivism: Theory, perspectives, and practice*. New York: Teachers College Press.

Foster, P., Senay, B., & Barney, H. (2017, March). Dutch election result: Mark Rutte sees off Geert Wilders challenge as Netherlands rejects far-Right. *Telegraph*. http://www.telegraph.co.uk/news/2017/03/15/dutch-election-results-geert-wilders-andmark-rutte-vie-power/. Accessed March 16, 2017.
Frones, I. (2016). *The autonomous child: Theorising socialisation*. Cham: Springer.
Fukuyama, F. (2006). *The end of history and the last man*. New York: Simon and Schuster.
Galstan, W. A. (2018). *The rise of European populism and the collapse of the centre-left*. Brookings Institution.
Golder, M. (2016). Far right parties in Europe. *The Annual Review of Political Science, 19*, 477–497.
Grabow, K. (2016). PEGIDA and the Alternative für Deutschland: Two sides of the same coin? *European View, 15*(2), 173–181.
Griffin, R. (2000). Interregnum or endgame? The Radical Right in the 'post-fascist' Era. *Journal of Political Ideologies, 5*(2), 163–178.
Guide to nationalist parties challenging Europe. (2016, May). *BBC News*. http://www.bbc.com/news/world-europe-36130006. Accessed February 2, 2017.
Gutteridge, N. (2017, May 10). Populism isn't over' Eurocrats urged to rein in gloating over Macron victory. *Express*. http://www.express.co.uk/news/politics/802744/European-Union-Eurocrats-warned-populism-not-dead-despite-Macron-victory. Accessed January 2, 2018.
Hahnel, R. (2002). *The ABCs of Political Economy: A Modern Approach*. London: Pluto Press.
Hameleers, M. (2018). A typology of populism: Toward a revised theoretical framework on the sender side and receiver side of communication. *International Journal of Communication, 12*, 2171–2190.
Heffer, G. (2015, December). Switzerland defies EU diktat pledging to bring in immigration controls. *Express*. http://www.express.co.uk/news/politics/624326/Switzerland-EU-freedom-of-movement-immigration-migrant-crisis. Accessed February 2, 2017.
Hirschman, O. A. (1970). *Exit, voice, and loyalty: Responses to decline in firms, organizations, and states*. Cambridge: Massachusetts.
Hurrell, A. (1995). Regionalism in theoretical perspective. In L. Fawcett & A. Hurrell (Eds.), *Regionalism in World politics: Regional organisation and international order* (pp. 38–73). Oxford: Oxford University Press.
Janssen, J. (2017, January). Close-up: Geert wilders. *Berlin Policy Journal*. http://berlinpolicyjournal.com/close-up-geert-wilders/.jornhocke.html?mtrref=undefined&gwh=5E36432569613EFB24053FD1185DCDFA&gwt=pay.
Kallis, A. (2013). Breaking taboos and 'mainstreaming the extreme': The debates on restricting Islamic symbols in contemporary Europe. In R. Wodak, K. Majid, & M. Brigitte (Eds.), *Right-wing populism in Europe: Politics and discourse* (pp. 55–71). London: Bloomsbury.
Kaltwasser, C. R., Paul, T., Paulina, O. E., & Pierre, O. (2017). *The oxford handbook of populism*. Oxford: Oxford University Press.
Katsas, G. (2012). Anomie, social changes and dysfunctional socialisation. *ENCEPHALOS, 49*, 98–102.
Kelstrup, M. (2012). Denmark's relation to the European Union: A history of Dualism and Pragmatism. In L. Miles, & A. Wivel (Eds.), *Denmark and the European Union*. New York: Routledge.
Khan, M. (2018, March). New Dutch 'Nexit' party threatens Rutte. *Financial Times*. https://www.ft.com/content/98f94164-2cca-11e8-a34a-7e7563b0b0f4. Accessed September 20, 2018.
Krasteva, A. (2016). The Post-communist rise of National populism: Bulgarian paradoxes. In G. Lazaridis, G. Camoani, & A. Beneveniste (Eds.), *The rise of the far-right in Europe* (pp. 161–200). London: Palgrave Macmillan.
Liang, C. S. (2007). *Europe for the Europeans: The foreign and security policy of the populist radical right*. Aldershot, Hampshire: Ashgate.
Lidegaard, B. (2015, June). Denmark's far-right kingmakers. *New York Times*. https://www.nytimes.com/2015/06/22/opinion/denmarks-far-right-kingmakers.html. Accessed February 2, 2017.
Lopatka, J. (2016, October). Czech Finance Minister's Party wins Regional Elections. *Reuters*. http://www.reuters.com/article/us-czech-election-idUSKCN1280R7. Accessed October 9, 2016.

Markovi, N. (2017). *Muslim citizens in the West: Spaces and agents of inclusion and exclusion*. New York: Routledge.

Martinelli, A. (2016). *Populism on the rise: Democracies under challenge*. Milano: Italian Institute for International Political Studies.

McLellan, D. (1995). *Ideology*. Buckingham: Open University Press.

Melissa, E. (2017, May). Pro-Nazi soldiers in German Army raise alarm. *New York Times*. https://www.nytimes.com/2017/05/10/world/europe/germany-military-far-right-extremists-terror-plot-nazi.html. Accessed May 10, 2017.

Mentzer, T. J. (2001). *Supply chain management*. New Delhi: Sage Publications.

Milne, R. (2015, July). Denmark to cut immigrant benefits in half. *Financial Times*. https://www.ft.com/content/5fe8095c-1ffb-11e5-aa5a-398b2169cf79. Accessed June 2, 2017.

Mudde, C., & Kaltwasser, C. R. (2017). *Populism: A very short introduction*. Oxford: Oxford University Press.

Mudde, C. (1996). The war of words defining the extreme right party family. *West European Politics, 19*(2), 225–248.

Mudde, C. (2000). *The ideology of the extreme right*. Manchester: Manchester University Press.

Muller, J. W. (2016). *What is populism*. Pennsylvania: University of Pennsylvania Press.

Nwabuzo, O. (2014). *Racist crime in Europe ENAR shadow report 2013–2014*. Brussels: European Network against Racism.

O' Brien, T. (2016). Populism, protest and democracy in the twenty-first century. *Journal of the Academy of Social Sciences, 10*(4), 337–348.

Odmalm, P., & Hepburn, E. (2017). *The European mainstream and the populist radical right*. London: Routledge.

Ojeaku, N. (2014). *Racist crime in Europe ENAR Shadow Report 2013–2014*. Brussels: European Network Against Racism.

Oltermann, P. (2016, December). Austria rejects far-right candidate Norbert Hofer in presidential election. *The Guardian*. https://www.theguardian.com/world/2016/dec/04/far-right-party-concedes-defeat-in-austrian-presidential-election. Accessed December 5, 2016.

Pirro, A. L. P. (2015). *The populist radical right in Central and Eastern Europe: Ideology, impact, and electoral performance*. New York: Routledge.

Rankin, J., & Philip, O. (2017, March). Europe's right hails EU court's workplace headscarf ban ruling. *The Guardian*. https://www.theguardian.com/law/2017/mar/14/employers-can-ban-staff-from-wearing-headscarves-european-court-rules. Accessed March 14, 2017.

Rettman, A. (2015, June). Far-right parties form group in EU parliament. *Euobserver*. https://euobserver.com/political/129129. Accessed May 16, 2017.

Reus-Smit, C. (2005). Constructivism. In S. Burchill, D. Richard, L. Andrew, & P. Matthew (Eds.), *Theories of international relations*. New York: Palgrave Macmillan.

Reuters. (2017, April 27). German Lawmakers Aim to Impose Some Limits on Full-Face Veils. https://www.nytimes.com/2017/04/27/world/europe/germanyparliament-veils.html?mtrref=undefined&gwh=D69E5C1EEC1A46348D221B925F54505F&gwt=pay.

Rubin, J. A. (2017a, March). Netherlands considers a new relationship to Muslims with coming election. *New York Times*. https://www.nytimes.com/2017/03/13/world/europe/netherlands-election-muslims.html. Accessed March 13, 2017.

Rubin, J. A. (2017b, March). Geert Wilders Falls Short in Election, as Wary Dutch Scatter Their Votes. *New York Times*. https://www.nytimes.com/2017/03/15/world/europe/geert-wilders-netherlands-far-right-vote.html. Accessed March 15, 2017.

Rubin, J. A. (2017c, May). Angela Merkel's party scores big win in Key German state election. *New York Times*. https://www.nytimes.com/2017/05/14/world/europe/german-elections-angela-merkel-martin-schulz.html?emc=edit_th_20170515&nl=todaysheadlines&nlid=49519343&mtrref=undefined&mtrref=www.nytimes.com. Accessed May 14, 2017.

Rubin, J. A. (2017d, May). Emmanuel Macron Is inaugurated as France's President. *New York Times*. https://www.nytimes.com/2017/05/14/world/europe/emmanuel-macron-inauguration-france.html. Accessed May 14, 2017.

Rubin, J. A. (2017e, May). Macron decisively defeats Le Pen in French presidential race. *The New York Times*. https://www.nytimes.com/2017/05/07/world/europe/emmanuel-macron-france-election-marine-le-pen.html. Accessed May 7, 2017.
Ruzza, C. (2017). Populism and euroscepticism: Towards uncivil society. *Journal of Policy and Society, 28*(1), 87–98.
Sakellartou, A. (2015). Golden dawn and its appeal to greek youth. *Friedrich Ebert Stiftung Perspective*, July, 1–19.
Sandford, A. (2017, December). Rise of populism in Europe 'a real threat to democracy. *Euronews*. http://www.euronews.com/2017/12/29/rise-of-populism-in-europe-a-real-threat-to-democracy. Accessed December 29, 2017.
Şandru, D. (2013). The ideological components of populism. In G. Sergiu, M. Sergiu, & S. Sorina (Eds.), *Contemporary populism: A Controversial concept and its diverse forms* (pp. 53–83). Newcastle: Cambridge Scholars Publishing.
Sargent, L. T. (2009). *Contemporary political ideologies*. Mexico: Wadsworth Cengage Learning.
Schopflin, G. (2015). Europe: An epistemological crisis. In J. Jody & M. Ferenc (Eds.), *Reframing Europe's future: Challenges and failures of the European construction* (pp. 7–15). New York: Routledge.
Selby, J. A. (2014). France. In J. Cesari (Ed.), *The oxford handbook of European Islam* (pp. 23–64). Oxford: Oxford University Press.
Sen, I. (2015, January). Greeks have handed a huge election win to a far-left anti-austerity party. *Quartz*. https://qz.com/332995/greece-syriza-anti-austerity-far-left-party-has-swept-elections/. Accessed August 12, 2017.
Shuster, S. (2017, January). Europe's far-right leaders unite at Dawn of the Trump Era. *TIME*. http://time.com/4643051/donald-trump-european-union-koblenz/. Accessed August 12, 2017.
Skolkay, A. (2000). Populism in Central Eastern Europe. *Thinking Fundamentals, 9*(10), 77–103.
Smale, A. (2016, December). Angela Merkel Calls for Ban on Full-Face Veils in Germany. *New York Times*. https://www.nytimes.com/2016/12/06/world/europe/merkel-calls-for-ban-on-full-face-veils-in-germany.html?emc=edit_th_20161207&nl=todaysheadlines&nlid=49519343. Accessed August 27, 2017.
Smith, A. D. (1992). National identity and the idea of European Unity. *International Affairs, 68*(1), 55–76.
Stone, J. (2017, September). German elections: Far-right wins MPs for first time in half a century. *Independent*. https://www.independent.co.uk/news/world/politics/german-election-results-exit-poll-2017-live-latest-afd-mps-merkel-alternative-a7964796.html. Accessed September 24, 2018.
Stratfor. (2013, July 18). Hungary seeks a multidimensional foreign policy. https://www.stratfor.com/geopolitical-diary/hungary-seeks-multidimensional-foreignpolicy.
Szczerbiak, A., & Taggart, P. (2008). 'Theorizing party-based Euroscepticism': Problems of Definition, measurement and causality. In A. Szczerbiak & P. Taggart (Eds.), *Opposing Europe?: The comparative party politics of euroscepticism* (pp. 225–230). Oxford: Oxford University Press.
Taub, A., & Fisher, M. (2017, January). Germany's extreme right challenges guilt over Nazi Past. *New York Times*. Retrieved from https://www.nytimes.com/2017/01/18/world/europe/germany-afd-alternative-b.
Taylor, J. P., & Flint, C. (2000). Locality politics. In P. J. Taylor & C. Flint (Eds.), *Political geography, world economy, nation-state and locality*. Pearson Education Limited: Patparganj Delhi.
Tharoor, I. (2018, March). Italy's election is another blow to the European establishment. *Washington Post*. www.washingtonpost.com/news/worldviews/wp/2018/03/05/italys-election-is-another-blow-to-the-european-establishment/?noredirect=on&utm_term=.9bb6b93b598f. Accessed March 5, 2018.
Tillerson, C. (2017). *The alt-right a reference for the far-right political movement*. Morrisville, North Carolina: Lulu Press.
Topaloff, K. L. (2012). *Political parties and euroscepticism*. New York: Palgrave Macmillan.

Traynor, I. (2009, November). Swiss vote to ban construction of Minarets on Mosques. *The Guardian*. https://www.theguardian.com/world/2009/nov/29/switzerland-bans-mosque-minarets. Accessed March 5, 2018.
Van Leeuwen, J. (2006). *Towards a radical right Europe? A theory for the explanation of the success of Radical Right Populist Parties in North-Western Europe*. Lund: Lund University Press.
Vasilopoulou, S. (2011). European integration and the radical right: Three patterns of opposition. *Government and Opposition, 46*(2), 223–244.
Viviani, L. (2017). A political sociology of populism and leadership. *SOCIETÀMUTAMENTOPOLITICA, 8*(15), 279–303.
Vorlander, H., Maik, H., & Steven, S. (2016). *PEGIDA and New Right-Wing populism in Germany*. Cham: Palgrave Macmillan.
Vossen, K. (2017). *The power of populism: Geert Wilders and the party for Freedom in the Netherlands*. New York: Routledge.
Wallace, W. (1990). *The transformation of Western Europe*. London: Pinter.
What does Alternative for Germany (AfD) want?. (2016, September). *BBC News*. http://www.bbc.com/news/world-europe-37274201. Accessed August 13, 2018.
Why are thousands of Germans protesting and who are Pegida?. (2015, January). *BBC Newsbeat*. http://www.bbc.co.uk/newsbeat/article/30694252/why-are-thousands-of-germansprotesting-and-who-are-pegida. Accessed August 13, 2017.

Europe in Times of Crisis

The Resilient Governance of the EU: Towards a Post-democratic Society

Marco Baldassari

> *"The euro is more than just a currency. It is a political and economic project"*
> Jean-Claude Juncker

1 Resilience and Market Adaptation

The buzz word "resilience" (like "sustainability", "good governance", and "accountability") belongs to the EU vocabulary and is part of a consolidated neoliberal discourse that shapes and drives the public choices at the European level. The keyword resilience can be found in numerous official European Commission documents and finds application in various areas and sectors of transnational public intervention (Baldassari et al. 2017). Resilience, for example, is the guiding principle of the EU external action and a part of the new approach towards neighbouring countries. It is a key term for renewable energy systems and for environmental protection. It is used in documents dealing with education infrastructures, in the urban sector, as well as for conceptualising "smart cities". In the economic epistemic discourse, resilience is conceived as the adaptability to the external shocks, i.e. a constant concern of the post-modern institutions, such as the EU, linked with the new risk and conflict management. In particular, this paper will focus on the political use of the term resilience in times of crisis, applied to the new Euro governance.

The EU Commission defines "resilience" as "the capacity of societies, communities, and individuals to manage opportunities and risks in a peaceful and stable manner, and to build, maintain, or restore livelihoods in the face of major pressures"

M. Baldassari (✉)
The European College of Parma Foundation, Parma, Italy
e-mail: m.baldassari@collegioeuropeo.it

© Springer Nature Switzerland AG 2020

M. Baldassari et al. (eds.), *Anti-Europeanism*,
https://doi.org/10.1007/978-3-030-24428-6_5

(European Commission 2015).[1] Therefore, it must be highlighted that a key requirement of the European governance is a demand for a constant adaptation through the managing of a negative situation by absorbing it in a variety of different sectors and situations. Moreover, as it has been shown by several studies (Jessop 2006, 2016; Georgakakis 2017), the technical language used in public administrations is not neutral and it reflects, especially in the recursive use of certain expressions, a number of doctrines, ideologies, scientific and social fields (Bourdieu 2014) which constitute the product of power relations, an hegemonic logic (Laclau 2003), power discourse (Foucault 1981), or strategic-relational dimension. (Jessop 2014, 2016). The epistemic communities and the scientific discourse, as well as the public authority, are not neutral. We can find many interconnections with politics. For instance, the term resilience has been used since the late 1990s and 2000s to manage society as an organic body, with the attempt to "naturalise", or normalise political relations (Chandler 2012). Resilience, in the same way as the term "functionalism" (a grand theory conceived as a guiding doctrine of EU integration), is borrowed from natural sciences, readapted for social sciences, and then transferred to politics.

As Jonathan Joseph pointed out, the concept of resilience could be interpreted ideally through the lens of a neoliberal form of governance. We find this path of research and reading the governmental character of the EU and its political jargon as a neoliberal discourse particularly interesting to follow. For instance, the adaptive behaviour and the capacity of the system to tolerate shocks enshrine "the ability of people to adapt to changing conditions through learning, planning, or reorganisation" (Joseph 2013: 39).[2] We can find the same key elements in EU policy-making: individual adaptation, self-responsibility (for private citizens as well for the states), and the capacity to change by "being flexible". Adaptation to the market forces, as well as to external shocks, is essential for this dynamic institutional framework. Therefore, the institutionalisation of the market—or the marketisation of the state—should be the guiding principle of a new conception of public management. Power should progressively abandon its rigidity and the typical counterbalances, ideologies, "thick" constitutional elements, claims of legitimacy, and hierarchies linked to a classical liberal institutional construction. Power should move to a neoliberal self-regulation of a spreading web of differentiated functions. For this reason, the dynamic nature of the European Union needs to find a constant adaptability and sustain a continuous negotiating effort with its partners, be they the Member States, or the so-called stakeholders or social agents, who must be continuously involved in the decision-making process. This, as we will try to demonstrate, is not always an advantage from the standpoint of a genuine process of democratisation, but rather a depoliticisation of the decision-making process (De Nardis 2017: 39). Joseph correctly argues that "part of this process is the neoliberal assault on the institutions of the post-war settlement and the promotion of the norms and values of the market as a means of destatification.

[1]EU Commission Brussels, 7. 6. 2017 JOIN(2017) 21 final JOINT COMMUNICATION TO THE EUROPEAN PARLIAMENT AND THE COUNCIL A Strategic Approach to Resilience in the EU's external action.

[2]See also the World Resource Institute, *World Resources 2008: Roots of Resilience*.

[…] Neoliberalism's promotion of free market norms is therefore much more than the simple ideology of free-market economics. It is a specific form of social rule that institutionalises a rationality of competition, enterprise individualised responsibility" (Joseph 2013: 39). EU institutions are part of this process, based on the social market economy and competitive ordoliberal model of society, bringing the *pouvoir-Europe* (Joly 2017) towards a de-nationalisation of the *function-publique*. This de-nationalisation pushes towards the resizing of distributive policies which gave primacy—during the "glorious years" of the capitalism system—to the elimination of social disparities. The resilient governance is one of the pillars of the hybrid and dynamic nature of the European Union, the objective of which is to regulate markets by making the society and the state adaptable to them (Somma 2017). Several scholars and practitioners have traced this complex institutional system back to an ordoliberal matrix (Dardot and Laval 2013). For example, it should not be ignored that the social market economy has profoundly influenced the construction of the community, contributing to "constitutionalise" an authority that contains the features of a regulatory state (Majone 2014), non-interventionist and adaptable to the market logic, embedding at the same time high competitiveness and social cohesion. The dynamism and the variable character of the Union has been identified by Leo Tindemans, who in the Seventies was the first to speak about a "differentiated Europe", in order to emphasise the impossibility of proceeding linearly at the same speed towards a single model of political unity (i.e. the federalist idea of the United States of Europe). The need to conceive Europe as a "variable geometry" or as "concentric circles" was also advanced by one of the most important political figures for the EU, Jacques Delors, the forerunner of what is now called multi-speed Europe.

Differentiated integration is, according to A. Stubb, "a model of integration strategies that tries to reconcile heterogeneity within the European Union and allows different groupings of Member States to pursue an array of public policies with different procedural and institutional arrangements" (Stubb 1996: 283). Therefore, the only way to bring this heterogeneity back—the impossibility to adopt a "one-size-fits-all" approach—is to assume the resilience as a founding principle of post-crisis Europe. To conclude, differentiated or flexible integration, disintegration or re-integration are the new paradigms for a conception of a multifaceted system of governance (Schmitter and Lefkofridi 2016; Hooghe and Marks 2008; Zielonka 2014). Bob Jessop has correctly described the latter as a strategic-relational dimension of a new form of statehood conceived as a "multispatial metagovernance". This institutional fragmentation is a consequence of the post-sovereign systems that are modifying the state and the role of the state in the economic field, as we will see later in this paper.

2 The External "Resilient Constraint" of the Euro

The Five Presidents' report, published in June 2015 by Jean-Claude Juncker in cooperation with other apical figures of the EU institutions, represents a decisive cornerstone in the acknowledgement of the strategy on how to ameliorate the integration process. Such process suffered not only from the abrupt halt caused by the economic and political crisis, but also from the frequent jumbled intergovernmental bargaining required by the adoption of extraordinary measures to face the crisis. The Five Presidents' strategic report and the further documents issued by the European Commission are extremely important to understand the strategy towards the so-called management of the crisis. First of all, it is worth providing an introduction of what the "external constraint" entails, its implications, and the critical positions about it. In Italy, one of the first scholars who have developed a critical legal analysis of it, linked to the euro system, is Giuseppe Guarino, Minister of Finance in 1987 and Minister of Industry in 1992–93. The Italian jurist moved from a pro-European position to a substantially negative commentary about the evolution of the European construction. He indicates 1999 as the date of an "obscure *coup d'État*", the year in which the EC Regulation 1466/97[3] was approved. This was the first community act introducing the imposition of a medium-term balanced budget constraint (apparently incompatible with the provisions of the Maastricht Treaty). It was an act which, according to Guarino, represented an unprecedented usurpation of sovereignty through a "fraudulent cunning". This fraudulency consisted in: 1. The tacit violation of the constitutional law of the Member States. 2. The limitation of sovereignty, by means of the misappropriation of the "exclusive" function to promote the development of the EU through the economic policies of the Member States. 3. The imposition of obligations on the Member States that their constitutions do not provide.

In other words, starting from the introduction of Reg. 1466/97 the possibilities for a Member State to effectively implement economic policies were gradually weakened. How does this process actually work? Simply through the abrogation by the law of the possibility for a state to resort to debt. "The target of growth was substituted with the achievement of the medium-term balanced budget" (Guarino 2014: 47). To a certain extent, Guarino can even refer to a "fake-Euro", as the monetary union deranged from the original provision of the Treaties. He argued that "the Euro has cancelled the powers and the means that States usually used to produce development. The problem lies in the fact that this regulation did not replace them with more powers and resources" (Guarino ibid.). Although such reasoning tends to a "*reductio ad unum*" and to a sort of an "original sin" inherent to the (dubious) incompatibility of the derived act with the provisions of the Treaty (i.e. with primary law), the analysis—from a pro-European perspective—is interesting because it can grasp precisely the contradictory aspects of the post-Maastricht European construction. In fact, the rigidity of the Stability Pact—later modified with Euro Plus—may lead to the implicit condemnation and to a possible disintegration of the European project itself (see Zielonka 2014).[4] In my view, the main contradiction lies in having accelerated the construction of governance, insisting on the primacy of the "M" of EMU, the monetary part, without adequately having provided the "E", the economic part, "the means to produce development". The European legislators have considered it

[3]COUNCIL REGULATION (EC) No 1466/97 of 7 July 1997 on the strengthening of the surveillance of budgetary positions and the surveillance and coordination of economic policies.

[4]See for the notion of "disintegration" Zielonka (2014).

as a natural outcome, achieved through an incremental method: a closer economic policy coordination. However, these fundamental economic policy instruments are still lacking and, in any case, they cannot be truly put in the framework of what Marcello Degni and Paolo De Ioanna have rightly described as the "episteme of the corporate-legal order" (Degni and De Ioanna 2019: 29, my translation). What is lacking—and almost incompatible with the Treaties, in the end—is a real mutualisation of debts through an effective federal budget, a deficit spending capacity (especially in economic conjunctures that require anti-cyclical policies) and a re-launch of a neo-Keynesian industrial plan on a continental scale (a sort of European New Deal). Not only does the adoption of these tools collide with Member States' resistance to "transfer" sovereignty to supranational institutions in specific sectors, but it is also at odds with the same DNA of the European construction, the economic pillars of which rely on ordoliberalism and monetarism.[5] The latter is not simply doctrinal expressions. They also concretely indicate the economic governance choices that are at the core of the "structural reforms" (Mitchell and Fazi 2017). These doctrines assume the "economic reality" as something objectively "natural" and "neutral": a presumed objectivity founded on the centrality of the competitive markets as the main tool for growth and employment, by ensuring the control of price stability (the "supply-side" economic doctrine). On the contrary, these elements, falsely considered as scientifically "neutral" and "objective", respond to a specific axiological system and refer to precise ordoliberal values. They are principles that are "almost-constitutionalised" and to which "full employment", solidarity, and social justice are subordinated. Moreover, these techno-political choices lead inevitably to a deconsolidation of "economic democracy", in the sense that the executive and the judicial side will be accentuated to the detriment of participatory democracy and redistribution policies. This is to be accompanied by a growing weakening of the welfare systems. Guarino (1997: 85) noticed: "the level of implementation of the welfare state, along with the productive potential of the country's system and the quality of life, was the superb result of the policy of the past decades. This fruit is going to dry out today under the pressure of convergence measures" (my translation).

This new "economic constitution" works on a variable geometry and on a multi-level system of governance. It seems to act as a kind of "automatic pilot" and it is based on the fundamental assumption that the Member States must be highly limited in resorting to the increase of public spending. Therefore, they are impeded from using debt leverage for investment in order to stimulate aggregate demand. But we should not forget that even the EU is not allowed to resort to similar counter-cyclical policies. The EU cannot operate in that way first of all because it has no real competences in the fiscal domain, but even in the future it would not be able to do that. This is so because the ECB's statutorily independent position is bound to the exclusive task of price stability and, secondarily, because the financing resources and the budget are not even to be conceived as instruments for the equalisation of incomes

[5] See for an excellent historical reconstruction of the ordoliberal economic and juridical thought and its influence in Europe, Somma (2014).

among the Member States, and therefore, as we will see, they are always subject to the convergence objectives.

Further confirmation of the contradictions within the EMU was detected even by the former Vice President of the ECB, Vítor Constâncio. The ECB's economist pointed out that mainstream interpretations of the euro crisis were completely insufficient. They frequently tend to remove the structural problems of the euro and explain the Euro-system malfunctioning only through the lens of the lacking convergence between the Member States, i.e. with the fact that they do not respect the Stability Pact and they have accumulated large debts (Constâncio 2013). Therefore, from these mainstream considerations, it follows that it is necessary to consolidate primarily national budgets, especially those of PIGS countries. However, as the economic literature largely confirms, there is not a direct correlation between the respect of the Stability Pact before the crisis and the financial performances required today (Bagnai 2016; Cesaratto 2018; Stiglitz 2016). For example, Germany and France did not respect the parameters in 2002–03, while Spain and Ireland respected them up to 2007, but the excessive deficit procedure was not launched.

Constâncio argued that in the early years of the Euro there was not a significant rise in public debt in those states that are now under pressure, such as Spain and Greece. It is therefore first of all necessary to adopt a new narrative of the crisis, which does not identify the public debt as the primary problem. We can conclude that the crisis is not a problem of the public budget, but of private expenditure and cross-border bank activities, i.e. it concerns the relationship between commercial and credit imbalances between the core areas and peripheral ones. The problem therefore relies on these asymmetries determined by the German mercantilism (i.e. external credit to Greece to dope its demand and internal social dumping, with the Hartz reforms) that cannot be solved simply by appealing to greater competitive efforts by those Member States that are currently in difficulty.

Moreover, these structural problems of the EMU are not separated from the democratic question and from the effective exercise of popular sovereignty. Although in the EU system, the fundamental freedoms of movement and circulation are still guaranteed—despite increasing difficulties—they still remain "negative" freedoms: while they are indeed necessary, they cannot be sufficient. Furthermore, the liberal representative democratic framework appears less and less effective and purely formal. It now becomes difficult for citizens to be really part of the decision-making process, since the people and political participation are dissolving in a post-democratic regulatory system enshrined in a self-mirroring spectator society. On this point, I agree with Colin Crouch's thesis on post-democracy described as the exhaustion of the welfare-parable (Crouch 2004). This represents the "divorce" between capitalism and democracy, the break-up of the pact between capital and labour and the realisation of what Friedrich Hayek advocated in the 30s: democratic choices should not interfere with market forces.

3 The Strategic Ordoliberal Reform for a Self-founded (Post)Democracy

The Five Presidents' report "Completing the EMU" is a long-term vision (2025) for a reconsideration of the European project. The strategy paper is the result of the encounter of the apical élite representatives of the EU: Jean-Claude Junker, President of the European Commission, Donald Tusk, President of the European Council, Jeroen Dijsselbloem, President of the Euro Group, Martin Schulz, President of the European Parliament, and Mario Draghi, President of the European Central Bank. It entails an ambitious project towards the completion of the EMU, integrated progressively in a wider multiple-dimensional system of unions. The institutional origins of this document could be traced back to the 2011 Euro Plus Pact on stronger economic policy coordination for competitiveness and convergence,[6] which set the basis for strengthening the control on the budgetary procedures of the Member States by adding a mechanism of sanctions. The weakness of the Euro Plus Pact consisted in its "intergovernmental" character and in the fact that the scope of the new plan is to bring the entire process within the realm of the so-called Community method (thus, giving the monopoly of the legislative initiative to the truly supranational institution: the European Commission, in co-decision with EP and the Council). In the Five Presidents' opinion, the "community method", at the very base of the European integration process, suffered, during the crisis management period, from a "lack of application", due to the urgency of the measures to be adopted. The strategy was a kick-off proposal to be implemented and properly institutionalised with a white paper that the commission issued in 2017, followed by the six reflection papers, which completed the strategy.

The core of the plan is the assumption that the Euro, or the Monetary Union, is not simply a currency, but it represents a political project and the highest level of integration reached so far. The crucial point is in fact the typical ordoliberal synthesis, in which the "economic" moment is not disjointed from the "political" one. Therefore, the European construction is not something purely economic (the "Europe of markets and banks", against the "Europe of peoples", as something to realise). It is not "economic integration" that is lacking—or awaiting—its political and democratic realisation. The "market" *is* political, according to ordoliberal thinking. It is an order founded not merely on the principle of free market, considered as a self-sufficient, autonomous, and independent interplay of forces and interests, but rather a system in which the spirit of competitiveness, together with a state and institutional regulation, can build up a *society*, a community in which the idea of "market" is enshrined. In a rhetorical discourse, the EMU is perceived as a vehicle for growth and progress, even though it must be considered not an end in itself, but a piece of the "constitution" of the Political Union.

---

[6]The "Blueprint for a Deep and Genuine EMU" of 2012 remains an essential reference for completing the EMU as well as the Analytical Note "Preparing for Next Steps on Better Economic Governance in the Euro Area" of 12 February 2015.

> Europe's Economic and Monetary Union (EMU) today is like a house that was built over decades but only partially finished. When the storm hit, its walls and roof had to be stabilised quickly. It is now high time to reinforce its foundations and turn it into what EMU was meant to be: a place of prosperity based on balanced economic growth and price stability, a competitive social market economy, aiming at full employment and social progress. To achieve this, we will need to take further steps to complete EMU.[7]

In this excerpt, we can find all the key concepts linked to the European ideology: the EMU as a "common house" to be built through a functionalist approach, an incremental view of the gradual approximation to the fullness of the political moment. A "place of prosperity", which is based on (1) "price stability", the obsession of the control of the inflation; (2) "competition", between individuals and between the Member States; (3) "full employment". The latter appears only once in the whole document,[8] but it is interesting, because a "Keynesian" reference formally remains, even though it is subordinated to the first element, and clearly in contrast with the second. In fact, it seems extremely difficult to achieve "full employment" while at the same time upholding the competitive principle, which does not necessarily imply an increase in the number of jobs, but rather their reduction and a pressure on wages. The technological lever of the R&D in this respect can only work in the short run, and it appears optimistic that it will spontaneously generate growth, as private enterprises firstly aim at the maximisation of profits, not at a general "social progress".

After having pointed out the aim of the EMU, the document focuses on the problem of the "crisis management". Of course, the language is important. Using the word "management" does not imply an idea of "overcoming" the crisis. Unconsciously (and perfectly in line with Marx's thought), the crisis is considered as a consubstantial element of capitalism in itself. But the idea of "change" is transposed into the idea of "resilience" and adaptability. How should the Member States manage the crisis?

> First, through high quality governance at European and national level, sustainable fiscal and economic policies, and fair and efficient public administrations. Second, they must be able to absorb shocks internally through having suitably resilient economies and sufficient fiscal buffers over the economic cycle. This is because, with monetary policy set uniformly for the whole Euro area, national fiscal policies are vital to stabilise the economy whenever a local shock occurs. And with all countries sharing a single exchange rate, they need flexible economies that can react quickly to downturns. Otherwise they risk that recessions leave deep and permanent scars.[9]

The notions of "flexible economies" and "resilient economies" imply a new concept of European capitalism, based on the assumption that the institutionalisation process is not a mere reflection of the mode of production and a passive subject in the hands of a transnational class. The Eurocratic élite has its own role in building a capitalist structure through the European discourse and does so by inventing a new form of state-building (even if we cannot properly speak neither of a "state" in the

[7]Report "Completing Europe's Economic and Monetary Union": https://ec.europa.eu/priorities/sites/beta-political/files/5-presidents-report_en.pdf, p. 4.

[8]The word "convergence" compares 28 times, "competitiveness" 46 times and "resilience" 8 times.

[9]Ibidem.

classical form, nor of a "super-state", which is not the case of the European Union). The European discourse—through the speech of the Five Presidents—reinvents a new "assemblage" of states and their roles. "Economies" must be resilient: solid, but responding quickly to the "guidelines" and recommendations of Brussels, capable of adjusting to macroeconomic imbalances and to autonomously face local shocks, without waiting for a financial intervention from the top. The best way is then to fully accept the rule of "benchmarking" competition, for individuals, as well as for the states.

This "institutional innovation" is revealed, for example, through the intent to create a new system of "competitiveness authorities", by establishing the rule that what is decided in Brussels should be then implemented at the national level. Since national apparatuses are often inadequate to pursue the scope of Europeanisation, these new bodies should sustain their activities through a system of controls and monitoring. One of the principal aims of these authorities is to "assess whether wages are evolving in line with productivity". This is particularly tricky, since macroeconomic data show that they progressively diverge, as the wage quota is subordinated to productivity and to the market rule. So, wage deflation is the key element of policy-making based on the interplay of competitiveness with other countries, as the best wage performances must be achieved through the confrontation with the "developments in other Euro area countries and in the main comparable trading partners". This comparison is based on fixing benchmarks and measuring the degree of competitiveness, taking for granted that it is possible to guarantee growth and technological progress only by creating a functioning market as a struggle between competitors.

What is important to notice is this particular multilevel institutional articulation. The aim of the "competitiveness authorities" is neither to "harmonise" the national legislation, nor to define a common "wage policy". This task would be almost impossible, since the social and labour sectors are still largely ruled by the nation-state. The new European approach on harmonisation is not to impose a common rule, or the standardisation of the production processes, commercial regulation, etc., at the European level (the "vertical" approach was already abandoned in the Eighties.). Rather, the new system is based on the subsidiarity principle that considers the national level as an integral and active part of the system. According to this conception, national bodies are not unresponsive subjects, but they are constantly involved. The new system is based on a common template shared by the Member States and prepared by the European institutions. This template leaves a certain margin to countries, but it only regards the "means", while the "end" is rigidly fixed.

> Each Member State should decide the exact set-up of its national Competitiveness Authority, but they should be democratically accountable and operationally independent. National actors, such as social partners, should continue to play their role according to the established practices in each Member State, but they should use the opinions of the Authorities as guidance during wage setting negotiations.[10]

The point is to maintain a simulacrum of formal democracy, but under the condition that it must be an "embedded democracy", which subsumes the ordoliberal

[10]Ivi, p. 8.

"guidance" and the principles of unavoidable convergences criteria: "the notion of convergence is at the heart of our Economic Union: convergence between the Member States towards the highest levels of prosperity; and convergence within European societies, to nurture our unique European model". Therefore, we can conclude that the grammar of democracy is re-written in this new "convergence" framework. The democratic claims have to be managed by the Member States, which can remain the phantoms (or the wrecks) of democracy, the field in which it is possible to play the old liberal game of elections, representations, party system, electoral campaigns, etc. Even though it is impossible to modify the entire framework of the Treaties, the "*Grundnorm*" of the European construction as it was settled in the ordoliberal framework (that is, a governance with an automatic pilot) cannot be put into discussion neither by the people nor by politics. As some authors have pointed out, we are experiencing, in this new post-democratic system, a sort of "bureaucratic caesarism" (see Durand and Keucheyan 2015).

4 Strengthening the Macroeconomic Imbalance Procedure and Flexicurity

The way to create a vast competitive field in the Euro-zone must be achieved through a rigid control system, i.e. the implementation of the so-called (MIP) macroeconomic imbalance procedure, a part of the device of surveillance settled with the European semester (the *ex-ante* control procedure concerning the national budgets). The scope of the MIP is, first of all, to ensure and foster "structural reforms" and, second, to avoid the intervention of the state in financial crisis situations, by decoupling public risk from private risk (i.e. to prevent the state dealing with the market failures). These two aims are crucial. Firstly, "structural reforms" mean more flexible labour market, privatisations of services and capital liberalisations, as well as wage pressure containment. Secondly, decoupling the risk means that national governments, even by popular demand, should not substantially interfere with the EU political decision-making, where it is acting to preserve and build the competitive market dimension.

The response is always to promote "efficient labour market" which means, in neoliberal language, to convert national collective labour contracts into individual bargaining, by reducing the trade unions to "*mitbestimmung*" agencies and, consequently, achieving the full adaptation of the labour to the market forces. The prescription is well known: "striking the right balance between flexible and secure labour contracts; avoiding the division between 'insiders' with high protection and wages and 'outsiders'; shifting taxes away from labour; delivering tailored support for the unemployed to re-enter the labour market, improving education and lifelong learning". This is also confirmed by the Reflection paper that states the necessity of "building resilience through better sharing of benefits and promotion of long-term competitiveness [...] Even if Europe already has the most equal and inclusive societies in the world, we need to continuously *strengthen* and *adapt* our policies for the future and address inequalities through fair and modern tax policies. A modern and effective labour market should *facilitate access* for all to the job market".[11] One of the most frequent instruments used by the EU institutions is "benchmarking", by activating a sort of comparison and adaptation to the "best practices" among the Member States. For example by highlighting that "Germany's dual vocational training ensures that students learn the skills that are really needed by companies", or that "the Scandinavian flexicurity welfare state model strikes a balance between flexible job markets and secure transitions between jobs", or "the use of digital technology has enabled Estonia to come top in the EU Member States ranking in the OECD's programme for international student assessment (PISA)". The active ageing programme is one of the best examples of this ideology: the aged must continue to "learn" and be actively involved in order to support legislations that increase the retiring levels. But the more advanced strategy about labour policy in the EU is the well known "flexicurity"—a perfect ordoliberal synthesis of "competition" and "cohesion". The flexibility of the labour market remains, of course, the key element, but it is combined with "security", even though the concept is completely overturned by modifying the original social-democratic meaning linked to the economic stability, fair level of wage, and permanent work. The new meaning of "security" is turned into an idea of stability that guarantees only the "conditions" of employability, thus the emphasis is now put on employability and not on employment as such. Flexicurity deals with conditions that are embedded in the valorisation of the individual "human capital". Everybody should treat him or herself not as a part of the collective workforce, or as an element of the society, but rather as an "individual enterprise" that must improve its capacities and skills and should ameliorate its performance. This leads to imagine society not as a collective body, but as a collection of isolated individuals free to move in the flat market society in which the worker is plunged. Therefore, society does not exist as a whole (Margaret Thatcher *docet*), a proper "community" does not exist and there is no common collectively oriented horizon. Individuals should not—as in the Italian Constitution, for example—contribute, independently by their talent and capacities, to the wellness of the entire society. Consequently, it is not necessary to set programmatic provisions to remove the economic obstacles of the inequalities (see Barra Caracciolo 2015; Giacché 2015). On the contrary, individuals must act autonomously, pursuing their economic interest. First of all, in the European ordoliberal construction, one has to 'emerge' and think about maximising one's "human capital"; the role of the institutions then is simply to clear the field, to create a social opened dimension that puts individuals in the best position to operate in the free market (you have to be educated, therefore there must be a lifelong learning programme to guarantee the adaptation of your skills to the technological progress of the market; you have to be free to circulate in order to guarantee labour mobility and movement to the areas in which capital concentrations need your work; you should be against national labour contracts because it hinders smart and more suitable individual solutions, etc.). Of course, a safety social net, in order to create what is called the "cohesion policy", and a "social protection floor" are provided as a last resort

[11] European Commission Reflection Paper on harnessing globalisation, COM (2017) 240 final.

(and possibly privatised), but the crucial point is to de-link "employment" from the "deficit spending" policy, and therefore to minimise the role of the nation-state in the economy, as a possible key player for the investments and long-term industrial plans, etc.). The nation-state is reduced to a decentralised vehicle of the supranational "bureaucratic ceasarism".

Another point that could not be ignored is then the question of the "statehood". This does not mean that the state has disappeared, or that we should consider it simply the realisation of the Hayekian theory of the "minimal state" (with the market substituting the state). We are rather moving to a sort of regulatory state (Majone 2014), which is a new form of statehood without the state, functionally articulated in a multilevel system of governance. With regard to this, it is interesting to consider the analysis carried out by Bob Jessop, who argued that the EU is moving towards a *multi-scalar metagovernance in the shadow of postnational statehood* (Jessop 2006). He suggested a sort of "third way" in the interpretation of the nature of the EU, neither a supranational entity that subsumes nationalities, nor a mere intergovernmental bargaining between Member States, but a system of interconnections capable of creating new forms of "state-building" out of the classical frameworks. In this sense, the notion of "ideology" remains, to a certain extent, still important and functional to this institutional "invention", which cannot be reduced simply to the Foucaultian idea of "governmentality" or technocracy.

5 Formalising the Convergence Process with a Multiple "Union"

In order to complete and formalise the "convergence" and "resilience" process, the strategy of the Five Presidents' document is to tie up together the four dimensions of the EU (the Monetary Union, the Financial Union, the Fiscal Union, and the Political Union): all these functional spaces should be conceived as a unique system, in which the Market is the political fundamental of politics itself, as they are self-determined by the inner logic of the combination of sharing sovereignty and supranational dimension. Therefore, the Monetary Union could not be thought without the macroeconomic coordination. It could not be separated from a truly common financial framework, which embraces first of all a Banking Union, which is a decisive cornerstone of the entire system. "Completing the Banking Union requires first and foremost the full transposition into national law of the Bank Resolution and Recovery Directive by all Member States. This is crucial for sharing risk with the private sector. Indeed, the Banking Union is a way to better protect taxpayers from the cost of bank rescues".[12] The Banking Union is based on three pillars: a single supervisory mechanism (an instrument for a preventive control of the "non-performing loans" of the banks), a single resolution mechanism (a device for the bail-in and intervention when bankruptcy occurs) and a deposit scheme (a sort of a common European

[12]Report *Completing Europe's Economic and Monetary Union*, p. 11.

insurance, in case of emergency). The entire system should not foresee neither a state intervention, nor a proper European intervention. A "backstop should be fiscally neutral over the medium term by ensuring that public assistance is recouped by means of ex-post levies on the financial industry".[13] So apparently the costs of the "market failures" rely on the private sector. The purpose is to break-up with the "sovereign-bank nexus" at national level, in order to avoid the involvement of the State in the financial rescue for the insolvency of the private banks, according to the free-market principle. The point, anyway, is that this system does not impede the basic functioning of the capitalist logic: "privatisation of profits and socialisation of costs". The scope is to share the "public risk" with the "private risk". In addition to the "divorce" from the state by its Central Bank—already achieved in the Eighties (in Italy, for instance, in the 1981 with the former Minister of Treasure Beniamino Andreatta)—the next step will be to entirely separate the national bank system from the state intervention, reputed as a sort of "state aid", incompatible with the competition law settled in the Treaty (the recent Etruria case is a very pertinent example). At any rate, the "socialisation of costs" operates at a higher level with the Banking Union, since every money saver is directly involved in the financialisation process of the economy. The role of the EU, on this respect, is absent—because the only effective means available, the (EDIS) European Deposit Insurance Scheme, "would be privately funded through ex-ante risk-based fees paid by all the participating banks in the Member States".[14] In addition to that, we should remark on all the difficulties in creating this third pillar, based on a common insurance: Germany, for instance, is still reluctant to its adoption and more generally, reluctant to create an effective federalised order capable of reconfiguring the entire bank system unlikely.

Another important aspect of the "multiple Union" is Fiscal Union. The thorny issue of a "European budget" has generated eternal animated debates regarding the possible federalisation of the EU. The premises for the creation of a "Fiscal Union" are—apart from the academic refrain of a creation of truly federation of the Europe of peoples—the risk of "contagion", due to the differences in the national budgets, tax policies, etc. The Five Presidents' report argues, on this regard, "it is important to ensure also that the sum of national budget balances leads to an appropriate fiscal stance at the level of the euro area as a whole. This is key to avoiding *pro-cyclical* fiscal policies at all times".[15] The monetarist vision of the European construction is clearly and explicitly underlined here. From an institutional point of view, the proposal for a creation of an "Advisory European Fiscal Board" is remarkable: a sort of supranational entity in charge of the coordination of the Fiscal council, in order to help the governments to strengthen the convergences of the fiscal policies. This board "should be pluralistic and draw from a wide range of *expertise*".[16] But what interests most, in my opinion, are the conditions under which this Fiscal Union should be settled. And this, to a certain extent, will frustrate every willingness to pursue a sort

[13]Ibidem.

[14]Ibidem.

[15]Ivi, p. 14.

[16]Ibidem.

of "more Europe", or "Europe of people", by repeating the eternal mantra of "we need a real common European budget". The conditions for Fiscal Union are clearly underlined in the guidelines: "It should not lead to permanent transfers between countries or to transfers in one direction only [...] It should also not be conceived as a way to equalise incomes between the Member States".[17] This is very important, because it explicitly says that not only counter-cyclical policies are prohibited, and therefore Keynesian measures are not admitted, but also a sort of "federal budget" is prevented, since it would be impossible to conceive it as a system of macroeconomic re-equilibrium through which resources from the richest areas in the Euro-zone could be centralised and redirected to the poorest or disadvantaged regions. Secondary, a Fiscal Union should "neither undermine the incentives for sound fiscal policy-making at the national level, nor the incentives to address national structural weaknesses".[18] This means of course that such "soundness" requirement must be in line with the structural reforms and compatible with the provisions of the Fiscal compact that impose the reduction of the deficit and the debt, and therefore the reduction of public expenditure, application of austerity measures, etc. The ordoliberal principle of the competitiveness between Member States (instead of all rhetorical solidarity) is once again confirmed. The point is that all the Member states must have a commercial surplus and "Germanise" their attitude towards inflation and debt.

The final part of the document is devoted to the "democratisation" process. The end of the functional logic is a truly Political Union which is a confirmation of what already exists, not a decisive popular moment of a "*pouvoir constituent*". The word "democracy" is in fact suddenly accompanied by the word "accountability". The utilisation of this term is particularly interesting for the ordo-analysis. "Accountability" as well as "governance" is the terms derived from corporate economics that deals with enterprises. The tendency to treat Institutions and democracy like private entities is actually a symptom of the ordoliberalisation of Europe. Accountability, in fact, represents the reduction of the democratic moment to a matter of transparency, the fact that politics coincides with the activity of policy-makers as technical expertise and that "democratic" procedure consists of giving response to the voters about their technical activities, with respect to the "outcome democracy" principle. It is not a simply a top-down approach, as many critics tend to argue, because the "bottom-up" exists, and it is completely absorbed in a post-democratic system. The problem is not a lack of democracy, but the transfiguration of democracy itself. We could use the term "real democracy", just like in the Soviet system the term "real" was applied for socialism. For instance, the point is not that the European Parliament has no effective power, which is false, since the EP has augmented its powers increasingly with the Europeanisation process. What we should focus on is how this new and distorted democratic principle works in a post-democratic system. For instance, in the document we find a reference to "a new form of inter-parliamentary cooperation to bring together European and national actors. This takes place within the European Parliamentary Week organised by the European Parliament in cooperation with National

[17] Ivi, p. 15.

[18] Ibidem.

Parliaments, which includes representatives from National Parliaments for in-depth discussions on policy priorities".[19] In this new multilevel framework, national representatives are involved, and pieces of national sovereignty are assembled together with supranational elements. Of course, the involvement of the National Parliaments is functional to the acceleration of "reforms" ("As a rule, national Parliaments should be closely involved in the adoption of National Reform and Stability Programmes"[20]) and must be aligned to the European semester procedure (the "synchronisation" of the national budgets). As Gian Domenico Majone pointed out, "unfortunately, the steady growth of the powers of this supranational assembly [European Parliament] has been accompanied by an equally steady decline in the turnout of voters at European elections. The fact is that both politicians and academics are reluctant to admit that the root cause of the phenomenon they deplore lies not so much in the failure to replicate at the supranational level the legislative institutions of the nation-state, but rather in the mismatch between expanding supranational powers and the limited, even shrinking, popular support of the European project" (Majone 2012: 19). The point is what Majone called the "end of permissive consensus". Since competences were limited, an indirect legitimacy of the Union was acceptable. Now permissive consensus has imploded and what remains is a sort of simulacrum of democracy. The more "democracy" you put in the machine, the less popular legitimacy you obtain. The distance between popular democracy, people claim, and participation is growing steadily (as the data from Eurostat can confirm). To a certain extent, the Institution boosts "accountability", not exactly democracy. It is what Gustavo Zagrebelsky correctly called the "democratic mask of the oligarchy" (Zagrebelsky and Canfora 2015), another expression of the "bureaucratic Caesarism".

To conclude, as the Italian jurist Luciano Barra Caracciolo correctly stated, "sovereignty, in this "unperceived" process, is "fragmented", i.e. it is rejected, precisely in the regulatory automatism of a supranational authority, without centralisation. Sovereignty and democracy, which is its complement in the modern constitutionalism, simply disappears" (Barra Caracciolo 2013: 157). The "back stage" forces acting behind the formal framework of democracy seem to escape the control of the people, who are now further and further away from the space of decisions. Even internal and critical interpretations of European law seem to have grasped this incontrovertible fact (Baldassari and Quintavalla 2015). But if this concern is not transferred into popular democracy, élites may come ultimately to embrace more and more closely Bertold Brecht's adage: "if people do not agree, dismiss the people and appoint a new one".

[19]Ivi, p. 17.

[20]Ibidem.

References

Bagnai, A. (2016). *Il tramonto dell'euro. Come e perché la fine della moneta unica salverebbe democrazia e benessere in Europa*. Reggio-Emilia: Imprimatur.
Baldassari, M., & Quintavalla, A. (2015). The dark side of the moon. *L'euroscetticismo nel diritto europeo, Lessico di Etica Pubblica*, n. 2.
Baldassari, M., Melegari, D., & Zai, S. (2017) *L'Europa resiliente: Plasticità e irreformabilità della governance, Il Ponte*, Vol. LXXIII, n. 5–6.
Barra Caracciolo, L. (2013). *Euro e (o?) democrazia costituzionale. La convivenza impossibile tra costituzione e trattati europei*. Reggio-Emilia: Imprimatur.
Barra Caracciolo, L. (2015). *La Costituzione nella palude. Indagine su trattati al di sotto di ogni sospetto*. Reggio-Emilia: Imprimatur.
Bourdieu, P. (2014) *On the State: Lectures at the Collège de France, 1989–1992*. In P. Champagne et al. (Eds.). Cambridge: Polity Press.
Cesaratto, S. (2018). *Chi non rispetta le regole. Italia e Germania le doppie morali dell'euro*. Reggio-Emilia: Imprimatur.
Chandler, D. (2012), *Resilience and human security: The post-interventionist paradigm*.
Constâncio, V. (2013). *The European Crisis and the role of the financial system*. Speech at the Bank of Greece conference Athens 23 May 2013: http://www.ecb.europa.eu/press/key/date/2013/html/sp130523_1.en.html. An excellent comment of this article by Bagnai, A. (2013). *Lessons from the crisis*, speech at the conference "Should we die for the euro?, organized by the EFD group at the European Parliament on 3rd December 2013: http://goofynomics.blogspot.it/2013/12/lessons-from-crisis.html.
Crouch, C. (2004). *Post-democracy*. Cambridge: Polity Press.
Dardot, P., & Laval, P. (2013). *The new way of the world*. London: Verso.
De Nardis, F. (2017). The concept of depoliticization and its consequences PArtecipazione e COnflitto. *The Open Journal of Sociopolitical Studies* http://siba-ese.unisalento.it/index.php/paco ISSN: 1972-7623 (printversion) ISSN: 2035-6609 (electronic version) PACO, *10*(2), 340–356.
Degni, M., & De Ioanna, P. (2019). *Il vincolo stupido. Europa e Italia nella crisi dell'euro*. Roma: Castelvecchi.
Durand, C., & Keucheyan, R. (2015). Bureaucratic Caesarism. A gramscian outlook on the crisis of Europe. *Historical Materialism, 23*(2), 23–51.
European Commission. (2015). "Completing Europe's Economic and Monetary Union". https://ec.europa.eu/priorities/sites/beta-political/files/5-presidents-report_en.pdf.
Foucault, M. (1981). The *order of discourse*. In R. Young (Eds.), *Uniting the text. A post-structural reader*, Routledge & Kegan: Boston.
Georgakakis. (2017). *European civil service in (Times of) Crisis. A political sociology of the changing power of eurocrats*, Palgrave.
Giacché, V. (2015). *Costituzione italiana contro Trattati europei. Il conflitto inevitabile*. Imprimatur: Reggio-Emilia.
Guarino, G. (1997). *Verso l'Europa ovvero la fine della politica*. Milano: Mondadori.
Guarino, G. (2014). *Cittadini europei e crisi dell'euro*. Napoli: Editoriale scientifica.
Hooghe, L., & Marks, G. (2008). A postfunctionalist theory of European integration: From permissive consensus to constraining dissensus. *British Journal of Political Science, 39*(1).
Jessop, B. (2016). *The State. Past, present and future*. Cambridge: Polity Press.
Jessop, B. (2006). State-and regulation-theoretical perspectives on the European Union and the failure of the Lisbon Agenda'. *Competition and Change, 10*(2), 145–165.
Jessop, B. (2014). Repoliticising depoliticisation: Theoretical preliminaries on some responses to the American fiscal and Eurozone debt crises. *Policy & Poltics, 42*(2), 2017–2023.
Joly, M. (2017). *L'Europe de Jean Monnet*, Biblis.
Joseph, J. (2013). *Resilience as embedded neoliberalism*: A governmentality approach. In Resilience: International policies, practices and discourses (Vol. 1, Issue 1).
Joseph, J. (2018). *Varieties of resilience. Studies in governmentality*. Cambridge University Press.

Laclau, E. (2003). *On populist reason*. London: Verso.

Leruth, B., & Lord, C. *Differentiated integration in the European Union: A concept, a process, a system or a theory.*

Majone, G. (2012). *Rethinking European integration after the debt crisis*. Working paper No 3/2012, June, UCL, European Institute.

Majone, G. (2014). *Rethinking the Union of Europe Post-Crisis. Has integration Gone Too Far?*, Cambridge University Press.

Mitchell, W., & Fazi, T. (2017). *Reclaiming the State: A Progressive Vision of Sovereignty for a Post-Neoliberal World*. London: Pluto Press.

Schmitter, C. P., & Lefkofridi, Z. (2016). *Neo-functionalism as a theory of disintegration.*

Somma, A. (2014). *La dittatura dello spread. Germania, Europa e crisi del debito*. Roma: DeriveApprodi.

Somma, A. (2017). *L'Europa a due velocità. Post-politica*. Reggio-Emilia: Imprimatur.

Stiglitz, J. (2016). *The euro. How a common currency threatens the future of the Europe*. New York: W. W. Norton & Company.

Stubb, A. (1996). A categorization of differentiated integration. *Journal of Common Market Studies, 34,* 283.

Zagrebelsky, G., & Canfora, L. (2015). *La maschera democratica dell'oligarchia*. Roma-Bari: Laterza.

Zielonka, J. (2014). *Is the EU doomed?*. Cambridge: Polity Press.

Euroscepticism in Times of European Crises: The Role of Solidarity

Ann-Kathrin Reinl

1 Introduction

Solidarity within the European Union (EU) emerged as a "super issue" from Europe-wide crises, reaching the continent from 2009 onwards. Starting with the onset of the European sovereign debt crisis at the end of 2009, solidarity within the European Union became a highly discussed topic among politicians, in the media as well as in scientific research. For instance, politicians appealed to European solidarity when discussing bailout packages and austerity measures for debt-ridden EU member states (e.g. Giannopoulou 2016). This trend perpetuated over the course of the European migrant crisis.

Solidarity within a state has been described as "the preparedness to share resources with others by personal contribution to those in struggle or in need and through taxation and redistribution organized by the state" (Stjernø 2004: 2). Existing research on the field of European solidarity either focused on the clarification of the theoretical concept (Ferrera and Burelli 2019; Kankaras and Moors 2009; Knodt and Tews 2014; Nicoli 2015; Sangiovanni 2013) or concentrated on single dimensions of EU-wide solidarity to empirically capture the term (Bechtel et al. 2014; Hobolt and de Vries 2016; Kuhn et al. 2017; Verhaegen 2017). This chapter builds on the previous work but studies multiple instead of single aspects of European solidarity in times of the European financial and migrant crises. Therefore, I analysed citizens' solidarity values as well as their support for EU-wide solidarity actions.

European solidarity builds on attitudes towards the European Union and EU fellow member states. Over the course of the European "polycrisis" (Nicoli and Zeitlin 2019), solidarity between European Union member states seems to have been an important factor affecting individual attitudes towards European integration.

A.-K. Reinl (✉)
GESIS Leibniz Institute for the Social Sciences, Cologne, Germany
e-mail: Ann-Kathrin.Reinl@gesis.org

© Springer Nature Switzerland AG 2020

M. Baldassari et al. (eds.), *Anti-Europeanism*,
https://doi.org/10.1007/978-3-030-24428-6_6

In the early days of the European Community, public endorsement for the European integration project was strong. This phenomenon was commonly described as a "permissive consensus" (Down and Wilson 2008; Hooghe and Marks 2009). However, with the ratification of the Maastricht Treaty in 1991, public opinion towards the EU worsened and turned into a "constraining dissensus" (Down and Wilson 2008; Hooghe and Marks 2009). Since the outbreak of the European financial crisis, populist anti-EU parties have gained increased support all over the European Union and continued to be successful during the migrant crisis.

In the past research, solidarity either served as an explanation for Eurosceptic voting (Hobolt and de Vries 2016) or as a consequence of European identity and cosmopolitanism (Bechtel et al. 2014; Kuhn et al 2017; Verhaegen 2017). Moreover, solidarity's role in the European asylum policy was discussed in the scientific literature (Langford 2013). However, so far no study has analysed the effect of solidarity on attitudinal Euroscepticism. As a consequence, lots of information on public attitudes towards the European Union has remained uncharted.

This chapter fills the academic void by studying multiple facets of European solidarity and its link to Eurosceptic sentiments in times of the European financial and migrant crises. I expect that the importance of solidarity as a value for the EU only changed marginally over the course of European crises, as values are known to be relatively stable over time. In contrast, I hypothesize that citizens' support for solidarity measures has changed during crises and, as a consequence, might have affected respondents' attitudes towards the European Union to a greater extent.

By using data provided by selected Eurobarometer waves, the development of transnational solidarity and Eurosceptic attitudes is demonstrated over the period of the European sovereign debt crisis and the climax of the migrant crisis from 2009 to 2015. The chapter applies descriptive statistics as well as multilevel regression analysis.

The empirical results are in line with my predictions. Overall, the evidence suggests that value-based solidarity marginally affected Euroscepticism. On the contrary, support for solidarity measures exhibited a strong influence on Eurosceptic attitudes. Respondents who supported transnational solidarity actions less likely represented EU critical positions. Hence, European solidarity matters more for citizens and generates greater opposition to the EU when it becomes costly for the member states of the European Union. Time will tell if opposition to the European Union continues to remain high in less turbulent times when European solidarity plays a subsidiary role.

2 European Solidarity—a Broadly Used Concept

Over the course of the financial crisis, the term solidarity was frequently used by European politicians (European Council 2011; Giannopoulou 2016). However, solidarity in the European context is not new in any sense. Since its foundation, solidarity has constituted a part of the European Community. On the 9th of May in 1950, the former French Foreign Minister Robert Schuman stated that "Europe will not be made all at once, or according to a single plan. It will be built through concrete achievements which first create a de facto solidarity" (Communication Department of the European Commission 2018). Following this, just to name a few, solidarity was mentioned in a range of European treaties like the Single European Act (1986), the Maastricht Treaty (1992) as well as in the Lisbon Treaty (2009). Nevertheless, until the outbreak of the financial crisis, European solidarity had never taken action and the concept of solidarity had remained rather fuzzy in the European sphere (Kontochistou and Mascha 2014; Pantazatou 2015). European solidarity existed on paper only (Bendiek and Neyer 2016: 3). The European Community supported economically weak regions through the European structural and cohesion funds. This financial assistance intended to catalyse convergence of the regions in the European Union (Ederveen et al. 2006). However, EU member states never actively asked for solidarity and assistance provided by the EU or fellow states before the Euro crisis, excluding disaster relief funds. With the introduction of bailout packages for economically struggling EU countries during the Euro crisis, the situation completely changed. Solidarity now implemented in reality went beyond the pure support for solidarity as a value of the European Union. For the first time in history, European solidarity became an actual cost and EU member states were pegged to "collective burden sharing" (Genschel and Hemerijck 2018: 2). In a speech given in the middle of the Euro crisis, Herman van Rompuy, the then president of the European Council, described the situation as follows: "Solidarity is a duty, not a right. Solidarity within the Euro Area now is a matter of necessity and survival" (European Council 2011).

Solidarity in the European Union appears at various levels. Literature distinguishes between member state solidarity, national solidarity and transnational solidarity (Sangiovanni 2013). During European crises, research on all three kinds of solidarity has been published. On the aspect of national solidarity, scientific work studying solidarity actions within EU countries has been conducted (Arampatzi 2016). Other papers analysed parliamentary debates on financial redistribution between countries (member state solidarity) (Closa and Maatsch 2014) and citizens' willingness to show financial solidarity towards other EU member states served as an indicator for transnational solidarity (Kuhn et al. 2017; Verhaegen 2017). The research focus of this chapter builds on former work on transnational solidarity. In a working paper published by Lahusen in 2016, the author originates a framework for analysing transnational solidarity within the European Union. This chapter's understanding of transnational solidarity refers to Lahusen's definition which states that "European' solidarity is consequently any attitude and behaviour striving to help Europeans (be that residents or citizens) in struggle or in need, regardless of their national origin" (Lahusen 2016: 8).

3 Europe in Times of Crises—Euroscepticism on the Rise

The definition of Euroscepticism adopted in this chapter is originally from Taggart (1998) and is widely used in current Eurosceptic literature. Back then, the author described Euroscepticism as "contingent or qualified opposition, as well as incorporating outright and unqualified opposition to the process of European integration" (Taggart 1998: 366). Over the course of the European financial crisis, Euroscepticism rose in many EU member states. This development manifested itself in electoral gains for Eurosceptic parties all over the continent. In the 2014 European Parliament Election, anti-EU parties received votes in 23 EU member states. In comparison with the preceding 2009 European election, Eurosceptic parties increased their vote share by eight percentage points (Treib 2014: 1542–1543). In addition, Eurosceptic parties achieved success on the national and sub-national level. Greece, a country that was known to be one of the most EU-supporting nations (Clements et al. 2014) elected two Eurosceptic parties in its government in 2015. In 2017, the Austrian electorate gave 26% of their votes to the EU critical Freedom Party of Austria (FPÖ) which joined a government coalition with the Austrian People's Party (ÖVP). Furthermore, Eurosceptic parties also gained influence in EU states which still have moderate political parties in government as, for instance, in France and Germany, the two core countries of the European Union. In France, the EU critical party Front National (FN) with its candidate Marine Le Pen ran for the final ballot of the French Presidential Election in 2017 and gained 33.9% of votes. Just a few months later, the right-wing Eurosceptic party Alternative for Germany (AfD) entered the German Bundestag for the first time.

This chapter takes a look at Eurosceptic attitudes of European citizens. Studying respondents' attitudes has, in contrast to electoral Euroscepticism, the advantage that attitudes can be measured at any time independent from election dates. Further, Eurosceptic attitudes do not always turn into Eurosceptic voting decisions. Hence, studying EU critical sentiments enables to react to Eurosceptic public voices before the ballot box.

Former research already examined the effects of national and European identity (Risse 2014; Serricchio et al. 2013; van Klingeren et al. 2013), trust rates (Abts et al. 2009; McLaren 2007) and economic performances (Hobolt and de Vries 2016; Nicoli 2016) on Euroscepticism. However, in this study, I tested one mechanism that was often overlooked in previous studies: the connection between Euroscepticism and transnational solidarity. The following paragraph develops the theoretical argument of the chapter.

4 European Solidarity and Euroscepticism

Previous work on the link between Euroscepticism and European solidarity has been conducted bidirectionally. On the one hand, solidarity within the EU has been described as a consequence of the European Community (Preuss 1999: 286–287).

Kuhn and her colleagues (Kuhn et al. 2017) analysed the effect of cosmopolitanism on support for transnational redistribution. Their results show that citizens with cosmopolitan attitudes more likely favour financial assistance provided for EU fellow states. These results are confirmed by a study published by Verhaegen (2017), which demonstrates a positive effect of European identity on support for financial solidarity.

On the other hand, transnational solidarity measures have been used to explain Eurosceptic voting. Hobolt and de Vries (2016) found a significant and negative impact of support for financial assistance for other EU member states on Eurosceptic vote choice in the European Parliament Election in 2014. Citizens who support cross-country redistribution are less likely to give their voice to anti-EU parties.

The research interest of this chapter aims to explain the rise of Eurosceptic attitudes over the course of the European financial and migrant crises. Hence, the multiple facets of transnational solidarity serve as explanatory variables for Eurosceptic sentiments. In this way, the chapter overcomes the one-dimensional reflections on transnational solidarity applied in former research and studies its effect on attitudinal Euroscepticism.

I expect to find different effects of support for solidarity actions and support for the value itself on Eurosceptic sentiments. Values do not change overnight but over longer time periods, like intergenerational changes (Inglehart 2008). Consequently, it is assumed that citizens' support for value-based solidarity within the European Union did not significantly change during the last decade. However, the value might have gained importance for citizens' opinion on European integration. Support for value based solidarity is expected to have weakened attitudinal Euroscepticism. My first two research hypotheses therefore read as follows:

H1a: Citizens' support for value-based European solidarity did not change over the course of European crises.
H1b: Citizens' support for value-based European solidarity decreased Eurosceptic attitudes.

In contrast, it is hypothesized that the support for solidarity actions changed during European crises as cross-country burden sharing gained importance during these days, for instance, through the implementation of bailout packages over the course of the European sovereign debt crisis.

H2a: Citizens' support for transnational solidarity actions changed over the course of European crises.

Voters might listen to good reasons for cross-national solidarity in the EU, when governments talk about it (Genschel and Hemerijck 2018: 8). Otherwise, there is a risk that citizens who oppose European solidarity start opposing European integration too. We know that citizens' attitudes towards the EU depend on their cost-benefit calculations of European integration (Hobolt 2015; Kuhn and Stoeckel 2014). In times of European crises, the costs of European integration might have become too high for some EU citizens compared to the benefits they gained from EU membership. As a result, I expect that support for EU-wide burden sharing lowered Eurosceptic sentiments of EU citizens.

H2b: Citizens' support for transnational solidarity actions decreased Eurosceptic attitudes.

For the period of the financial crisis, former research on public support for financial redistribution policies within the EU either concentrated on the provision of financial help for EU member states facing economic or financial problems (Hobolt and de Vries 2016; Kuhn et al. 2017; Verhaegen 2017) or on the endorsement of Eurobonds (Daniele and Geys 2015; Kuhn and Stoeckel 2014; Nicoli 2018). Backing financial assistance for fellow member states might be bound to conditions for debtor countries. For instance, providing financial help for fellow states could depend on the implementation of harsh austerity programs on the debtor side. On the contrary, the introduction of Eurobonds, implicating mutual guarantees on the EU level (European Commission 2011), signalizes more unconditional solidarity.

Hence, public support for Eurobonds seems to be an adequate way to capture support for European solidarity actions. Measures which have been implemented to save the common European currency raised public opposition towards the European integration project (Auer 2014). My third research hypothesis therefore predicts that

H2c: Citizens who support the introduction of Eurobonds are less likely to show Eurosceptic attitudes.

Moreover, transnational solidarity during the European migrant crisis is analysed. Here, I define the willingness to financially assist countries receiving high numbers of asylum seekers as transnational solidarity. In addition, support for the introduction of binding asylum quotas for all EU member states is judged as another important sign of transnational solidarity.

H2d: Citizens who want to financially assist member states receiving high numbers of asylum seekers are less likely to show Eurosceptic attitudes.
H2e: Citizens who want to introduce binding asylum quotas within the EU are less likely to show Eurosceptic attitudes.

5 Database, Variables and Analyses Methods

To test the research hypotheses of this chapter, Eurobarometer data from 2009 to 2015 are analysed. Since not all Eurobarometer waves include questions on transnational solidarity and Euroscepticism, I used the most comprehensive ones. With this data, it is possible to trace back the development of transnational solidarity and Euroscepticism over the course of the European financial and migrant crises (its peak in the year 2015). Eurobarometer data claim various advantages in comparison with other comparative survey programs or electoral data. In contrast to most international survey programs, Eurobarometer data are ascertained every few months in all member states of the European Union. This provides the possibility to monitor public opinion on a regular basis and independent of election dates.

Previous research already analysed Eurobarometer data to study the proceeding rise of Euroscepticism (see, for instance, van Klingeren et al. 2013; Verney 2015). However, Eurobarometer data do not directly measure the concept of Euroscepticism. Subsequently, different strategies have been applied to overcome the measurement problem. The dependent variable of this work depicts attitudinal Euroscepticism. The theoretical concept is captured via several variables on European integration. Whereas previous studies either used single questions of Eurobarometer data to capture Euroscepticism (Clements et al. 2014; Radu et al. 2014; Serricchio et al. 2013; Verney 2015) or only built an additive index over variables capturing attitudes towards EU membership (van Klingeren et al. 2013), this chapter calculates two multiplicative indexes to capture distinctive aspects of Eurosceptic sentiments.

The first index is captured using two variables to measure citizens' sentiments towards the current shape of the European Union. One question captures respondents' trust in the European Union[1] and the other captures their image of the EU.[2]

The second index measures respondents' evaluation of their country's EU membership and is likewise measured using two variables. The first variable asks for respondents' support for their country's EU membership[3], and the second enquires about the perceived benefits the country has gained from EU membership.[4]

All variables are first converted into dummy variables before they are integrated into the multiplicative indexes. Unfortunately, no Eurobarometer wave captures both these measurements of attitudinal Euroscepticism in one survey. Hence, due to a restriction in data, I applied index one in my regression analyses for the period of the financial crisis and drew on index two when it came to the European migrant crisis.

The aim of this chapter is to measure the effect of transnational solidarity on Euroscepticism. Consequently, the concept of transnational solidarity needs to be operationalized too. Since transnational solidarity is a multifaceted phenomenon, several variables are utilized for its measurement.

On the one hand, mentioning solidarity as a core value of the EU[5] and support for defending solidarity by the European Parliament (EP)[6] are used as proxies for value-based solidarity in this chapter. On the other hand, support for solidarity actions is

---

[1] I would like to ask you a question about how much trust you have in certain institutions. For each of the following institutions, please tell me if you tend to trust it or tend not to trust it. 4: The European Union. 1-Tend to trust, 2-tend not to trust, 3-dk.

[2] In general, does the European Union conjure up for you a very positive, fairly positive, neutral, fairly negative or very negative image? 1-Very positive, 2-Fairly positive, 3-Neutral, 4-Fairly negative, 5-Very negative, 6-dk.

[3] Generally speaking, do you think that (OUR COUNTRY)'s membership of the European Union is…? 1-A good thing, 2-A bad thing, 3-Neither good nor bad, 4-dk.

[4] Taking everything into account, would you say that (OUR COUNTRY) has on balance benefited or not from being a member of the European Union? 1-Benefited, 2-Not benefited, 3-dk.

[5] Which three of the following values best represent the EU? 8-Solidarity, support for others.

[6] In your opinion, which of the following values should the European Parliament defend as a matter of priority? 4-Solidarity between EU member states.

metered. To that end, variables asking for the support of Eurobonds,[7] binding asylum quotas within the EU[8] and support for financial assistance provided for EU countries facing high asylum flows[9] are integrated into the statistical models. For the statistical analyses, the variables measuring solidarity are converted into dummy variables.

Finally, several control variables frequently used in the literature on Euroscepticism are included in the statistical models when available in the respective datasets. Sociodemographic variables like gender, age and education as well as self-positioning on the economic left-right scale are considered. Additionally, questions asking for closer cooperation within the EU during the financial crisis, respondents' assessment of the current direction of the EU, EU's performance during the financial crisis, respondents' satisfaction with democracy within the EU, attachment to the EU, identity feelings towards the community, if the respondent discusses about EU matters and personal evaluation of the economic situation on the European, national and household level are introduced (besides sociodemographics, all other controls are transformed into dummy variables).

On a final note, two variables, which are metered at the country level, are added to the datasets. The first variable (dichotomous) depicts if a country received financial assistance from the European Union during the European financial crisis (European Commission 2018). The second macro level variable constitutes the number of asylum applications per 1000 inhabitants (data provided by Eurostat). Both country level variables are calculated on an annual basis. By inserting these variables in my statistical models, I am able to capture the context effects of the European financial and migrant crises. Countries that are not EU member states are excluded from the samples.

I first present descriptive analyses on the development of attitudes towards the EU and transnational solidarity over the course of recent European crises. Then, I employ multilevel logistic regression analysis to identify the effect of transnational solidarity on attitudinal Euroscepticism while considering country level differences.

6 Results

6.1 Descriptive Analyses

At first, the development of Euroscepticism over the course of European crises is retraced. Figure 1 demonstrates the trends of support for European integration within the European Union (all member countries together) from 2009 to 2015.

[7] The introduction of Eurobonds (European bonds). 1-strongly in favour, 2-fairly in favour, 3-fairly opposed, 4-strongly opposed, 5-dk.

[8] The distribution of asylum seekers should be decided at EU level on the basis of binding quotas. 1-totally agree, 2-tend to agree, 3-tend to disagree 4-totally disagree, 5-dk.

[9] The EU has recently decided to allocate financial support as a matter of priority to the member states currently facing the most migratory flows on their coasts and borders. Do you think it is…? 1-A good thing, 2-A bad thing, 3-Neither good nor bad, 4-dk.

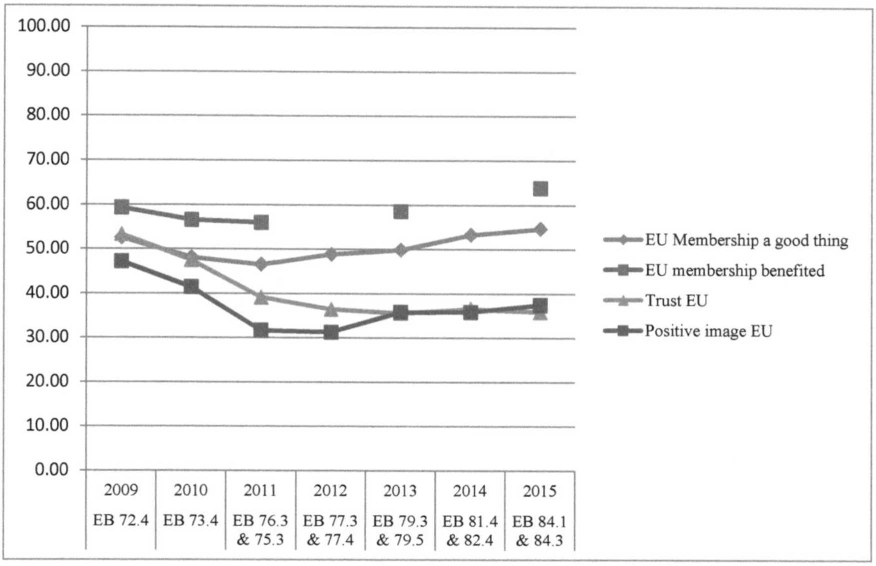

Fig. 1 *Source* Eurobarometer data (EB 72.4, EB 73.4, EB 75.3, EB 76.3, EB 77.3, EB 77.4, EB 79.3, EB 79.5, EB 81.4, EB 82.4, EB 84.1, EB 84.3)

The orange line portrays support for a country's membership in the European Union. We see that the approval for this variable only minimally changed over the years. During the Euro crisis, its value dropped under 50% but already recovered from 2012 onwards.

A similar trend manifests for the variable measuring perceived benefits from EU membership. Unfortunately, no values for the years 2012 and 2014 are available from Eurobarometer data. In the year 2015, over the peak of the migrant crisis, perceived EU benefits exceeded the value of 2009. Between these years, agreement on the statement that the country benefited from EU membership slightly decreased.

The light blue curve depicts the respondents' trust in the European Union. From 2009 onwards, trust rates continuously declined until 2013. Starting with a trust rate of 53% in 2009, only 35% of respondents indicated to trust the EU in 2013. After 2013, it slightly increased again. Hence, trust levels eroded with the outbreak of the Euro crisis. After a short period of recovery from 2013 to 2014, levels of trust in the EU marginally dropped again at the climax of the refugee crisis in 2015.

The dark blue line captures the public image of the EU and reveals an almost similar trend compared to the development of public trust rates. The percentage of respondents stating to have a positive image of the EU already increased again after 2012 and another growth became visible in the year 2015. Once again, the migrant crisis, in contrast to the financial crisis, did not mar the positive image of the EU, but the values slowly seem to recover towards the pre-crises numbers.

Taken together, Fig. 1 demonstrates that the support for EU membership and European integration dropped during the years of the Euro crisis but started to recover afterwards. By comparing the developments of attitudes towards the current shape of the EU and respondents' evaluations of EU membership, we see a much more pronounced downturn in public trust rates and EU evaluations than we see for respondents' opinion on EU membership.

Figure 2 portrays the progress of European solidarity in the years of European crises. For the variables measuring support for solidarity actions during the European migrant crisis, only one point in time is available (questions were not asked prior to 2015).

The percentage of respondents naming solidarity as a value best representing the EU scaled fewer than 20% in 2009. Afterwards, it eroded from 2010 to 2014. With an already low popularity in 2010, slightly over 20% of respondents mentioned solidarity, approval further decreased to 14% in 2014. After the year 2014, it increased again.

In contrast, the percentage of citizens naming solidarity as a value that should be defended by the European Parliament remained relatively stable during the years of the financial crisis as well as in times of the migrant crisis. Hence, the first research hypothesis H1a, stating that citizens' support for value-based European solidarity

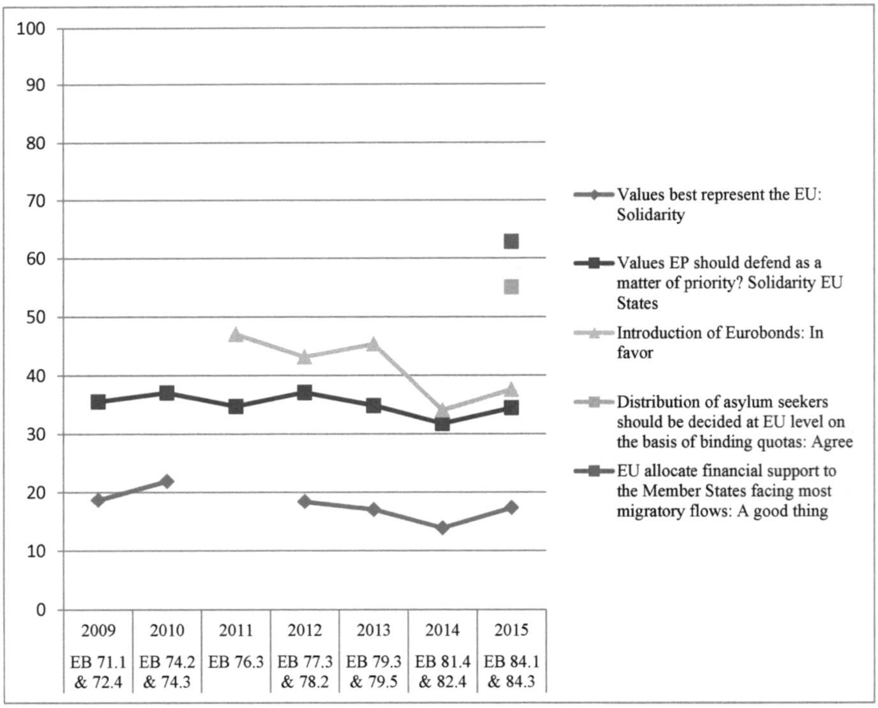

Fig. 2 *Source* Eurobarometer data (EB 71.1, EB 72.4, EB 74.2, EB 74.3, EB 76.3, EB 77.3, EB 78.2, EB 79.3, EB 79.5, EB 81.4, EB 82.4, EB 84.1, EB 84.3)

did not change over the course of European crises, is supported through my results as public support for solidarity values only varied to minor extents.

Support for the introduction of Eurobonds started with an agreement of over 45% of respondents in 2011. Thereafter, it decreased and increased again. The lowest amount of support was seen in 2014, when only 34% of survey participants favoured the implementation of Eurobonds.

Contrary to the endorsement of solidarity actions over the course of the financial crisis, support for transnational solidarity actions during the migrant crisis was much higher. Over half of the respondents agreed on introducing binding quotas for the distribution of asylum seekers on the European level. On top of this, more than 62% of citizens favoured financial assistance for European countries facing high migration flows. Hence, EU citizens' willingness to demonstrate transnational solidarity is higher in times of the migrant crisis compared to the preceding years of financial depression.

To sum up, public support for Eurobonds changed during the financial crisis. Hence, in line with hypothesis H2a, citizens' support for transnational redistribution policies has changed over the years. Since only one data point measuring support for solidarity actions in times of the migrant crisis exists, hypothesis 2a can only be tested during the Euro crisis.

7 Multilevel Logistic Regression Analyses

The next paragraph presents the multilevel logistic regression results. Through the conduction of multilevel logistic regression analyses, it is possible to examine the effect of transnational solidarity on attitudinal Euroscepticism while considering cross-country variance.

Since no Eurobarometer survey from the year 2009 asked questions on attitudes towards the EU and European solidarity at the same time, it was not feasible for us to perform regression analyses for this year. Moreover, due to an irregular set of variables contained in Eurobarometer surveys, the Eurobarometer waves studied in this chapter do not include questions on Eurobonds and respondents' evaluation of EU membership (Index 2) at the same time. On the contrary, Eurobarometer waves that entail issues concerning solidarity actions during the European migrant crises just asked for respondents' sentiments towards the current shape of the EU (Index 1). Hence, the analyses on solidarity actions during the financial crisis are limited to attitudes towards the EU; whereas, the regression analysis for the year of European migrant crisis' peak (2015) is restricted to citizens' opinion on their country's EU membership.

Table 1 portrays the multilevel regression results separated per year. Once again, since not all variables were ascertained simultaneously, the set of value-based solidarity and control variables slightly varies from year to year.

Generally speaking, the results show that value-based solidarity issues affected Euroscepticism negatively. My first measurement of value-based solidarity—citizens

Table 1 *Source* Eurobarometer data (EB 74.2, EB 76.3, EB 77.3, EB 79.3, EB 81.4, EB 84.1)

Eurobarometer	EB 72.4	EB 76.3	EB 77.3	EB 79.3	EB 81.4	EB 84.1
Year	2010	2011	2012	2013	2014	2015
	Euroscepticism (Index 1)					Euroscepticism (Index 2)
Values which best represent the EU: Solidarity	**−0.286 (0.055)*****		**−0.095(0.058)**	**−0.179 (0.058)*****	**−0.183 (0.076)****	
Values the EP should defend as a matter of priority? Solidarity between EU member states		**−0.195(0.041)*****				**−0.120(0.069)***
Introduction of Eurobonds: In favour		**−0.329(0.043)*****	**−0.217(046)*****	**−0.334(0.044)*****	**−0.305(0.055)*****	
EU allocates financial support to the member states facing most migratory flows: A good thing						**−0.892(0.066)*****
Distribution of asylum seekers should be decided at EU level on the basis of binding quotas: Agree						**−0.420(0.075)*****
Crisis: EU should work together more	−0.999(0.077)***	−0.334(0.082)***	−0.448(0.078)***	−0.589(0.073)***	−0.429(0.084)***	

(continued)

Table 1 (continued)

Eurobarometer	EB 72.4	EB 76.3	EB 77.3	EB 79.3	EB 81.4	EB 84.1
Year	2010	2011	2012	2013	2014	2015
	Euroscepticism (Index 1)					Euroscepticism (Index 2)
Present direction EU: Right	−2.133(0.075)***	−1.537(0.054)***	−1.201(0.075)***	−1.424(0.066)***	−1.425(0.079)***	−1.677(0.124)***
Political discussion, EU matters: Yes	−0.128(0.049)**	−0.297(0.045)***	0.224(0.052)***	0.239(0.048)***	0.079(0.058)	−0.178(0.069)**
Satisfaction with democracy, EU: Satisfied		−1.468(0.040)***	−1.059(0.049)***	−1.212(0.047)***	−1.483(0.059)***	
EU citizenship: feel to be EU citizen					−1.060(0.055)***	
Attachment to the EU: not attached			0.895(0.051)***			1.931(0.081)***
Feeling future: also European			−0.603(0.047)***			

(continued)

Table 1 (continued)

Eurobarometer	EB 72.4	EB 76.3	EB 77.3	EB 79.3	EB 81.4	EB 84.1
Year	2010	2011	2012	2013	2014	2015
	Euroscepticism (Index 1)					Euroscepticism (Index 2)
Crisis performance EU: effective			−0.616(0.054)***			
Situation economy EU: good	−0.735(0.067)***	−0.481(0.057)***	−0.608(0.071)***	−0.555(0.064)***	−0.70(0.065)***	
Situation economy nation: good	−0.344(0.068)***	−0.357(0.057)***	−0.216(0.067)***	−0.347(0.064)***	−0.289(0.076)***	
Situation economy household: good	−0.479(0.051)***	−0.302(0.046)***	−0.318(0.051)***	−0.326(0.048)***		
Left-right position	−0.039(0.010)***				0.010(0.011)	0.016(0.014)
Female	−0.154(0.044)***	0.039(0.039)	−0.102(0.044)**	−0.081(0.042)**	−0.211(0.051)***	−0.058(0.062)
Age	0.067(0.014)***	0.043(0.012)***	0.037(0.014)***	0.057(0.013)***	0.046(0.016)***	0.041(0.019)**
Education	−0.017(0.008)**	−0.019(0.022)	0.008(0.026)	0.038(0.025)	−0.009(0.029)	−0.070(0.032)**

(continued)

Table 1 (continued)

Eurobarometer	EB 72.4	EB 76.3	EB 77.3	EB 79.3	EB 81.4	EB 84.1
Year	2010	2011	2012	2013	2014	2015
	Euroscepticism (Index 1)					Euroscepticism (Index 2)
Assistance (country received from EU)	−0.230(0.224)	−0.272(0.201)	0.099(0.163)	0.167(0.212)	−0.109(0.175)	0.215(0.232)
Asylum applications (per 1000 inhabitants)	0.166(0.109)	−0.014(0.074)	0.126(0.056)**	0.101(0.071)	0.074(0.044)*	0.036(0.22)
_cons	0.687(0.198)***	1.982(0.179)***	0.141(0.176)	1.038(0.186)***	1.106(0.192)***	−2.286(0.258)***
N (individuals)	17110	14901	15205	16501	12927	13891
N (groups)	29	29	29	29	30	30

Significance level: ***<0.01<**<0.05<*<0.10; Standard errors in parentheses; Index 1: Multiplicative index of trust in the EU and respondent's image of the EU; Index 2: Multiplicative index of respondent's support for country's EU membership and perceived benefits of country's EU membership naming solidarity as a value best representing the European Union—ascertained a significant and negative impact on Eurosceptic feelings, except for the year 2012. For 2012, a control variable on European identity was incorporated in the regression analysis (not available for other years). By admitting this variable to the statistical model, the effect of value-based solidarity became insignificant. This might be an indication that feelings of solidarity within the EU are related to European identity (Kuhn et al. 2017; Verhaegen 2017) and I only found a spurious correlation between value-based solidarity and Euroscepticism when I excluded identity measurements from analyses.

Agreeing on the statement that the European Parliament should defend solidarity between EU member states as a matter of priority, negatively and significantly impacted Euroscepticism in 2011 (measured through Index 1). By contrast, it only negatively affected Euroscepticism (measured through Index 2) at a ten per cent significance level during the migrant crisis.

Based on these results, the data show evidence for hypothesis H1b (except for the year 2012). On average, citizens' support for value-based solidarity negatively affected Eurosceptic attitudes.

In reference to public support for solidarity actions and its meaning for Euroscepticism, I found significant effects over all the years. Support for the introduction of Eurobonds always shows significant and negative influence on Euroscepticism. Subsequently, research hypothesis 2c is endorsed by the regression results. Citizens who support the introduction of Eurobonds are less likely to be Eurosceptic.

This trend proceeds in the year 2015 for transnational solidarity measures during the migrant crisis. Both support for financial assistance for EU states facing high numbers of asylum seekers as well as support for redistribution of migrants via binding quotas within the EU showed negative and highly significant impressions on Euroscepticism. Referring back to the postulated research hypotheses, I found empirical support for hypotheses H2d and H2e. Citizens who want to financially assist member states receiving high numbers of asylum seekers less likely show Eurosceptic attitudes. Moreover, citizens who want to introduce binding asylum quotas within the EU less likely possess Eurosceptic attitudes.

To sum up, over the course of both European crises the regression results approve hypothesis H2b as citizens' support for Europe-wide redistribution policies negatively affected Eurosceptic attitudes.

8 Discussion

This chapter aims to study the development of transnational solidarity and its effect on Eurosceptic attitudes in times of the European financial and migrant crises. Therefore, selected Eurobarometer waves were analysed. The results of the conducted multilevel logistic regression analyses supported my predictions. Support for solidarity measures within the European Union negatively impacted Eurosceptic attitudes of survey respondents. The more citizens are in favour of the introduction of Eurobonds, the less likely they show Eurosceptic attitudes. The same influence was discovered for the fair redistribution of refugees between EU member states and the approval of financial assistance provided for refugee host countries. Those respondents who supported the introduction of binding refugee quotas and wanted to financially assist refugee host states were less likely to have Eurosceptic attitudes.

In contrast, solidarity as a value for the European Union shows much weaker effects on personal Euroscepticism and the impact even diminishes with the introduction of European identity measurements in the statistical model (see regression results for the year 2012). Future studies should control for the influence and interdependency between value-based European solidarity and European identity on Euroscepticism for all the years under investigation. Due to a lack of data, this was not feasible within the scope of this chapter.

In conclusion, solidarity is likely of higher importance for Europeans when the EU takes action. Before the outbreak of the European financial crisis, member states of the EU had never actively asked for assistance provided by fellow states or the European Union before. This change in the embodiment of European solidarity might have produced or intensified negative sentiments towards policies of the European Union as well as towards the community as a whole. Solidarity within the European Union matters for citizens to a greater extent when it becomes costly. I have demonstrated that support for value-based solidarity did only marginally change over the course of European crises but approval of solidarity actions did shift from time to time. Hence, solidarity as a value within the EU continued to exist at a certain level almost unperturbed by any crises; whereas, public support for solidarity measures varied and highly impacted attitudes towards the European Union. This was true for the Euro crisis as well as for the migrant crisis.

Time will show if support for solidarity actions likewise impacts Euroscepticism after the end of European crises. It is expected that other aspects dominate attitudes towards the EU in less turbulent periods. Since no community can survive without solidarity (Auer 2014: 8), studying transnational solidarity's development and its political consequences is relevant for the future existence of the European Union. Academic research should continue working on the topic to afford an opportunity to react to eroding levels of transnational solidarity before it puts the European Union's persistence at risk.

References

Abts, K., Heerwegh, D., & Swyngedouw, M. (2009). Sources of Euroscepticism: Utilitarian interest, social distrust, national identity and institutional distrust. *World Political Science, 5*(1), 1–26.

Arampatzi, A. (2016). Constructing solidarity as resistive and creative agency in austerity Greece. *Comparative European Politics, 16*(1), 50–66.

Auer, S. (2014). The limits of transnational solidarity and the Eurozone crisis in Germany, Ireland and Slovakia. *Perspectives on European Politics and Society, 15*(3), 322–334.

Bechtel, M. M., Hainmueller, J., & Margalit, Y. (2014). Preferences for international redistribution: The divide over the Eurozone Bailouts. *American Journal of Political Science, 58*(4), 835–856.

Bendiek, A., & Neyer, J. (2016). Europäische Solidarität: die Flüchtlingskrise als Realitätstest. *SWP-Aktuell*, 20. Berlin: Stiftung Wissenschaft und Politik -SWP- Deutsches Institut für Internationale Politik und Sicherheit. http://nbn-resolving.de/urn:nbn:de:0168-ssoar-46541-3.

Clements, B., Nanou, K., & Verney, S. (2014). We no longer love you, but we don't want to leave you: The Eurozone crisis and popular Euroscepticism in Greece. *Journal of European Integration, 36*, 247–265.

Closa, C., & Maatsch, A. (2014). In a spirit of solidarity? Justifying the European Financial Stability Facility (EFSF) in National Parliamentary Debates. *Journal of Common Market Studies, 52*(4), 826–842.

Communication Department of the European Commission. (2018). *The Schuman Declaration*. May 9, 1950 from https://europa.eu/european-union/about-eu/symbols/europe-day/schuman-declaration_en.

Daniele, G., & Geys, B. (2015). Public support for European fiscal integration in times of crisis. *Journal of European Public Policy, 22*(5), 650–670.

Down, I., & Wilson, C. J. (2008). From 'permissive consensus' to 'constraining dissensus': A polarizing Union? *Acta Politica, 43*, 26–49.

Ederveen, S., de Groot, H. L. F., & Nahuis, R. (2006). Fertile soil for structural funds? A panel data analysis of the conditional effectiveness of European Cohesion Policy. *Kyklos, 59*(1), 17–42.

European Commission. (2018). *EU financial Assistance*. https://ec.europa.eu/info/business-economy-euro/economic-and-fiscal-policy-coordination/eu-financial-assistance_en.

European Commission. (2011). *European Commission Green Paper on the feasibility of introducing stability bonds*. http://europa.eu/rapid/press-release_MEMO-11-820_en.htm.

European Council. (2011). *The economic and political challenges for Europe*, Speech by President Herman Van Rompuy at the opening of the Academic Year 2011–2012, European University Institute. http://europa.eu/rapid/press-release_PRES-11-425_en.htm.

Ferrera, M., & Burelli, C. (2019). Cross-national solidarity and political sustainability in the EU after the crisis. *JCMS Journal of Common Market Studies*, forthcoming.

Genschel, P., & Hemerijck, A. (2018). Solidarity in Europe. European University Institute, School of Transnational Governance, *Policy Brief*, May 2018.

Giannopoulou. A. (2016). *Main points of Alexis Tsipras speech at the Conference Alliance against austerity—for democracy in Europe*. Transform! Europe. https://www.transform-network.net/en/focus/overview/article/strategic-perspectives-of-the-european-left/alliance-for-democracy-and-against-austerity-in-europe/.

Hobolt, S. B. (2015). The 2014 European Parliament Elections: Divided in Unity. *The JCMS Annual Review of the European Union in 2014, 53*(1), 6–21.

Hobolt, S., & de Vries, C. (2016). Turning against the Union? The impact of the crisis on the Eurosceptic vote in the 2014 European Parliament elections. *Electoral Studies, 44*, 504–514.

Hooghe, L., & Marks, G. (2009). A postfunctionalist theory of European integration: From permissive consensus to constraining dissensus. *British Journal of Political Science, 39*(1), 1–23.

Inglehart, R. F. (2008). Changing values among western publics from 1970 to 2006. *West European Politics, 31*(1–2), 130–146.

Kankaras, M., & Moors, G. (2009). Measurement equivalence in solidarity attitudes in europe insights from a multiple-group latent-class factor approach. *International Sociology, 24*(4), 557–579.

Knodt, M., & Tews, A. (2014). Einleitung: Solidarität im Europäischen Mehrebenensystem. In M. Knodt & A. Tews (Eds.), *Solidarität in der EU* (pp. 7–18). Baden-Baden: Nomos.

Kontochistou, M., & Mascha, E. (2014). The Euro crisis and the question of solidarity in the European Union: Disclosures and manifestations in the European Press. *Review of European Studies, 6*(2), 50–62.

Kuhn, T., & Stoeckel, F. (2014). When European integration becomes costly: The Euro crisis and public support for European Economic Governance. *Journal of European Public Policy, 21*(4), 624–641.

Kuhn, T., Solaz, H., & Van Elsas, E. (2017). Practising what you preach: How cosmopolitanism promotes willingness to redistribute across the European Union. *Journal of European Public Policy*.

Lahusen, C. (2016). *Transnational solidarity within the European Union: Towards a framework of analysis*. Paper presented at the 8th Pan-European Conference on the European Union, The Union's Institutional and Constitutional Transformations: Stress or Adaptation? Trento, June 15–18, 2016.

Langford, L. M. (2013). The other Euro crisis: Rights violations under the common European Asylum System and the Unraveling of EU Solidarity. *Harvard Human Rights Journal, 26,* 217–264.

McLaren, L. (2007). Explaining mass-level Euroscepticism: Identity, interests, and institutional distrust. *Acta Politica, 42*(2–3), 233–251.

Mudde, C. (2014). Fighting the system? Populist radical right parties and party system change. *Party Politics, 20*(2), 217–226.

Nicoli, F. (2015). Eurocrisis and the myths of European redistribution: Illegitimate, unsustainable, inefficient? *Perspectives on Federalism, 7*(3), 19–48.

Nicoli, F. (2016). Hard-line Euroscepticism and the Eurocrisis: Evidence from a Panel Study of 108 Elections Across Europe. *Journal of Common Market Studies, 55*(2), 312–331.

Nicoli, F. (2018). Integration through crises? A quantitative assessment of the effect of the Eurocrisis on preferences for fiscal integration. *Comparative European Politics*, Online Preprint.

Nicoli, F., & Zeitlin, J. (Eds.) (2019). Europe beyond the polycrsis? Politicization and integration in the age of shifting cleavages. *Special Issue for the Journal of European Public Policy (JEPP)*, scheduled to appear in Q1/2019.

Pantazatou, K. (2015). Promoting solidarity in crisis times: Building on the EU Budget and the EU Funds. *Perspectives on Federalism, 7*(3), 49–76.

Preuss, U. (1999). National, supranational, and international solidarity. In K. Bayertz (Ed.), *Solidarity* (pp. 281–289). Dordrecht: Kluwer Academic Publishers.

Radu, L., Negrea-Busuioc, E., & Bârgăoanu, A. (2014). The rise of Euroscepticism in times of crisis. Evidence from the 2008–2013 Eurobarometers. *Romanian Journal of Communication and Public Relations, 16*(1), 9–23.

Risse, T. (2014). No Demos? Identities and public spheres in the Euro Crisis. *Journal of Common Market Studies, 55*(6), 1207–1215.

Sangiovanni, A. (2013). Solidarity in the European Union. *Oxford Journal of Legal Studies*, pp. 1–29.

Serricchio, F., Tsakatika, M., & Quaglia, L. (2013). Euroscepticism and the global financial crisis. *Journal of Common Market Studies, 51*(1), 51–64.

Stjernø, S. (2004). *Solidarity in Europe: The history of an idea*. Cambridge: Cambridge University Press.

Taggart, P. (1998). A touchstone of dissent: Euroscepticism in contemporary Western European Party Systems. *European Journal of Political Research, 33*(3), 363–388.

Treib, O. (2014). The voter says no, but nobody listens: causes and consequences of the Eurosceptic vote in the 2014 European elections. *Journal of European Public Policy, 21*(10), 1542–1543.

Van Klingeren, M., Boomgaarden, H. G., & De Vreese, C. H. (2013). Going soft or staying soft: Have identity factors become more important than economic rationale when explaining Euroscepticism? *Journal of European Integration, 35*(6), 689–704.

Verhaegen, S. (2017). What to expect from European identity? Explaining support for solidarity in times of crisis. *Comparative European Politics*, pp. 1–34.

Verney, S. (2015). Waking the 'sleeping giant' or expressing domestic dissent? Mainstreaming Euroscepticism in crisis-stricken Greece. *International Political Science Review, 36*(3), 279–295.

European Integration and the Economic Crisis: The Changing Positions of Left Parties in Spain and Italy

Valeria Tarditi and Davide Vittori

1 Introduction

From the beginning of the Great Recession (2008), the issue of European integration acquired increasing salience in many European polities (Cramme 2011). Extremist and niche parties have been the main agents of the politicization of the European issue; accordingly, mainstream parties have been forced to deal with a crisis of legitimacy of the European project and an increasingly dissatisfied citizenry (Hutter and Kriesi 2019). In the public discourse, the "responsible" pro-EU political forces were counterposed to Eurosceptic or populist parties, with the main line of division represented by the European Union as a larger project. In this chapter, we shed light on the radical left (RLPs) and social democratic (SDPs) party families, which have been either governing allies, partners, or external supporters several times in the two countries both at the national and sub-national levels, but whose positions on the European Union are divergent. RLPs have been more sensitive to the issue of a social Europe and have opposed an integration of the EU dominated by neoliberal logic, thus coming to be defined as a Eurosceptic party family; SDPs, on the other hand, have been supportive of EU integration and of the European Social Model. Despite the ever-increasing importance of the politicization of the EU, the literature on Euroscepticism has not tackled this issue insofar. Our main research question is therefore the following: to what extent do SDPs and RLPs diverge in the political and socio-economic field with regard to the European Union? Based on a diachronic analysis of party manifestoes, our guiding hypotheses are: (a) the crisis predominantly impacted the SPDs pro-European identity, while the RLPs Eurocritical (see below)

V. Tarditi (✉)
Università di Bologna, Bologna, Italy
e-mail: valeria.tarditi2@unibo.it

D. Vittori (✉)
Università Luiss, Rome, Italy
e-mail: dvittori@luiss.it

© Springer Nature Switzerland AG 2020

M. Baldassari et al. (eds.), *Anti-Europeanism*,
https://doi.org/10.1007/978-3-030-24428-6_7

pre-crisis position was strengthened; (b) while SDPs have moved leftward vis-à-vis the social Europe issue, the economic and political issues are still divisive for the two families.

We propose a binary comparison between Italy and Spain (see Tables 1 and 2), in particular, examining the Partido Socialista Obrero Español (Spanish Socialist Workers' Party—PSOE) and the Partito Democratico della Sinistra/Democratici di Sinistra/Partito Democratico (Democratic Party of the Left/Democrats of the Left/Democratic Party—PDS/DS/PD) (on this party's historical transformations see Marinelli 2017) in the SD family and Izquierda Unida (United Left—IU)-Podemos (We Can) and the Partito della Rifondazione Comunista (Party of the Communist Refoundation—PRC)-Sinistra Ecologia Libertà (Left, Ecology and Freedom—SEL) for the RLPs.

We start by briefly addressing the relative Eurosceptic/Pro-European attitudes of the RLPs and SDPs; then, we provide methodology and case selections. Finally, we analyze the parties' attitudes toward the European project, identifying the main similarities and differences.

2 The EU According to the Left: A Comparison Between Radical Left Parties and Social Democratic Parties

The politicization of the European issue in recent years (Ares et al. 2017) and the electoral growth of the so-called populist parties all around Europe in both national and European elections (Akkerman et al. 2016) reinvigorated the debate on Euroscepticism. Without reviewing the literature in-depth here (for a review see Leconte 2015), we will create a heuristic framework of analysis as a way to locate our case studies on the pro-EU/anti-EU continuum. By relying on the various typologies elaborated by scholars (see among others Hix and Lord 1997; Ray 1999; Kopecky and Mudde 2002; Conti and Verzichelli 2002), we can identify four categories along the aforesaid continuum. At the positive pole, we find *identity Europeanism*, meaning that parties express their unconditional support for Europeanization; instead, at the negative pole, *Euroscepticism* describes references against EU integration, aimed at reducing or totally rejecting (such as in the case of UKIP) the intervention of EU institutions in the national polity. In between these two poles, *functional Europeanism* is support for EU integration in various dimensions as long as it explicitly permits reaching domestic goals. On the other hand, *Eurocriticism* identifies those parties which accept the EU integration process while expressing criticisms of both the current configuration of the EU and the policies pursued by European supranational institutions. We use these heuristic categories to locate the parties under investigation on the continuum and to investigate the diachronic evolution of their attitudes vis-à-vis EU integration. Historically, RLPs and SDPs have adopted different stances toward the EU and the integration process. The former have generally criticized the process of European integration for its neoliberal character, emphasizing the weakness of the EU's social

Table 1 Social democratic and radical left parties competing in the national elections (Italy and Spain, main parties)

National election year	2000	2001	2004	2006	2008	2011	2013	2015	2016
Social democracy (ESP)	PSOE		PSOE		PSOE	PSOE		PSOE	PSOE
Radical left (ESP)	IU		IU		IU	IU		IU/Podemos	Unidos Podemos

(continued)

Table 1 (continued)

National election year	2000	2001	2004	2006	2008	2011	2013	2015	2016
Social democracy (ITA)		ULIVO		UNIONE[a]	PD		PD		
Radical left (ITA)		PRC		UNIONE[a]	SA		SEL/RC		

[a]L'Unione was an electoral coalition comprised of centrist, social democratic, and radical left parties

Table 2 Social democratic and radical left parties competing in the European elections (Italy and Spain, main parties)

European election year	2004	2009	2014
Social democracy (ESP)	PSOE	PSOE	PSOE
Radical left (ESP)	IU	La Izquierda[a]	IU/ Podemos
Social democracy (ITA)	ULIVO	PD	PD
Radical left (ITA)	PRC	PRC	AEcT[b]

[a]La Izquierda was an electoral coalition comprised of several radical left parties
[b]L'Altra Europa con Tsipras was an electoral coalition comprised of several radical left parties. Now, it is an independent association with its own internal bodies

dimension (Hudson 2012). RLPs have been often classified as Eurosceptic parties, i.e., opposing further integration (Hooghe et al. 2002; Marks et al. 2006; De Vries and Edwards 2009; Charalambous 2011). SDPs, however, were among the main supporters of the supranational project from the beginning of the 1980s and throughout the 1990s (Featherstone 1988). For SDPs, the integration process was an opportunity for the construction of a European social democratic project (Bailey 2005; Escalona and Vieira 2014).

The difference between the two families is unsurprising. Opposition to European integration is generally identified as the "touchstone of dissent" (Taggart 1998), the protest topic of peripheral or ideologically extremist parties (Hooghe et al. 2002). According to Hooghe et al. (2002), the party positioning on European integration can well be interpreted as an inverted U curve, where the opposition comes from the ideological poles—the radical left and the radical right—while parties in the middle are generally more supportive of European integration. In particular, radical left parties oppose the EU because of their refusal of capitalism, while the radical right do so because of their defence of national sovereignty; center-left parties see in deeper integration new possibilities for regulating capitalism, while center-right parties are favorable to supranational market integration.

The 2008 crisis has shown, however, the imbalances between the economic and social dimensions in the architecture of the EU, and the latter especially has been an important aspect for both families under analysis: the SDPs and the RLPs. Austerity measures, stemmed from a political will to follow EU economic criteria, have led to increasing social inequalities in the Eurozone, especially in the southern countries (Schmidt 2015).

3 Methodology: The Parties' Positions on the EU Through Their Manifestos

The party manifesto is the most relevant instrument that parties possess to present their programs, define priorities, and articulate their policy proposals. Since our longitudinal analysis goes back to a period in time when use of the Web was underdeveloped, an analysis based on sources such as social media would be non-comparative. This investigation applies qualitative content analysis (QCA) as its methodology. QCA can be defined as "a research method for the subjective interpretation of the content of text data through the systematic classification process of coding" (Hsieh and Shannon 2005: 1278). Our coding scheme proceeds as follows: firstly, we have selected party manifestos for the legislative and the European elections from 2000 to 2016. Secondly, we coded the manifestos and thirdly, we subjected the resulting coded texts to interpretative analysis. In each document, the unit of analysis is the paragraph; since we are focused on a qualitative analysis, a full sentence allows for the reconstruction of the most complete meaning. When the topic changes within the space of one paragraph, that paragraph is split into two units. Every unit of analysis is coded, first by categorizing it as either a 1, meaning the period tackles one of the EU-related issues we selected, or a 0 (the period refers to other issues). If a period is coded as 1, then the coder decides whether to assign the paragraph to one of four categories: (A) Political Integration (*Pol. Int.*), (B) Single Currency Defence (*Sin. Cur. Def.*), (C) Social Europe (*Soc. EU*), and (D) Economic Integration (*Ec. Int*). The coding of the paragraphs is structured as follows:

(A) *Pol. Int.* refers to positive/negative/neutral (hereafter p./n./n.) mentions of political integration (enlargement of the European Union, deeper integration among Member States, and democratization of EU institutions toward a shared management of the EU).
(B) *Sin. Cur. Def.* refers to p./n./n. mentions of the EURO (EURO as market stabilizer, a country's improved economic performance under Euro, EURO as the only currency for EU).
(C) *Social Europe* refers to p./n./n. mentions of any provisions regarding welfare state economic policies at the European level (European unemployment benefit schemes, European basic income, European minimum wage, maintenance of public services, free access to public national healthcare schemes, and European harmonization of wages among genders).

(D) *Ec. Int.* refers to p./n./n. mentions of economic integration (fiscal and financial integration, introduction of supranational taxes, liberalization of the market, and integration of the single market with a shared European budget).

The four categories are further split into three sub-categories: positive, negative, and neutral paragraphs. Positive paragraphs refer to the promotion of further integration at the EU level for a given policy; in this sense, all the reforms proposed aimed at modifying the status quo at the EU level are coded as positive, even when a party criticizes the status quo. On the contrary, a paragraph is coded as negative when the party criticizes the status quo without promoting a supranational solution or when the criticism is coupled with a call for retrenchment of EU competencies in a given policy. In neutral paragraphs, either there are no positive or negative comments, or the coders cannot clearly identify the positive/negative direction of the paragraph. What we expect and what we will discuss is an increase in the negative references toward EU in all aspects: the more a political party negatively refers to the EU in one of the dimensions under analysis, the more it turns to either a Eurocritical or Eurosceptic position. The extent to which a party turns to more critical positions toward the EU is described by the coder in the analysis, as our QCA methodology does not provide a scaling method to measure Euroscepticism, Eurocriticism, functional Europeanism, and identity Europeanism.

4 Spain (2000–2008)

In Spain, European integration and the country's role in the European Community (EC) have been among the most uncontroversial and cross-cutting topics across political parties. Although IU rejected the Maastricht Treaty, the Spanish Communist Party and, after 1992, IU advocated a critical support of supranational integration (Benedetto and Quaglia 2007). In line with a Euro-enthusiast public opinion (Barreiro and Sánchez-Cuenca 2001; Áviles 2004), the PSOE unconditionally backed European integration both politically and economically.

It is thus unsurprising that Europe is framed as a dream come true for the socialists. As the PSOE puts it in their manifesto for the 2000 legislative elections (2000: 78), "Spain fulfilled the dream of generations of progressives, who saw in Europe not only the guarantee for freedom and rights that were lacking here, but also the occasion to modernize our country […]". The overwhelming majority of the references in both the 2000 and 2004 PSOE manifestos frame both political and economic integration positively, in particular, the enlargement of the EU and commercial agreements with non-EU countries. From 2000 to 2004, the positive references to European integration increase, especially in the European manifesto (PSOE 2004b), due to the forthcoming referendum on the European constitution (February 20, 2005),[1] which the PSOE had

[1] PSOE, Partido Popular (PP) and the Greens—along with other regionalist parties, Convergència i Unió, Partido Nacionalista Vasco and Coalición Canaria—campaigned for the 'YES' to the European Constitution; IU, Esquerra Republicana de Catalunya, the Catalan Greens and other regionalist

previously supported at the European level. The emphasis on social Europe is much less pronounced: in the three manifestos for the legislative elections from that period (2000, 2004a, and 2008), 43 paragraphs are coded as positive mentions of economic integration, 13 as positive references to social Europe.

IU demonstrates a very critical position toward the single currency project and the stability pact associated with the Economic Monetary Union. Nonetheless, IU criticism is mainly focused on economic integration, especially on the "neoliberal" soul of the EU. Several paragraphs (IU 2000: 26–28) are dedicated to the imbalances produced by the economic union and by the 2000 Lisbon agenda; at the same time, IU (negatively) targets the absence of both a European social dimension and the introduction of supranational schemes aimed at contrasting unemployment and social exclusion. These critical stances are somewhat nuanced in the following legislative election (2004), but the IU posture toward neoliberal Europe remains critical and is accompanied by a strong preference for a social Europe (IU 2004a).The paragraphs dedicated to economic and political integration in the IU European election manifesto (2004b) show that the party has a radically different view on the European constitution compared to the PSOE: "The text [i.e., the draft of the Constitution] is far away from what the majority of the Europeans need now [...] [The draft] sanctifies the neoliberal economic model, which supports privatization, deregulation, flexibilization of the job market, the dismantling of the national social protection's policies and the no-deficit dogma" (2004b: 11).

5 Spain (2009–2016)

When the building sector's bubble burst, Spain's economic growth collapsed (Royo 2009). The political system was jeopardized by the entrance of Podemos (2014), a new left competitor to the PSOE and IU. Starting from 2009, the reduction of the impact of the crisis has been at the core of all manifestos. In the PSOE's case, the crisis is framed as a critical juncture for the EU. While the coding shows that social Europe acquired a greater importance vis-à-vis economic integration (eleven positive mentions for the former vs. "only" six for the latter), the economic model within the EU remains unquestioned. The Lisbon Strategy, which was rejected by IU and supported by the PSOE in the previous election, is regarded as the starting point for a new employment and competitiveness pact based on proactive policies, social dialogue, and fiscal incentives (PSOE 2009: 5). The emphasis on reforming European economic integration is crucial in the 2011 manifesto (PSOE 2011), while most of the proposals regarding the welfare state are related to Spain rather than to Europe. In the 2009 and 2011 manifestos, there are only six negative paragraphs related to economic integration and social Europe. During the Spanish economic tempest (2011–2014), the PSOE shifted to the left in the socio-economic field. As the party

and niche parties for the NO. The participation was 42.32%; the YES won with 81.65%. The NO voters were 18.35%.

states in its 2014 manifesto (PSOE 2014: 24), “the path of Europe’s rebuilding, as a whole, is an unequivocal success story. However, nowadays in the midst of a socio-economic and political crisis, the European Union risks losing the very meaning of its identity.” In the 2014 and 2015 manifestos (PSOE 2014, 2015), the growth of the paragraphs focused on the necessity of a reform of social Europe and on criticism of an economic integration based only on supply-side control is significant. The paragraphs with negative references to political integration increase significantly as well. In 2016, the number of paragraphs devoted to social Europe and to economic integration as well as the ratio between positive and negative references remain stable; however, for the first time since 2000, the PSOE (2016: 249–250) raises the question of the sustainability of the fiscal and monetary union as it was conceived after Maastricht.

Since the outbreak of the crisis, IU has reiterated its critical stance toward neoliberal Europe (IU 2008, 2009, 2015; IU-LV 2011). On the one hand, IU advocates replacing the Stability and Growth Pact with a Solidarity Pact based on high social protection and full employment as well as the democratization of the EU governance, especially within the European Central Bank (ECB). On the other hand, it proposes a defence of all public services against the liberalization proposed by the EU (IU 2009: 20–22); in particular, eight paragraphs in the 2009 manifesto are dedicated to the negative repercussions of the Bolkestein Directive. The negative references to economic integration are counterbalanced by a proactive attitude toward anti-neoliberal measures such as the Tobin Tax. Moreover, IU actively campaigns in support of several proposals related to European unemployment protection schemes and the minimum wage, and against the flexibilization of the job market. In the 2014 manifesto, three main parts can be identified in the coding process: the first regards criticism of economic integration (IU 2014: 5–10); the second comprises positive references to a European welfare state (IU 2014: 10–14) with similar characteristics to those in the 2009 manifesto; the third focuses on an alternative economic model to be developed in contrast to the privatization and liberalization process that took place after Maastricht (IU 2014: 14–19).

Podemos presented its first manifesto on the occasion of the 2014 European elections. In the following legislative elections, it proposed two similar programs, the latter of which was shared with IU.

Podemos’ program lacks the analytical introductory chapter that characterized the IU manifestos, in which IU has usually described the status quo in Spain and Europe and where several references to the EU can be found. The coding shows a more reformist attitude vis-à-vis the EU and a less critical stance (only five paragraphs present a negative reference to economic integration). However, in two paragraphs, Podemos criticizes the configuration of the European institutions: the party calls for a democratic refoundation of the EU, which Podemos defines as neoliberal and anti-democratic because of the liberalization and commodification of public services (Podemos 2014: 28). Accordingly, Podemos rejects both the EU’s proposed Free Trade Treaties and the Memorandum of Understanding signed by European and international institutions and some Member States. The 13 paragraphs, which include positive references to economic integration, focus exclusively on the redefinition of

EU crisis management and the reform of EU institutions such as the ECB. Podemos' (2015) manifesto follows the same pattern: it is composed of a list of 394 proposals without any overarching political premise. Nonetheless, Podemos' negative attitude toward the EU's trade policy manifests in seven paragraphs that the party is critical of economic integration and, in particular, of the TTIP, TISA, and CETA.

Finally, the pact between Podemos and the IU for the 2016 election has a shorter program than the others, with few paragraphs on the EU (11). The official Podemos program is identical to the 2015 manifesto, revealing the two parties' shared scepticism of the EU's austerity programs as well as the fiscal policies suggested by the Eurozone Member States (Unidos Podemos 2016: 3).

6 Italy (2001–2008)

In Italy, elites, political parties, and citizens have long been considered pro-European. However, on the center-left, there was a clear distinction between the PRC and the PDS, the heirs of the Partito Comunista Italiano (PCI). Simply put, the PRC was against the Maastricht Treaty and the single currency. Subsequently, while it remained extremely critical toward the EU's economic and social model, it proposed radical changes to the supranational project (Charalambous 2008; Quaglia 2008). The PDS, on the other hand, appeared to espouse a "principled Europeanism" (Conti and Verzichelli 2002). Between 1996 and 2001, Italy had three different center-left governments, each of which introduced policies oriented to reducing the budget deficit and allowing Italy to meet the Maastricht criteria and enter into the Euro area (Vampa 2009). In the 2001 elections, the Ulivo's (the coalition between the PDS and various smaller center-left smaller parties) EU-related economic and political policies are centered around deepening European integration (Ulivo 2001: 19). In the thirty-nine paragraphs coded, no negative evaluation has been identified. In contrast, the European issue is used to emphasize the coalition's distance from the center-right, which is composed of parties that are considered supporters of "extremist nationalism" and anti-European positions. The economic constraints and the related Stability and Growth Pact are defined as the "economic constitution" (Ulivo 2001: 20) of the country and the basis for building a model of regulated capitalism at the European level. For the PRC, Europe is instead a field of action and political struggle (Charalambous 2008). In its program, there are several paragraphs (40) about the EU: unlike those of the Ulivo, half of them are negative. However, the party is in favor of the European integration process as long as it is oriented by the principles of solidarity and equality. According to the PRC, the aim of the EU should be the realization of a social Europe capable of fostering employment and establishing cooperative relations with foreign countries (PRC 2001).

In the 2004 European elections, the Ulivo dedicates twenty-six paragraphs to economic issues, pointing out once again the need to respect EU economic criteria, inflation control and the usefulness of further liberalization in different economic and job market sectors. Still, there are more references to the social dimension (twenty-six paragraphs compared with five in 2001) which, according to the Ulivo, has to be strengthened in order to counteract the negative effects of globalization (Ulivo 2004). The Ulivo coalition enthusiastically supports the European Constitution, which according to the PRC is an "attempt to provide dignity and constitutional form to neoliberalism, to a Europe of markets and merchants" (PRC 2004: 6). For this reason, the PRC voted against the ratification of the Constitutional Treaty, as it had previously voted against the Maastricht Treaty and the Treaty of Nice (Conti and De Giorgi 2011).

In 2006, the DS, the PRC and other minor forces formed the vast Unione coalition, led by Romano Prodi. The coalition's manifesto was the outcome of a difficult process of compromise between the various parties. The general orientation is clearly pro-EU, but acknowledges the weaknesses of the supranational project. According to the coalition, it is necessary to use the European achievements as a starting point: the single market, economic integration, the single currency, and enlargement (Unione 2006: 87). Nonetheless, it also proposes new goals in the social and political dimensions: the Unione backs a new constitutional process aimed at elaborating a new European Constitution to be ratified by a referendum on a supranational scale. This issue and the more general democratization of the EU are particularly important for the PRC, which has a much more critical position than its coalition partners.

The end of the center-left government (2006–2008) caused a split between the moderate left and the radical left. The former was represented by the PD (a new party originated from the merger of DS, La Margherita (The Daisy), and other centrist parties); the latter by Sinistra Arcobaleno (Rainbow Left, SA), an electoral cartel led by the PRC's leader, Fausto Bertinotti. The PD's manifesto radically departs from the previous Unione's program: it is shorter (only 49 pages) and it is focused on abstract concepts such as "innovation" and "change." Five paragraphs on the first page are dedicated to European integration and its political, economic, and internal dimensions. There are no negative mentions, but the party's commitment to revitalizing European integration after the failure of the draft constitution is reiterated. The EU is therefore identified as a tool for managing globalization (PD 2008: 1).

The SA also presents a shorter program than in the past. The paragraphs about the EU are concentrated mostly in one section (SA 2008: 25–26) and contain criticisms about the strict budgetary constraints, the excessive separation of the economic sphere from the political one, and the harsh consequences in terms of social inequality. However, references to an idealistic Europeanism can be found in this manifesto, including SA's support for a federal Europe based on labor rights, civil liberties, and solidarity.

7 Italy (2009–2014)

The effects of the international economic crisis emerged in Italy starting, in particular, in 2011. However, the topic of the crisis was already present in the public debate and in the parties' programs in 2009. Both the PD and the PRC advocate a general reform of the EU in many areas, especially in the economic field. However, for the PD, which defines itself as "the most coherently Europeanist Italian political force" (PD 2009: 18), the EU is still a lifeline able to limit the consequences of the crisis in a globalized world. According to the PRC, the EU actively contributes to those neoliberal policies which are at the origin of the crisis (PRC/FdS 2009: 10).

On the front page, the PD describes the achievements of the European project in terms of peace-keeping and economic well-being. Only two paragraphs can be classified as negative. In the first of these, the EC is criticized for its incapability to coordinate the member countries' economic policies and to adequately address the crisis (PD 2009: 6). In the second, the PD addresses the EU's democratic deficit, sustaining the need to expand citizens' political participation (PD 2009: 15). Four paragraphs focus on the promotion of social policies aimed at ensuring a greater redistribution of resources (PD 2009: 7–8, 10). The PRC and its coalition partners (the PDCI, Socialismo 2000 and Consumatori Uniti) see the EU as the outcome of decisions adopted over the years by all the mainstream European parties. The PRC declares itself in favor of a democratic Europe of the people, opposing the "technocratic Europe" that (according to the party) was built through the Maastricht and Lisbon Treaties (PRC/FdS 2009: 10). The program is very synthetic (only five pages), but tackles the main economic and social topics.

The distance between the two parties has increased even more in the last years. At the end of 2011, Silvio Berlusconi resigned as Prime Minister and was replaced by a technocratic government led by ex EU-Commissioner Mario Monti and supported by the mainstream parties, i.e., the PD and FI. In the 2013 political elections, the RC allied with other minor left parties, while the SEL was part of the PD-led *Italia Bene Comune* coalition. The PD and the SEL drafted their own separate programs before the creation of the electoral alliance.

The PD manifesto is mainly focused on national politics and the four paragraphs dedicated to the EU concern the economic/fiscal and political dimensions. The party presents itself as a reliable actor in ensuring compliance with the recently approved Fiscal Compact. However, the European rules are no longer considered immutable: the PD advocates a new economic approach, focused on economic growth and on the emission of European bonds (Eurobonds). Furthermore, the party pursues the democratization of the supranational project in view of the future creation of the "United States of Europe" (PD 2013: 4).

The SEL also expresses the idea of a federal project. This party rejects austerity policies while favoring greater financial integration through a more active role for the ECB. According to the SEL, the EU's crisis is due to the prevalence of intergovernmental logic and national economic interests. Solutions should be found through further integration via a governmental architecture based on citizens' participation and a more powerful EP. The SEL advocates the substitution of the Fiscal Compact with a "citizens' pact for democracy" (SEL 2013: 45) as well as strengthened international cooperation.

In the vision espoused in the PD/SEL shared document, Italy's future is necessarily within the EU, while greater political, economic, and fiscal integration is also promoted (PD-SEL 2013).

According to the PRC and its allies in the Rivoluzione Civile (RC) cartel, the EU is responsible for the economic crisis because it promoted and imposed austerity policies that led to the dismantling of domestic welfare and to the rise of unemployment. Even in this program, the economic, political, and social dimensions are particularly fundamental (RC 2013).

In the 2014 manifesto, the PD shows a far more critical approach to the European economic policies introduced in recent years, highlighting the consequences of these in terms of social inequalities. However, the PD attributes responsibility to conservatives' poor management rather than to the policies themselves (PD 2014: 4).

The coding of the program shows a preponderance of paragraphs in the economic and social dimensions. In eight paragraphs, we find critical positions about the economic management of the EU; in thirteen paragraphs, the party promotes the EU's intervention in domestic welfare and employment policy. Moreover, a European minimum wage and the taxation of financial transactions are proposed (nine paragraphs are dedicated to Keynesian measures to be developed). Both the PRC and the SEL, which appear together on the list *l'Altra Europa con Tsipras* (Other Europe with Tsipras, AEcT), consider the EU to be a victim not only of the crisis but also of its own neoliberal policies (AEcT 2014: 1). Criticisms cover all the areas identified, with a focus on the economic and social models. At the same time, those parties acknowledge that the EU is the most appropriate forum in which to introduce anti-crisis policies.

8 Identity Europeanism Versus Eurocriticism

In the pre-crisis environment, both the PSOE and the PD incorporated an Identity Europeanism at political and socio-economic levels. The political integration (i.e., federalization) of Europe and the resulting political spill-over into foreign and defence policies are framed as a *conditio sine qua non* for deepening economic integration. In both countries, the main line of demarcation between the social democratic and radical left parties lies in their stances regarding political integration. SDPs support the Constitutional Treaty while RLPs are highly sceptical of the whole project, which they considered an instrument for the imposition of neoliberal policies on national constituencies. In this first phase, RLPs in both Spain and Italy explicitly recognize the necessity of political integration among MSs but also highlight the deficiencies of the peculiar integration pursued since Maastricht. The IU and PRC stress the neoliberal political design of the EU and emphasize the risk of political integration without a parallel social process.

These tendencies within RLPs are not Eurosceptic per se. Instead, RLPs in Italy and Spain can be considered Eurocritical, since they do not reject European integration *tout court*, nor do they advocate for disengagement or withdrawal from the EU or its institutions. The PSOE and the Ulivo defend economic integration and the financial requirements envisaged by EU institutions. Though both mention the necessity of more integrated social policies, neither advances a clear-cut negative judgment of the Lisbon Agenda or other European social schemes proposed during the relevant period.

9 Toward Functional Europeanism and the Radicalization of Eurocriticism

The economic and financial crisis jeopardized the previous pro-EU/EU-critic scheme. From 2008 onwards, Spain's social democracy amplifies criticism of the lack of Europeanized social protection schemes and emphasizes the complications inherent to the austerity measures imposed by European institutions. Nonetheless, for the PSOE, the answer to these multiple crises remains "more Europe" rather than "less Europe." Despite lamenting the weaknesses of Europe's social dimension, the PSOE stands for a greater political and economic integration. As far as they are concerned, the blame for this weakness lies with the center-right conservative majority, both at the European and national level. For its own part, the Italian PD defines itself as the most pro-European party in Italy, thus maintaining its pre-crisis Europeanist attitude. Like the PSOE, the PD highlights the deficiencies of the EU's social and economic management, focusing on conservatives' role in imposing severe budget retrenchment. However, because of its previous support of a grand-coalition government (2011–2013) responsible for several austerity measures, the PD can present itself as a responsible force in the Italian system, one able to guarantee greater flexibility in the budget restrictions. In the 2014 manifesto, criticism toward the EU increases substantially, especially regarding the economic and social spheres. At the time, the young and dynamic party secretary Matteo Renzi's promise of a new direction in EU affairs coincided with the newly emerged Five Star Movement's growing presence in the polls to induce the party to adopt a responsive electoral campaign based on radical change in EU economic and social policies.

In the social dimension, the PSOE and PD engaged in "blame shifting" onto the center-right parties, despite their own roles in having approved European austerity measures in their respective domestic contexts.

On the other hand, radical left manifestos highlight not only the pre-crisis opposition to neoliberal visions of Europe, but above all scepticism toward economic integration and the "constitutionalization" of austerity measures such as the balanced budget deficit. These critiques seem to be radicalized and appear to espouse a Eurosceptic stance. However, they advocate for a complete reversal of the EU's crisis management in the aftermath of the Greek bailout without anything so drastic as an exit from the EU. The democratization of Europe is inextricably linked to the protection of social rights as well as to the transformation of the ECB to an instrument in the service of the people rather than financial interests. All RLPs place greater emphasis on rejecting all free trade agreements (FTA) between the EU and other counterparts.

Thus, the main difference between SDPs and RLPs lies in the economic and political fields. According to IU, from 2008 onward, Europe has been facing a systemic crisis; Podemos and L'Altra Europa con Tsipras refer instead to the failures of the EU's neoliberal crisis management. On the other hand, the PSOE and the PD focus on the failure of the conservative solutions to the crisis, while nonetheless supporting several austerity-driven reforms as well as the most recent supranational treaties (see Table 3).

10 Conclusion

The Great Recession has shown the imbalances in the EU's economic and social dimensions as well as the EU's growing impact on domestic politics. This has influenced the positions expressed by moderate and radical left parties regarding the European project.

In the past, SDPs considered Europe to be the ideal sphere in which social democratic policy might be actualized, regardless of its actual feasibility in the EU institutional and economic context. The crisis has clearly highlighted the contradictions of the "Faustian pact" that induced SDPs to give full and unconditional support to European integration and to the construction of a neoliberal structure without even proposing any alternatives (Escalona and Vieira 2014; Cramme 2011). Our analysis shows that SDPs present an identity Europeanism in the pre-crisis environment that was in line with the SDPs Europeanist literature. This Europeanism is supportive of the integration process—and its attendant ideology—across the board. By attempting to adopt a more responsive approach to their electorate in the crisis environment, SDPs in Italy and Spain have shifted closer to a functional Europeanism. The EU has become the most effective arena in which SDPs can combat social austerity.

As for RLPs, our analysis shows that this family cannot be classified as pertaining to straightforward Euroscepticism either in the pre-crisis period or during the crisis itself. Rather, this family can be more comfortably located in the Eurocritical position. Still, criticism of the neoliberal character of EU institutions has continued to radicalize, especially with regard to the new economic treaties such as the Fiscal Compact. However, RLPs still look at the EU as a privileged arena in which to pursue radical changes in economic and social policies. In conclusion, since the beginning of the crisis, the similarities between the parties of the two families have increased in regard to the social dimension of the EU. With respect to the greater EU's political project and economic model, however, the distance still remains today and appears to be even greater than in the past. The analysis provided in this chapter has evidenced how the parties' positions on the EU are not immutable over time, but can change according to the evolution of the integration process and unexpected external shocks. In particular, the Great Recession caused growing criticism toward the EU management of the financial crisis in those party families, such as SDPs, which have been promoter of further European integration in several policy fields. This may be one signal of the mainstreaming of either Eurocritical or Eurosceptic

Table 3 Summary of the parties' positions on European integration issues

Party families and countries	Parties	Before the economic crisis 2000–2008	During the Great Recession 2009–2016
Spanish social democracy	PSOE	Identity Europeanism: – in favor of all dimensions (Pol. Int., Sin. Cur. Def., Social Europe, Ec. Int.)	Functional Europeanism: – supportive of the European integration – critical toward conservative parties in the management of the crisis – emphasis on the lack of social integration
Spanish radical left	IU	Eurocriticism: – critical to the neoliberal integration – support of Europeanization of social policies and of an alternative economic integration	Radicalization of Eurocriticism: – critical position toward neoliberal-oriented political integration – support of Europeanization of social policies and a treaties' change
	Podemos	Did not contested	Eurocriticism: – critical position toward neoliberal integration – support of Europeanization of social policies (treaty change)
Italian social democracy	PDS/DS/PD (Ulivo; Unione)	Identity Europeanism: – in favor of all dimension under analysis (Pol. Int., Sin. Cur. Def., Social Europe, Ec. Int.)	Between identity and functional Europeanism: – support of the European integration – more references to democratic deficit – critical toward conservative parties in the management of the crisis

(continued)

Table 3 (continued)

Party families and countries	Parties	Before the economic crisis 2000–2008	During the Great Recession 2009–2016
Italian radical left	PRC/SA	Eurocriticism: – critical to neoliberal integration – critical toward measures related to the adoption of austerity measures – support of Europeanization of social policies	Radicalization of Eurocriticism: – critical toward the EU economic integration (austerity) – critical toward political integration and new treaties – support of Europeanization of social policies
	SEL	Did not contested	Eurocriticism: – critical position toward neoliberal integration – support of political integration (Federal Europe) and of social rights – support of Europeanization of social policies
	Altra Europa	Did not contested	Eurocriticism: – critical position toward neoliberal integration – support of political integration – support of Europeanization of social policies (treaty change)

positions in Europe: in a nutshell, it is becoming more popular to criticize the EU, and mainstream party families are adapting to this new scenario. Due to the political and financial challenges that in the last years the EU has had to deal with, as for example that of the managing of the immigration flows or the growing economic difference between Northern and Southern European member states, further research is needed to asses if also other party families may have recently changed their position vis-à-vis the EU.

References

Akkerman, T., de Lange, S. L., & Rooduijn, M. (Eds.). (2016). *Radical right-wing populist parties in Western Europe: Into the mainstream?* Abingdon: Routledge.

Ares, M., Ceka, B., & Kriesi, H. (2017). Diffuse support for the European Union: Spillover effects of the politicization of the European integration process at the domestic level. *Journal of European Public Policy, 24*(8), 1091–1115.

Áviles, J. (2004). España y la Integración Europea: Partidos y Opinión Pública, 1977–2004. *Espacio, Tiempo y Forma, 5,* 409–442.

Bailey, D. J. (2005). Obfuscation through integration: Legitimating 'new' social democracy in the European Union. *Journal Common Market Studies, 43*(1), 13–35.

Barreiro, B., & Sánchez-Cuenca, I. (2001). La Europeización de la Opinión pública Española. In C. Closa (Ed.), *La Europeización del Sistema Político Español* (pp. 29–51). Madrid: Istmo.

Benedetto, G., & Quaglia, L. (2007). The comparative politics of communist Euroscepticism in France, Italy and Spain. *Party Politics, 13*(4), 478–499.

Charalambous, G. (2008). *Rifondazione and Europe: A party competition analysis.* Paper presented at the PSA Conference, Swansea, UK, April 1–3.

Charalambous, G. (2011). All the shades of red: Examining the radical left's Euroscepticism. *Contemporary Politics, 17*(3), 299–320.

Conti, N., & De Giorgi, E. (2011). L'Euroscetticismo a parole: Lega Nord e Rifondazione comunista, tra retorica e comportamento istituzionale. *Rivista Italiana di Scienza Politica, 41*(2), 266–289.

Conti, N. & Verzichelli, L. (2002). *The European dimension of political discourse in Italy: A longitudinal analysis of party preferences (1950–2001).* Occasional papers of CIRCaP, Centre for the Study of Political Change, Siena.

Cramme, O. (2011). *The power of European integration. Social democracy in search of a purpose.* Policy network paper, London.

De Vries, C. E., & Edwards, E. E. (2009). Taking Europe to its extremes. Extremist parties and public Euroscepticism. *Party Politics, 15*(1), 5–28.

Escalona, F., & Vieira, M. (2014). 'It does not happen here either': Why social democrats fail in the context of the great economic crisis. In D. J. Bailey, J.-M. De Waele, F. Escalona, & M. Vieira, (Eds.), *European social democracy during the global economic crisis. Renovation or resignation?* (pp. 19–41). Manchester: Manchester University Press.

Featherstone, K. (1988). *Socialist parties and European integration: A comparative history.* Manchester: Manchester University Press.

Hix, S., & Lord, C. (1997). *Political parties in the European Union.* London: Macmillan.

Hooghe, L., Marks, G., & Wilson, C. (2002). Does left/right cleavage structure party positions on European integration. *Comparative Political Studies, 35*(8), 965–989.

Hsieh, H. F., & Shannon, S. E. (2005). Three approaches to qualitative content analysis. *Qualitative Health Research, 15*(9), 1277–1288.

Hudson, K. (2012). *The new European left. A socialism for the twenty-first century?* Houndmills, Basingstoke: Palgrave Macmillan.

Hutter, S., & Kriesi, H. (2019). Politicizing Europe in times of crisis. *Journal of European Public Policy, 26*(7), 996–1017. https://doi.org/10.1080/13501763.2019.1619801.
Kopecky, P., & Mudde, C. (2002). The two sides of Euroscepticism. Party positions on European integration in East Central Europe. *European Union Politics, 3*(3), 297–326.
Leconte, C. (2015). From pathology to mainstream phenomenon: Reviewing the Euroscepticism debate in research and theory. *International Political Science Review, 36*(3), 250–263.
Marinelli, V. (2017). *Il Partito. Organizzazione, mutamenti e scissioni della sinistra maggioritaria italiana (PCI-PDS-DS-PD)*. Soveria Mannelli: Rubbettino.
Marks, G., Hooghe, L., Nelson, M., & Edwards, E. (2006). Party competition and European integration in the east and west. Different structure same causality. *Comparative Political Studies, 39*(2), 155–175.
Quaglia, L. (2008). Euroscepticism in Italy. In A. Szczerbiak & P. Taggart (Eds.), *Opposing Europe: The comparative party politics of Euroscepticism* (pp. 58–73). Oxford: Oxford University Press.
Ray, L. (1999). Measuring party orientations towards European integration: Results from an expert survey. *European Journal of Political Research, 36*(2), 283–306.
Royo, S. (2009). After the Fiesta: The Spanish economy meets the global financial crisis. *South European Society & Politics, 14*(1), 19–34.
Schmidt, V. (2015). Changing the policies, politics and processes of the Eurozone in crisis: Will this time be different? In D. Natali & B. Vanhercke (Eds.), *Social policy in the European Union: State of play 2015* (pp. 33–64). Brussels: ETUI.
Taggart, P. (1998). A touchstone of dissent: Euroscepticism in contemporary Western European party systems. *European Journal of Political Research, 33*(3), 363–388.
Vampa, D. (2009). The death of social democracy: The case of the Italian democratic party. *Bulletin of Italian Politics, 1*(2), 347–370.

Manifestos: Spain

IU. (2000). *Somos necesarios/as. Programa Electoral. Elecciones Generales 2000.*
IU. (2004a). *Programa Electoral de Izquierda Unida. Elecciones Generales 2004.*
IU. (2004b). *Programa de Izquierda Unida. Elecciones Europeas del 13 Junio 2004.*
IU. (2008). *Más Izquierda. Programa Electoral. Elecciones Generales 2008.*
IU. (2009). *Programa de Izquierda Unida a las elecciones Europeas 2009.*
IU. (2014). *Programa para las elecciones Europeas 2014.*
IU. (2015). *Por un nuevo país. Cuadernos programáticos para la unidad popular.*
IU-LV. (2011). *Propuestas electorales Izquierda Unida. Elecciones 2011.*
Podemos. (2014). *Podemos. Documento final del programa colaborativo.*
Podemos. (2015). *Podemos, sabemos, queremos. Un programa para cambiar nuestro país.*
PSOE. (2000). *Programa Electoral. Elecciones Generales 2000.*
PSOE. (2004a). *Merecemos una España mejor. Soluciones ahora. Programa Electoral Elecciones Generales 2004.*
PSOE. (2004b). *Elecciones Europeas 2004. Manifiesto.*
PSOE. (2008). *Motivos para creer. Programa Electoral Elecciones Generales 2008.*
PSOE. (2009). *Manifiesto. Programa Electoral PSOE Europeas 2009.*
PSOE. (2011). *Programa Electoral. Elecciones Generales 2000.*
PSOE. (2014). Tú mueves Europa. *Programa Electoral 2014.*
PSOE. (2015). El cambio que une. *Programa Electoral. Elecciones Generales 2000.*
PSOE. (2016). Sí. Sí por el cambio. *Programa Electoral. Elecciones Generales 2016.*
Unidos Podemos. (2016). *Cambiar España: 50 pasos para gobernar juntos.*

Italy

L'Altra Europa con Tsipras—AEcT. (2014). *Le proposte della lista 'L'altra Europa con Tsipras'*.
PD. (2008). *Un'Italia moderna. Si può fare.*
PD. (2009). *L'Europa che conviene. Le idee e gli impegni del PD per le elezioni europee. Più forte noi, più forte tu.*
PD. (2013). *L'Italia giusta.*
PD. (2014). *L'Europa cambia verso. 25 maggio/europee.*
PD-SEL. (2013). *Italia Bene Comune. Carta d'intenti.*
PRC. (2001). *Programma politico 2001 del Partito della Rifondazione comunista.*
PRC. (2004). *La sinistra, L'Altra Europa. Programma del Partito della Rifondazione Comunista-Sinistra Europea. Elezioni europee 13–14 giugno.*
PRC/Fds. (2009). *Un'altra Europa è possibile. Il programma per le elezioni europee di PRC, PdCI, Socialismo 2000 e Consumatori uniti. Elezioni per il Parlamento Europeo*, Giugno 6–7, 2009.
RC. (2013). *La nostra rivoluzione civile.*
SA. (2008). *Il programma de la Sinistra Arcobaleno. Fai una scelta di parte.*
SEL. (2013). *Benvenuta sinistra. Il programma.*
ULIVO. (2001). *Rinnoviamo l'Italia, insieme. Il programma dell'Ulivo per il governo 2001/2006 presentato da Francesco Rutelli.*
ULIVO. (2004). *Parole nuove per l'Ulivo.*
UNIONE. (2006). *Per il bene dell'Italia. Programma di Governo 2006–2011.*

Simplicity Versus Complexity in the European Debate: Identity, Responsibility, and the Dialogue Questioned

Kristina Khutsishvili

1 Words and Their Meanings

Current debates around populism, nationalism, anti-Europeanism, and related issues have gone beyond the space of academia. Moreover, it is not clear whether social sciences researchers are tackling the actual issues, trying to prevent the possible outcomes, or are just left to deal with inevitable consequences, being too late to work on the causes.

Populist and nationalist claims are supplemented with a phenomenon of anti-intellectualism. Although there is no common negotiated definition of this term—that is also an indicator of the social sciences following but not leading the debate—intuitively anti-intellectualism comprehends both distrust in experts and disregard of expertise. While populism and nationalism are not truly new features of political reality but, rather, have received an increased attention during political events over the last years, anti-intellectualism is less discussed. The issues, though, share a dimension of responsibility. In simple terms, the question may be: Who is responsible for the phenomenon we discuss at academic conferences, such as the rise of populist narratives, far-right movements (while far-left ones are less discussed), fake news, "alternative facts", multiple truths, nationalist and anti-Europeanist claims, and Brexit?

This issue's moral complexity exceeds the existing framework of the debate. In current emotional discussions, movements, parties, politicians, and public figures are often attacked, as they are seen as sources of populist and nationalist ideas and discourses, although behind the successful populist uprising there are voters, i.e. people who have made their choices, whether well informed or not, in favour of these movements. It is not an easy task to research whether the demand has caused the shift

K. Khutsishvili (✉)
DIRPOLIS Institute, Scuola Superiore Sant'Anna, Pisa, Italy
e-mail: k.khutsishvili@santannapisa.it

© Springer Nature Switzerland AG 2020

M. Baldassari et al. (eds.), *Anti-Europeanism*,
https://doi.org/10.1007/978-3-030-24428-6_8

of supply on the market of political ideas, or vice versa. Taking a moral stand towards the discourse of politicians cannot be an isolated action: the issue of responsibility of the voters should also be taken into consideration. Furthermore, the broader question of responsibility in the society is not very well discussed, for instance, the responsibility of academics and intellectuals in application to contemporary political and societal challenges.

Populist narratives are characterized by simplicity: simple answers are given to the questions that need a careful and thoughtful assessment, and words constituting these narratives are powerful, but not ethically considered. Populists approach words and construct claims with easiness, while voters, who appreciate these narratives, are making a choice in favour of simple versus complex. Nationalist claims have a clear identitarian nature: in the European context, nationalist and anti-European narratives are defining *us* versus *them* through *othering*. National identity starts to prevail on the sense of European belonging and Europeanness and since identity is defined through the process rather than being something stable or fixed, the relevant competition for identitarian space, once started, is ongoing.

With the emergence of the social networks and media outlets developing their online platforms, we have become both witnesses and participants of an incredible phenomenon of inclusivity and globalization. It is not yet well reflected in academic literature, but discourses appearing in the online comment sections of newspapers and magazines, both on the outlets themselves and on their social media pages, have a significant value for social scientists. While in the past we had to launch a survey in order to understand what people thought about a certain issue, now we only have to go to the comment sections to get an overview, albeit superficial.

Words matter, and it is not by chance that we started to pay so much attention to hate speech, fake news, and populist narratives. Powerful words, such as *the wall, invasion, us* versus *them, putting first, taking back*, are already written in the open-ended book of contemporaneity, yet we do not know where they will lead us, or which narratives will turn out to be more convincing and winning. The words constituting populist narratives appeal to features of identity, such as belonging, othering, and recognition. European nationalist claims are based on the presupposition that national identity is stronger than European or European Union identity. In turn, in attempts to tackle the challenges of populism and nationalism, we turn to identity, but that is not easy to shape or strengthen artificially. Even methodologically, identity is difficult to approach: one of the clearest ways is to discuss it through the narrative. Narrative is based on words, and also on images; thus, populist claims to identity—and identity itself—are all about words and their meanings.

2 Identity and Conditions for Dialogue

The interdisciplinary character of identity studies gives the opportunity to take various theoretical perspectives, trying to analyse current political and social trends. In claiming that issues of identity have an explanatory potential for Brexit, the rise of far-right movements, new waves of populism, and so forth, it is necessary to go deeper and reflect on the factors, those "sources" of identity-making, discussed by Charles Taylor (1989).

Current scholarship provides a common classification of identity, distinguishing individual or personal identity and collective or group identity. It sees identity as a constantly changing, fluid entity, somehow corresponding with Zygmunt Bauman's idea of liquidity—and, going further, liquid modernity (2012). Identity is a constantly changing result of an open-ended process, rather than something fixed or static; however, it can be described, "photographed" at a certain moment of time, but in other moments, it may already be different. This continuity and change of identity and its expression are brilliantly defined by Bakhtin (1984: 293), who primarily was a scholar in literature and semantics:

> The single adequate form for verbally expressing authentic human life is the open-ended dialogue. Life by its very nature is dialogic. To live means to participate in a dialogue: to ask questions, to heed, to respond, to agree, and so forth. In this dialogue a person participates wholly and throughout his whole life: with his eyes, lips, hands, soul, spirit, with his whole body and deeds. He invests his entire self in discourse, and this discourse enters into the dialogic fabric of human life, into the world symposium.

Narrative describes identity, and identity is shaped through dialogue. Words, therefore, are means of the identitarian process. In *The Politics of Recognition* (1992), Taylor approaches identity through the categories of recognition and misrecognition, alienation, and othering. He writes: "We define our identity always in dialogue with, sometimes in struggle against, the things our significant others want to see in us" (32–33). In 1916, reflecting on the issues of education, John Dewey states: "The moment when we recognize that the self is not something ready-made, but something in continuous formation through choice of action, the whole situation clears up" (2001: 358). Taylor does not include actions in his elaboration of the self, but speaks about significant others and shaping one's own identity in constant interactions: "Discovering my own identity doesn't mean that I work it out in isolation, but that I negotiate it through dialogue, partly overt, partly internal, with others. My own identity crucially depends on my dialogical relations with others" (1992: 34). The role of the dialogue in Bakhtin's and Taylor's writings may be compared with Dewey's stress on choice, while Dewey's and Taylor's writings are united by the common framework of moral philosophy. Michel Foucault is another thinker who took a narrative stand: in their works, both Bakhtin and Foucault directly link individual identity—the self—with a dialogical process and narrative.

In *Self Writing*, in Foucault's *Ethics: Subjectivity and Truth* (1997), he introduces the technique of hupomnēmata, aimed "to enable the formation of the self out of the collected discourse of others" (p. 217). Hupomnēmata includes notes, letters, and other discourses, in conversation either with somebody or with oneself; *the self* is written, a view that is also not far from Bakhtin's, where monologue is a form of dialogue, and dialogue is where the self is shaped. Taylor's self is also formed through the interactions with significant others, but there is a point of difference and confusion to be reflected upon in Foucault's writing (210–211):

> They (hupomnēmata) do not constitute a "narrative of oneself", the intent is not to pursue the unspeakable, nor to reveal the hidden, nor to say the unsaid, but on the contrary to capture the already-said, to collect what one has managed to hear or read, and for a purpose that is nothing less than the shaping of the self.

Words matter, and they both shape and describe identities. Personal identity may be influenced by words in both positive and negative ways: misrecognition and alienation may create conditions for radicalization, while recognition, on the contrary, may encourage further successful integration. Of course, there is no common rule when it comes to the complexity of an individual: in *Sources of the Self* (1989), Taylor explores the factors which have had an impact on contemporary identity, with certain sources having contradictory effects. However, the dialectic of identity comes with its definition: both recognition and misrecognition shaping personal identity are opposite vectors, predetermining the dialectic on the individual level. Contemporary identity scholarship does not clearly connect individual and collective identities. For instance, Anderson (2006) approaches collective identity through the "imaginary" dimension, describing nations as "imagined political communities" (6), while Smith (1999) defines the contemporary nation as "a cultural artefact of modernity, a system of collective imaginings and symbolic representations, which resembles a pastiche of many hues and forms, a composite patchwork of all the cultural elements included in its boundaries" (168).

Although quantitative methods and modelling are also used in identity studies, collective identity is not presented through aggregation as a simple sum of individual identities; this is different from, for instance, economic studies, where aggregation is a basis of analysis. Curiously, by studying broader identities, such as race or gender, we are able to aggregate for sociological reasons, but when it comes to personal identity as a whole complex unity, influenced by such peculiarities as gender, race, religious views, and other factors, aggregation does not make sense. There is another question concerning relationships between individual and collective: Are gender, race, ethnicity, and other broader collective identities imposing certain characteristics on a personal level? And where is the place for narrative here: Do we assess certain collective identities as scripts which can be imposed on our lives through *living accordingly* your gender, race, ethnicity, religion, and European citizenship? The common scholarly approach is to distinguish individual and collective and study them separately, but if we particularly speak about the European collective identity, we will face dialectic of the similar nature: we can distinguish a certain European collective identity, but also "individual" identities of the European nations, which differ from each other.

Dialectic of identity is also hidden in the dichotomy of belonging versus refusing to belong on the one hand, and in advantages of belonging versus restrictions coming from belonging to a certain group on the other. Appiah (2005) reflects on this in relation to solidarity (112):

> As a parameter, identities provide a context for choosing, for defining the shape of our lives, but they also provide a basis for community, for positive forms of solidarity. And it is perfectly consistent to consider your membership in an identity group as both parameter and limit: the Black Nationalist who deplores white supremacy is keenly aware of color as

> constraint, even as he seeks to make it the basis of a political mode of resistance. There is a two-way traffic between limits and parameters, then.

Applying such an idea to the European space, the shared European identity may be a basis for solidarity of the nations. Keeping in mind that belonging to such a collective identity as the European Union or Europe as a whole implies not only advantages but also limits, the feeling of belonging, strong identitarian sources on the individual level, and "the European imaginary" on the collective level should be prevailing in comparison with bureaucratic limitations. By assessing identity as a narrative and realizing that the identity-making process is open-ended, we still admit that different European scenarios are possible, as identity is a result of a competition of different narratives.

Cerutti and Rudolph (2001) made an attempt to describe European identity from various perspectives, combining literary, juridical, economic, philosophic, and other contributions. The attempt somehow had foreseen the challenges Europe is facing now: identitarian confusion and contradiction, re-emerging nationalisms, issues of solidarity, and harmony. The metaphor, linking identity to the soul, is not only poetic, but also well-reasoned. However, the defenders of the European unity are not alone in using metaphoric language to improve their connection with the public: such a tool is also used by populists and the far right. In the essay *Reflections on the Philosophy of Hitlerism*, Emmanuel Lévinas also mentions the soul, in this case the German soul, towards which Hitler's claims were addressed (1990: 64):

> The philosophy of Hitler is simplistic [primaire]. But the primitive powers that burn within it burst open its wretched phraseology under the pressure of an elementary force. They awaken the secret nostalgia within the German soul. Hitlerism is more than a contagion or a madness; it is an awakening of elementary feelings.

Appeals to personal narrative, references to recognition, belonging, othering, the whole language of identity is employed by current populists and nationalists; powerful words are used in a competition for the European identitarian space.

In *The Europe of Strangers*, Bauman reflects on the issue of European identity in a metaphorical way (1998: 1):

> Realities do not move easily; they resist push and pull, claim solid foundations and surround themselves with thick walls and closely guarded borders. If unity was Europe's spectre, nations were its realities. Over the years, nations proved to be the grandmasters of the exorcist art. They managed each time to sweep clean the haunted house, chasing the ghost of European unity away or forcing it to skulk and mope in a few dark and musty corners.

Current political agenda, such as Brexit, the questions around Catalonia, and the visible lack of solidarity in Europe while dealing with the refugee crisis, are all illustrating Bauman's metaphor. However, the deliberate scepticism of Bauman is of artistic nature: painting in the dark, in the end he comes to the necessity of "solidary (and confident) community" (14).

The idea of community is an essential pillar of the European project and has a strong identitarian dimension. Community framework involves a certain dualism: on the one hand, living in a community should be associated with better conditions than living individually; on the other hand, community encompasses a certain decline in freedom. Conditions here may be replaced by benefits: speaking about nations, among such benefits, may be a higher level of security and economic advantages. The decline in freedom implies a need to make collegial decision instead of individual ones. The identitarian dimension of a community refers to collective or group identity scholarship. As we see, complexity and dualism are characterizing European identity, contrasting the simplicity of populist narratives, appealing though to the same identitarian issues.

Problems of the European Union, and Europe as a whole, to a certain extent are internal, related to the complexity of its construction, and the historical and cultural differences on the European space. Some scholars see problems of the European identity as not emerging, but having a retrospective dimension (Smith 1999: 19):

> The ambiguities and nebulous character of European cultural identity contrast strongly with the dramatic and powerful diaspora nationalisms of the Greeks, Jews, and Armenians with their rich memories of golden ages of saints and heroes, their stark symbols of trauma and suffering, and their potent popular myths of glorious restoration in their age old homelands.

Facing external challenges such as the refugee crisis, all the problems inside the system resonate, and the consequent cumulative effect brings the issue of sustainability. From a theoretical point of view, the institutional framework of the European project may be considered as a system, with its dynamic and ongoing changes. According to Prigogine and Stengers (1984), crucial moments, points of the possible change of the system, are bifurcation points. It is impossible to say for sure in which direction the change is going to happen: Will the system disintegrate into chaos or leap to a new, higher level of order? Consequently, instability is not a negative term characterizing the system, since reality cannot be totally controlled. The ideas of Prigogine and Stengers may be applicable not only in science, but also in a broader context. Small fluctuations in physics influence the choice of scenario after the bifurcation point. Fluctuations form the outcome we observe, both the change and the final result. Since it is possible to influence the future of systems through small fluctuations, an individual action is important. In the political sphere, examples may be a personal voter's choice, human rights activism, a raised voice in the media, and an individual responsible narrative. The system develops according to its path, but besides the path dependence, which is not optimistic for the European project, there are bifurcation points, opportunities of change.

European space is neither homogenous, neither undoubtedly matching with the borders of the European Union. Multiple issues of belonging are related to this discrepancy: may Turkey be categorized as a part of the European space, is Russia a European country, can South Caucasus further join the Union, etc. These questions exceed the sphere of politics, and they are of a complex historical and cultural nature. One of the examples of complexity inside the current borders of the European Union is an imaginary division between Western and Eastern Europe that is not only a linguistic construct, but also a dimension of identitarian nature, based on the absence versus presence of the socialist past. The refugee crisis as a challenge for the European project illuminated a complex problem of the lack of solidarity, with a Western–Eastern dimension.

Defining yourself as a person, on a level of personal identity as well as defining the nation, may be accomplished through the mechanisms of alienation and othering used in describing a person or community that is different from myself or my community. The refugee crisis in this context provided a simple answer for complex identitarian questions and brought an image of "the other".

A new wave of nationalism, both in Eastern and Western Europe, may be conceptualized as giving easy answers on complex questions and unsolved identitarian issues which in different cases around Europe may vary, being hidden in the historical past, memories, and myths:

> To read the nation as a printed text to be decoded may reveal much of the recurrent imagery and language of nationalism, but it tells us little about the genesis and course of either particular nations and nationalisms or of nationalism in general. Nor does it help us to understand why only certain political and/or ethnic communities became nations, and which these are. (…) Finally, the idea that thousands, even millions, of men and women have let themselves be slaughtered for a construct of their own or others' imaginations, is implausible, to say the least (Smith: 100).

Nationalism versus globalism, this is an example of competitive narratives, both aspiring to fill identitarian space. Nationalism by its connotation is a powerful word, while globalism does not have such a connotation, and is vague and abstract. The competition between national and broader globalist identities may not have an ultimate winner. Moreover, a strong national identity, a sense of national belonging, does not necessarily contradict with belonging to the European space. For instance, Pultar (2014) argues that the contemporary context is challenging the national identity concept as well (155):

> Instability, distortion of meaning, and volatile identities seem to be rapidly spreading in the wake of globalization throughout the world in a multitude of forms. In such a scenario, the concept of national identity becomes inevitably a most vulnerable notion, subject to reformulations of different nature.

Speaking about the possibility of the UK to stay in the European Union after Brexit, Donald Tusk quoted John Lennon's song *Imagine* (*The Guardian* from 22 June 2017):

> I told them that in fact the European Union was built on dreams that seemed impossible to achieve. So, who knows? You may say I'm a dreamer, but I am not the only one.

A collective imaginary is built on a shared cultural code, memories, symbols, myths—feasible and less feasible elements uniting people in a nation and, more broadly, inside the European space. Understanding these symbolic meanings, their self-sufficient value not being necessarily related to the European institutions, may be a key for strengthening solidarity and coping with current challenges.

The challenges of the European space, such as the refugee crisis and the rise of the far right, are illustrating the lack of solidarity. One of the possible explanations of this is fear. Fears have identitarian features: both the rising popularity of nationalistic parties and unequal participation in the crisis resolution illustrate means of defence from the unknown, from the identitarian other. What are the differences which enable the alienation of the other? It seems that they are not related to the European institutions and judicial norms, but to symbols, values, and cultural codes. Following this reasoning, a solution here may be in a thoughtful response to these fears based on the narrative underlying the priority of the shared European values, codes, and culture on the European space, inviting for the dialogue. The refusal to face such fears and to work on inclusive solutions may strengthen the movements opposing solidarity. A lack of dialogue would encourage citizens facing non-recognized fears to express them through the democratic procedures, to be vocal, and to make themselves to be heard. This process is also of an identitarian nature, illustrating Taylor's idea of misrecognition.

3 The Issue of Responsibility

Who is responsible if things go wrong? This complex issue is inscribed into the democratic system: with an exercise of political expression accomplished through voting comes responsibility. In democratic contexts, politicians should not be perceived as gods on the Olympus, but as representatives of the will of the people. Moreover, it is crucially important to realize this responsibility and to make efforts to gain the necessary knowledge for a well-informed choice. A simple thesis outlining a causal relationship between people getting power on the political arena and our actions is not often clear; instead, we often hear "us" versus "them", and gods, coming from the Greek mythology, may easy to be blamed for possible outcomes.

Issues of responsibility of politicians and intellectuals are inscribed in both contexts of democracy and morality. If something goes wrong because of a political decision, action, or statement—with no specification whether it was made by a "far-right" or a "left-wing" politician—the democratic system itself does not imply a clear leverage of responsibility. At its best, a politician may lose popularity, and if there is a time gap between the action and the consequences, the political life of the actor may end sooner than the assessment of the consequences. How may we deal with the responsibility of those politicians whose actions influenced future generations? The same logic applies to citizens whose votes determine the context for other people, for the future generations. The importance of the political cycle in democratic regimes brings with itself moral challenges which need to be addressed.

Decades before our discussion around populism in Europe, Noam Chomsky wrote an essay called *The Responsibility of Intellectuals* (1967). Probably, the most quoted piece of this essay is "It is responsibility of intellectuals to speak the truth and to expose lies" (1). Provided outside the context, this powerful declaration of moral obligation matches up all the expert columns, commentaries, and blogs we are seeing today, aiming to tackle or even to attack the phenomenon of Trump, fake news, far-right, populist movements, etc. The context of Chomsky's statement is different:

he outlines that intellectuals are privileged to have access to knowledge, and as a consequence, they should transmit this knowledge further in society, in order to make people capable of tackling the issue, and of making a distinction:

> Intellectuals are in a position to expose the lies of governments, to analyze actions according to their causes and motives and often hidden intentions. In the Western world, at least, they have the power that comes from political liberty, from access to information and freedom of expression. For a privileged minority, Western democracy provides the leisure, the facilities, and the training to seek the truth lying hidden behind the veil of distortion and misrepresentation, ideology and class interest, through which the events of current history are presented to us.

This perspective of moral obligation should not be reduced to anti-Trump, anti-populist, and other anti-statements. Spreading knowledge and sharing expertise have different aims: appealing to the people with a free will, presenting arguments, focusing on facts, and giving them so that people can make their own, but now better informed, choices. These choices, though, may be made in favour of a populist party or political figure.

This stand is different to the situation when intellectuals attack populists using a hard language of shame, with references to the Nazi and Fascist European past. In both cases, it is the responsibility that encourages *to speak*, but the second situation is characterized by a certain moral ambiguity. We would not have dedicated time and effort trying to find a clue against populism if this phenomenon had not become so literally popular, and supported by votes. It is not clear whether shaming the intentions of populists can be done separately from shaming the voters exercising their democratic right in favour of populism. Taking an active position and speaking may be an example of the responsible behaviour of intellectuals, but what should this speech contain and to whom should it be addressed? These are questions to think about. The trend of anti-intellectualism that we observe today certainly has reasons that should be defined and reflected upon. It might be a lack of knowledge; thus, Chomsky's claim is suitable and should be supported, but it also might be that complexity of knowledge is not chosen over the attractive simplicity of popular solutions. If this is true, then Chomsky's stand would be helpless: the problem is not a lack of knowledge, but the rejection of the very same knowledge.

Chomsky himself had been a vocal opponent of the Vietnam War, having a strong moral ground on the case. The current situation in Europe, with the rise of populist and far-right movements, has a moral complexity due to unclear issues of responsibility and non-negotiated obligations towards refugees. While nationalist claims in the European states are addressed to Brussels, the support gained by populists may also be explained by the lack of inclusive communication and dialogue between European citizens and the centres of power.

4 Conclusion

Speaking the truth is the responsibility of the intellectuals, Chomsky says. Being vocal implies not only having the privilege of knowledge, but also having the privilege to speak and to be heard. Figures of the popular movements are enjoying this privilege, and so do some of their opponents who make moral claims against populism, nationalism, and lack of solidarity in Europe. At a certain point, the ideology of simplicity became attractive to voters, and populists and nationalists succeeded in providing their narratives, filling them with identitarian appeals, addressing identitarian issues, and speaking the language of identity.

Academics and public intellectuals, on the contrary, lost their positions. Reasons behind anti-expertise attitudes and anti-intellectualism may be debated, but this phenomenon just means that experts and intellectuals failed to involve the public in the dialogue, failed to convince, and maybe failed to listen. To address issues to the populists or nationalist themselves, including the people in power, making appeals to morality does not seem an effective strategy. Most probably, they also have possibilities to get knowledge, and their narratives are made on a very rational and cynical basis which will not be influenced by moral appeals. Moreover, the situations in which politicians are attacked and blamed on a basis of moral claims are ambiguous due to the support they received by their voters. Such a strategy is not inclusive, and it does not involve any dialogue with the voters, but only increases the gap between "us" and "them".

Democratic systems, based on political cycles and political figures replacing one another, have some issues regarding the position of responsibility. Thus, the basic question of who will be responsible if things go wrong should be addressed through the dialogue with the voters. Being concerned with the challenges of the European unity and solidarity, experts, intellectuals, and politicians have to improve the dialogue with people and establish an inclusive dialogical process, aiming to strengthen the sense of recognition and belonging. Besides identitarian claims, such a dialogue should cover the most problematic and sensitive issues existing in the European society, since the absence of complex dialogues creates the space for the same issues appearing in the narratives of populists, who propose very simple solutions.

References

Anderson, B. (2006). *Imagined communities: Reflections on the origin and spread of Nationalism*. London: Verso.

Appiah, K. A. (2005). *The ethics of identity*. Princeton: Princeton University Press.

Bakhtin, M. M. (1984). *Problems of Dostoyevsky's Poetics*. In Theory and History of Literature, Vol. 8. Minneapolis: University of Minnesota Press. Available online: https://monoskop.org/images/1/1d/Bakhtin_Mikhail_Problems_of_Dostoevskys_Poetics_1984.pdf.

Bauman, Z. (1998). *The Europe of strangers*. Available online http://www.transcomm.ox.ac.uk/working%20papers/bauman.pdf. Accessed on November 11, 2018.

Bauman, Z. (2012). *Liquid modernity*. Cambridge: Polity Press.

Boffey, D., & Rankin, J. (2017, June). Donald Tusk echoes John Lennon to suggest UK could stay in EU. *The Guardian* (June 22, 2017). Available online on https://www.theguardian.com/politics/2017/jun/22/donald-tusk-john-lennon-eu-summit-uk-britain-brexit. Accessed on November 9, 2018.

Cerutti, F., & Rudolph, E. (2001). *A Soul for Europe: On the Political and Cultural Identity of the Europeans.* Vols. 1 and 2. Leuven: Peeters.

Chomsky, N. (1967). *The responsibility of intellectuals.* Essay. In The New York review of books. Available online: https://chomsky.info/19670223/. Accessed on November 9, 2018.

Dewey, J. (2001). *Democracy and education.* Penn State Electronic Classics.

Foucault, M. (1997) Self writing. In *Ethics: Subjectivity and truth* (pp. 207–221). New York: The New Press.

Levinas, E., & Hand, S. (1990). Reflections on the Philosophy of Hitlerism. *Critical Inquiry, 17*(1), 62–71. Available online: http://users.clas.ufl.edu/burt/DisappearingMan/ReflectionsHitlerism.pdf. Accessed on November 10, 2018.

Prigogine, I., & Stengers, I. (1984). *Order out of Chaos: Man's new dialogue with nature.* New York: Bantam Books.

Pultar, G. (2014). *Imagined identities: Identity formation in the age of globalization.* Syracuse: Syracuse University Press.

Smith, A. D. (1999). *Myths and memories of the nation.* New York: Oxford University Press.

Taylor, C. (1989). *Sources of the self: The making of the modern identity.* Cambridge: Harvard University Press.

Taylor, C. (1992). *The politics of recognition.* Available online http://elplandehiram.org/documentos/JoustingNYC/Politics_of_Recognition.pdf. Accessed on November 9, 2018.

Cases

From the Clash of Cultures to the Culture of Clash: Normative Political Theory and the Question of Muslims' Citizenship in Europe and the USA

Giovanni Vezzani

1 The Domestic War on Terror: Mainstreaming Islamophobia

The Muslims Are Coming! The title of Arun Kundnani's book efficaciously denounces the paradox underlying the narrative of fear that dominates discourses about Muslims and Islam in Europe and the USA. Actually, Muslims *are not coming*, at least not in the sense that the exclamation seemingly implies. By and large, Muslims have already come, settled, and lived their lives within societies that they perceive (most of the times, one would venture to say) as their home. In the words of the well-known Muslim scholar and public intellectual Tariq Ramadan, the '[i]ntegration of Islam [and] of Muslims as European citizens is already accomplished: Islam is nowadays a European religion' (2008a: 326, my translation). However, negative perceptions about Islam and Muslims and the opinion according to which contemporary European societies are experimenting an ongoing process of invasion are more widespread than one may think. A 2016 PEW Research Centre's survey found that 72% of Hungarians, 69% of Italians, 65% of Greeks, 50% of Spaniards, but also 35% of Dutch people, 29% of Frenchmen and Germans, and 28% of British people hold an unfavourable view of Muslims (PEW Research Centre 2016: 23–27). A 2017 Chatham House's survey involving 10,000 people in ten European countries showed that 55% of the sample agreed to stop further immigration from Muslim-majority countries (Chatham House 2017).

For the sake of simplicity, let me borrow Robert Putnam's sharp definition of identity as '*our sense of who we are*' (Putnam 2007: 159). Symmetrically, in this chapter, I define perceptions as *our sense of how things are*. Indeed, what matters the most is the fact that perceptions and identities are relevant for political theory,

G. Vezzani (✉)
CSEIA (Center for Studies in European and International Affairs),
University of Parma, Parma, Italy
e-mail: gio.vezzani@gmail.com

© Springer Nature Switzerland AG 2020

M. Baldassari et al. (eds.), *Anti-Europeanism*,
https://doi.org/10.1007/978-3-030-24428-6_9

because they significantly contribute to shape reality, at least if one takes the Thomas theorem seriously, according to which 'if men define situations as real, they are real in their consequences' (Thomas and Thomas 1928: 572, quoted in Merton 1995: 380). Now, from the above-mentioned figures one may legitimately infer that the exclamation *The Muslims Are Coming!* voices the perception of Islam and Muslims as something alien to Europe and to some sort of European self-perception. In other words, as it will become clearer in the following pages, it seems that today Islam is perceived as a peculiar kind of religious-based *non-European* or even *anti-European* identity. This way of framing reality leads to the 'externalisation' of Muslims (Cesari 2013: xvii). That is, such views are functional to the *public* representation of Muslims as the paradigmatic 'other' in European and American societies.

Such an externalisation may occur in two ways. First, especially in the recent past, in Western Europe there has been an increasing overlap between the categories of 'immigrant' and 'Muslim' (Cesari 2009: 2) so that some authors maintain that there has been an 'Islamisation of immigration' (Allievi 2005: 3). In contrast to this European trend, in the USA the prototypical 'immigrant' is not the 'Muslim' but the 'low-skilled Mexican or Central American worker' (Cesari 2009: 3; see also Zolberg and Litt Woon 1999). Second, the externalisation of Muslims also occurs through their being portrayed as an 'enemy within', or an existential 'threat' to the core of basic liberal values and institutions. With reference to Europe, it has been observed that '[f]raming Islam as a set of values intrinsically incompatible with Europe implies that Muslims must choose between abandoning their religion and remaining outside the boundaries of the true European citizenry' (Bowen et al. 2014: 1). Clearly enough, such explicit or implicit public representations of Muslims pave the way to Islamophobic attitudes and acts of different kinds:

> Islamophobic acts manifest themselves in numerous ways. Some are explicit and obvious, some subtle and implicit. They take various forms and display varying degrees of aggression. Sometimes they come in the form of verbal and physical attacks on Muslim individuals. In some cases, mosques, Islamic centres, and Muslim properties are attacked and desecrated. In the workplace, health services, schools, and housing, Islamophobia takes the form of suspicion, staring, hazing, mockery, rejection, stigmatizing, and outright discrimination. In other public places, it may take the form of indirect discrimination, hate speech, or denial of access to goods and services (Kalin 2011: 9).

Therefore, the externalisation of Muslims has material consequences in terms of their social and political exclusion and discrimination, as the Report 'Muslims in the European Union: Discrimination and Islamophobia', published by the European Union's Monitoring Centre on Racism and Xenophobia, showed already a decade ago (European Monitoring Centre on Racism and Xenophobia 2006). In Chris Allen's words, 'Islamophobia has a very real impact on the daily experience of many European citizens' (2014: 34, my translation).

Kundnani's book *The Muslims Are Coming!* focusses on the second line of the argument for the externalisation of Muslims considered above. The first chapter of the book analyses the process through which 'Muslims became what Samuel Huntington described as the "ideal enemy," a group that is racially and culturally distinct and ideologically hostile' (Kundnani 2014: 10). In a crucial passage, the author illustrates the critical link between routinised daily forms of Islamophobia (e.g. on the workplace) and the more aggressive rhetoric of the war on terror. This juncture is represented by what the author calls the 'racialization of Muslimness' (ibid.: 11). Kundnani argues that:

> The war on terror –with its vast death tolls in Afghanistan, Iraq, Pakistan, Somalia, Yemen, and elsewhere– could not be sustained without the racialized dehumanization of its Muslim victims. A social body dependent on imperialist violence to sustain its way of life must discover an ideology that can disavow that dependency if it is to maintain legitimacy. Various kinds of racism have performed that role in the modern era; Islamophobia is currently the preferred one (ibid.).

According to Kundnani, the obvious objection that 'Muslims are not a race' is not of primary importance, since 'all racisms are socially and politically constructed rather than reliant on the reality of any biological race' so that 'it is perfectly possible for cultural markers associated with Muslimness (forms of dress, rituals, languages, etc.) to be turned into racial signifiers' (ibid.). The 'racialization of Muslimness' is thus a cornerstone of a broader strategy underlying the international and domestic war on terror: Kundnani claims that 'Islamophobia [is] a form of structural racism directed at Muslims and […] sustained through a symbiotic relationship with the official thinking and practices of the war on terror' (ibid.: 10–11). For him, this strategy aims at the bureaucratisation, normalisation, and mainstreaming of the narrative underpinning the war on terror. It must become as banal, internalised, and ordinary as possible. It must be deeply embedded in common discourses, attitudes, and practices so that it can result natural, almost instinctive. From this perspective, Kundnani maintains that '[a]ltough Obama was elected on a wave of opposition to Bush's war on terror, he then failed to take the U.S. in a fundamentally different direction' (ibid.: 6). Rather, Kundnani claims that Obama's administration 'made permanent what had been a "state of emergency"' (ibid.: 6) so that '[t]he very banality of counterterrorism discourse secured its ideological power much more effectively than the confrontational rewriting-the-rules strategy of the Bush years. Neoconservatives invented the terror war, but Obama liberalism normalized it, at which point, mainstream journalists stopped asking questions' (ibid.: 6–7). This strategy considerably relies on shaping perceptions. The result is that, although '[t]he majority of American Muslims […] do not attend mosques and have a secular outlook,' 'since 9/11 they have become "Muslim," because others perceive them as such' (ibid.: 48).

2 Two Approaches to Islamic Extremism

Kundnani takes into consideration two different approaches to the issue of the so-called Islamic extremism.

First, for him 'culturalists' ascribe extremism to the very nature of Islamic culture and religion: Bernard Lewis (1990) and Samuel P. Huntington (1993, 1996) would exemplify such a culturalist approach. However, Edward Said's critique of essentialism has demonstrated that similar positions are theoretically flawed in several important respects (Said 2003; for his critique of Huntington's clash of civilisations, see also Said 2001). Since culture is assumed as an all-embracing explanation for every predicament of the present, this perspective turns a blind eye on politics and material interests. As the Syrian philosopher Sadik Al-Azm perceptively puts it:

> As for the current tensions, suspicions, confrontations, and enmities that characterize the relationship of Islam to the West, they are certainly not purely affairs of the spirit, or simply clashes of religious ideas or theological interpretations, or merely matters of beliefs, values, images, and perceptions. They are normal affairs of history, power politics, international relations, and the pursuit of vital interests' (Al-Azm 2014: 99).

From a similar viewpoint, Kundnani convincingly argues that 'culturalists displace what are essentially political conflicts onto a more comfortable cultural plane. The problem is their culture, not our politics' (Kundnani 2014: 58–59).

The second perspective is more interesting from a theoretical point of view, and Kundnani devotes a great part of his book to its critique. The author calls it the 'reformist approach.' According to the latter, extremism is 'a perversion of Islam's message. Rather than the legacy of a premodern, Oriental religion, extremism is the result of twentieth-century ideologues who transformed Islam's essentially benign teachings into an antimodern, totalitarian, political ideology' (ibid.: 55). According to Kundnani, the reformist approach opposes and fights Islamic extremism by turning to 'cultural techniques that had been favoured in the early cold war, in which the CIA had sought to recruit the noncommunist Left in an ideological battle against Moscow' (ibid.: 69). In view of this 'cultural war' effort, the author continues, the reformists have recruited moderate Muslim intellectuals and leaders within their ranks. They were charged with a crucial task: since '[w]hat mattered [...] was not Islamic culture itself but the politicization of Islamic culture among an extremist minority,' and since 'the battle was between competing definitions of Islamic identity' (ibid.: 66 and 68), moderate Muslim intellectuals had to redefine Islamic identity in conformity with reformists' desiderata. Thus, the reformist approach includes three main strategic points. First, 'reformists [want] a mainstream Islam to be recognised as a valid identity within an official discourse of cultural tolerance' (ibid.: 76). Second, the legitimation of mainstream Islam must be associated with a strategy of containment and progressive eradication of (at least the most extreme) Islamist views. Third, reformists 'call for a public campaign to celebrate and promote the liberal values' (ibid.: 79). One could read Angela Merkel's declaration that the project of building a multicultural society 'has utterly failed' and David Cameron's call for 'a much more active, muscular liberalism' as two manifestations of such public promotion of common liberal values against some perceived risks of cultural and religious 'ghettoisation', especially with reference to Muslims (Merkel 2010; Cameron 2011). *En passant*, from a less political and more theoretical viewpoint, it could be observed that even some of the most prominent theorists of liberal multicultural citizenship acknowledge that, if one considers the specific case of Muslims with an immigrant background (including second and third generations), multicultural policies are not likely to work in the direction of inclusion in Western Europe, although there is no agreement in the literature about the effective existence of a backlash against multicultural policies and institutions (for this debate, see, among others, Bowen 2011; Brubaker 2001; Glazer 1997; Joppke 2004; Kymlicka 2010, 2012; Maffettone 2011; Taylor 2012; Vertovec and Wessendorf 2010). The reason for this is that 'certain conditions must be in place for [multicultural citizenship] to have its intended effects' (Kymlicka 2012: 21):

> [I]mmigrant multiculturalism has run into difficulties where it is perceived as carrying particularly high risks. Where immigrants are seen as predominantly illegal, as potential carriers of illiberal practices or movements, and/or as net burdens on the welfare state, then multiculturalism poses perceived risks to both prudential self-interest and moral principles, and this perception can override the forces that support multiculturalism (Kymlicka 2010: 46).

Building on the previous considerations about the externalisation of Muslims, one could legitimately venture to say that all these unfavourable conditions that work against multicultural inclusion seem to be present in contemporary Western Europe. By the same token, a consequence of the connection between negative perceptions and representations of Islam and Muslims on the one hand and the widespread criticism of multicultural policies and institutions on the other is that European '[a]ttacks on multiculturalism have become indirect attacks on Islam and Muslims' (Kalin 2011: 4). Attacking multiculturalism and attacking Islam have become interchangeable practices.

3 Critique of Radicalisation Theories

Coming back to the reformist approach, Kundnani argues that the view that Islamic extremism is the product of 'Islamism, a totalitarian ideology to be fought' (Kundnani 2014: 81), rather than of Islam as a religious or cultural identity in itself, leads to focussing on the concept of radicalisation, which he simply defines as 'the process by which a terrorist is made' (ibid.: 116). According to Kundnani, '[t]heories of radicalisation that purport to describe why young Muslims become terrorists are central to the counterterrorism policies on both sides of the Atlantic' (ibid.: 10). However, as in the case of the culturalist approach, he affirms that such an emphasis on the notion of radicalisation risks to stress the explanatory power of ideology too much, while at the same time it overshadows real political interests and conflicts. Kundnani maintains that 'these models make an unfounded assumption that "Islamist" ideology is the root cause of terrorism. To do so enables a displacement of the war on terror's political antagonisms onto the plane of Muslim culture' (ibid.: 10). Thus, in the eyes of the author the concept of radicalisation does not explain the difference between having an ideology (religious or political) and choosing terrorism as a tactic of political action.[1] Moreover, such a view of extremism and violence as by-products of a political ideology (Islamism) is silent—by its very nature—about 'the part played by Western states themselves in constituting the global conflict between the West and

---

[1] Kundnani defines terrorism as 'violence against innocent civilians designed to advance a political cause' (Kundnani 2014: 21).

radical Islam' (ibid.: 96). Instead, Kundnani claims that attention must be paid to the particular political circumstances in which specific actors find themselves, the conditions that lead them to embrace terrorist violence, and how they try to legitimise their political actions and behaviours. Therefore, he rejects radicalisation theories' 'a priori distinction [...] between the new terrorism, seen as originating in Islamist theology, and the old terrorism of nationalist or Leftist political violence, for which the question of radicalisation is rarely posed' (ibid.: 117). On this point, one could observe another convergence between Kundnani and Sadik Al-Azm's thought. Not unlike Kundnani, Al-Azm notes a similarity between contemporary and old forms of terrorism, rooted as they are in analogous historical conditions of political impasse.

> Although unique in its horror, in its desperation 9/11 can be compared to past terrorist acts that foretold the ends of the movements in whose names they were committed. [...] Looking back after 9/11 it seems to me that the left-wing terrorism of the 1970s in Europe was indeed a futile attempt to break out of the historical impasse and terminal structural crisis reached by communism [...] The terrorism of that period was the first visible manifestation of that impasse and the prelude to the final demise of those movements, including world communism itself. Today the hard-core Islamists' spectacular terrorist violence reflects a no less desperate attempt to break out of the historical impasse and terminal structural crisis reached by the world Islamist movement in the second half of the twentieth century. I predict this violence will be the prelude to the dissipation and final demise of militant Islamism in general' (Al-Azm 2014: 88–89).

Thus, Kundnani affirms that 'the key factor in becoming a terrorist' is *political* radicalisation, and not mere religious awakening or indoctrination (2014: 125). Notwithstanding this, he claims, radicalisation theories have provided the necessary framework for the domestic war on terror. Therefore, he analyses several counter-radicalisation policies, which are based on the idea that 'terrorism can only be prevented by systematically monitoring Muslim religious and political life and trying to detect the radicalisation indicators predicted by the model' (ibid.: 12). He then turns to the role played by those far-right political movements, parties, leaders, bloggers, and activists that more or less openly oppose the presence of Islam in Europe, such as Pim Fortuyn and Geert Wilders in the Netherlands, Vlaams Belang in Belgium, and the English Defence League in the UK (whom he calls 'Twenty-First-Century Crusaders'). Kundnani claims that their message is so popular and 'resonates because it aligns with significant elements of the war on terror's official discourse' (ibid.: 247). Thus, Kundnani apparently holds that the normalisation of Islamophobic attitudes and practices has finally succeeded. He pessimistically concludes his book by saying that

> The more the war on terror has emphasized [a] view of liberalism in which it becomes a transcendent identity politics of its own rather than a space where various identities come together, the less liberalism has been able to play the role of neutral mediator. Instead it appears to its interlocutors as a one-sided demand that they simply substitute one form of identity politics for another, giving up their current ethnic, racial, or religious affiliations [...] But while the extremist is positioned as an outsider, as a force alien and disruptive of liberal democratic capitalism, he is in fact a symptom of the very system he despises. The al-Qaeda wannabe is no more than the mirror image of the official discourse of the war on terror, simply inverting the terms in the culturalist clash of civilizations rhetoric' (ibid.: 287).

4 Political Theory and the Question of Muslims' Citizenship in Western European Societies

The power of Kundnani's analysis lies in its critical deconstruction of the war on terror's rhetoric, which is based on (and in turn reinforces) a broader context of everyday exclusion, discrimination, and mutual distrust. *The Muslims Are Coming!* convincingly argues that there is a deep and substantial connection between the most spectacular, discussed, and problematic policies adopted to fight Islamic radicalisation (such as extrajudicial targeted killings, provocation-based counterterrorism, and so on) on the one hand, and more routinised, ordinary, and 'banal' forms of discrimination towards Muslims on the other. They are both part of the same Islamophobic environment in which the domestic war on terror has flourished. One cannot understand the latter if one of the two elements is missed.

However, while the deconstructive side of Kundnani's approach is powerful, one may wonder whether it also provides a theoretical ground which is solid enough for a reconstruction. My answer is twofold. I answer 'yes' because he unambiguously formulates the conditions for the solution of the predicaments that he has exposed. As he points out: 'liberals will be unable to solve their problems with extremism unless they can construct forms of political identification that reach beyond questions of cultural identity and speak to the wider context of neocolonialism, social and economic inequality, and the collapse of working-class representation' (ibid.: 287). Notwithstanding such awareness, I must also answer 'no' to the previous question, because Kundnani does not provide any theoretical instrument for achieving those very conditions.

Indeed, the problems that Kundnani highlights can be framed from different perspectives. From what I have previously argued, it could be deduced that he would probably opt for an approach based on some contextual analysis of the actual economic, social, and historical paths of exclusion and discrimination. However, one could also consider these questions from a more general and abstract perspective. I would suggest that political theorists should be concerned with such a perspective, the goal of which is not to overlook actual inequalities and exclusions, but to ask why and how such phenomena have become possible in the first place. Once these questions have been answered, then one can deal with ongoing phenomena of exclusion and discrimination and prevent future ones.

I would like to develop some normative considerations for framing the problem in such wise. Due to space constraints, I cannot present my theoretical position in full detail here: I have systematically and comprehensively expounded it elsewhere (Vezzani 2016). In the next few pages, I merely sketch an alternative theoretical framework for trying to explain and solve the current predicaments between Western democracies and their Muslims citizens, but for a full argument I must refer the reader to my PhD thesis 'European Muslims and Liberal Citizenship. Reconciliation through Public Reason'. However, I do believe that even a preliminary analysis of this sort deserves attention, because it may urge political theorists to develop normative conceptions that address, more directly, the question of the relationships between

Western societies and their Muslim citizens. This is not to say that contemporary political theory is completely unaware of such topics. Some outstanding contributions in the literature openly deal with the issue of Muslims' citizenship in Western Europe and the USA (see in particular: Carens and Williams 1998; Laborde 2008; March 2009; see also Okin 1999; Phillips 2007). However, they conceptualise the question in various ways and offer different solutions. I have considered their merits and (in some cases) the problems that they raise in another work.[2]

Let me clarify some working assumptions. Firstly, in what follows I am mainly concerned with Western European societies. Secondly, here I adopt a broad philosophical (normative) definition of citizenship as the political relationship specifying the mutual rights and obligations of persons seen as free and equal, 'normal and fully cooperating members of society over a complete life' (Rawls 2005: 18), and not as a legal status. Thirdly, when I speak of 'Muslim citizens' I have in mind citizens of Muslim faith with an immigrant background from Muslim-majority countries (including second and third generations). Thus, here I do not consider the cases of Muslims who are not citizens (illegal immigrants, refugees, resident aliens, and so on), indigenous Muslim populations in Europe, and converted Europeans. These are obviously great simplifications: they do not take into account the fluidity and plurality of persons' attachments, the wide diversity of religious affiliations and practices, national and ethnic peculiarities, and the various degrees of individual religious commitment of real Muslims. I am aware that there is a thin red line between such assumptions and an oversimplifying essentialist approach. In the limited space of this chapter, what I can do to reject essentialism and its dominating effects is to be frank about the motivations that underlie the approach that I will concisely sketch out in the following pages. The latter arise from a deeply rooted concern: while there is reason to be sceptical about the actual existence of something like a clash of cultures (Soravia 2015), one can be legitimately worried by the emersion of what I shall call the 'culture of clash', the features of which Kundnani so efficaciously expounded. I believe that normative political theory can and should provide Muslim and non-Muslim citizens alike with effective theoretical means to neutralise such a risk and to actualise more just and inclusive forms of social cooperation and political participation.

As I have said at the beginning, Muslims are frequently represented as 'outsiders'. Even when they possess the legal status of citizenship, they are often presented as being outside or even against liberal citizenship. This perception of 'Muslims as a problem' is—in turn—deeply problematic. It seems that when these perceptions and representations are publicly evoked, the real problem at stake is the lack (or the

[2]See again (Vezzani 2016). In particular, my approach is close to Andrew March's one (March 2009). Both approaches are Rawlsian, but in my work I emphasise the role of the 'idea of public reason' and of public justification, while March focuses on the concept of an 'overlapping consensus' and the necessity of presenting an Islamic justification for stabilising the liberal conception citizenship in a proper way (or, as Rawls says, 'for the right reasons'). In my Ph.D. Thesis, I explain the distinction between March's comparative ethics and my own approach, that I define "justificatory evaluative political theory." For the notions of public reason, overlapping consensus, and stability for the right reasons, see John Rawls's *Political Liberalism* and "The Idea of Public Reason Revisited" (respectively, Rawls 1997, 2005).

extreme weakness) of a shared normative conception of citizenship, which should instead be firm enough to underpin citizens' mutual relationships within the same political community understood as a cooperative venture. I suspect that many of the issues that are so divisive today (e.g. wearing the veil in public schools) would be less contentious (even though they probably cannot be uncontroversial in a free and democratic public debate, characterised by 'the fact of reasonable pluralism'[3] about the conceptions of what is good) if there were not a wider and more fundamental predicament about the political status of Muslims as citizens. This is why I have said that the 'more general and abstract' (i.e. ideal and normative) perspective of political theory is needed more than ever in considering these questions. Such a 'citizenship crisis' (that is, the crisis of European societies' shared normative conception of citizenship) is connected to the fact that in the last decades Western Europe has been going through new forms of pluralism (Pace 2004: 58, 64, 118, and 121–122). Obviously, contacts, exchanges, hybridisations, and intersections have always existed. However, today's pluralism seems of a new kind for Europe because it combines three elements at the same time. First, with reference to its *character*, it is not confined within Christianity itself, it concerns (to different extents) all the continent, and it is likely to endure. Second, the *numbers* concerned are sizeable. Third, and most important, such pluralism has become *highly visible*, as proved by the often burning 'Muslim question' debates, such as the already mentioned *hijab* controversy in France.

If one takes seriously the fact that 'reasonable pluralism' is 'the work of free practical reason within the framework of free institutions' (Rawls 2005: 37), then it should be clear that the only liberal way for facing such pluralism is to reabsorb the latter within the framework of common political institutions without annihilating it. In other words, it seems that what political theory can and should do is to undertake an effort towards *political reconciliation*. John Rawls explains the meaning of political philosophy as an endeavour in political reconciliation in this passage, with an unusually emphatic tone:

> We try to show that the well-ordered society […] is indeed possible according to our nature and [the requirements of workable political institutions]. This endeavor belongs to political philosophy as reconciliation; for seeing that the conditions of a social world at least allow for that possibility affects our view of the world itself and our attitude toward it. No longer need it seem hopelessly hostile, a world in which the will to dominate and oppressive cruelties, abetted by prejudice and folly, must inevitably prevail. None of this may ease our loss, situated as we may be in a corrupt society. But we may reflect that the world is not in itself inhospitable to political justice and its good. Our social world might have been different and there is hope for those at another time and place' (Rawls 2001: 37–38).

Consider now the case of Muslim citizens in Western European societies. As I have said, it seems that mutual trust is lacking and that European Muslims' allegiance to a shared conception of citizenship is continuously called into question (see for instance,

---

[3]Rawls (2005: in particular xvi–xviii, xxv–xxvi, 36–37).

Ramadan 2010: ix; Kalin 2011: 16).[4] When we consider the question of Muslims' citizenship in contemporary European liberal democratic regimes, we apparently face a paradox. The paradox is that European pluralism seems to endanger social and institutional 'stability for the right reasons' (to use a Rawlsian terminology) for two opposite kinds of reasons. On the one hand, it seems that pluralism undermines citizens' mutual assurance of their commitment to principles of justice and to the requirements of liberal citizenship, because diversity produces centrifugal forces (for the mutual assurance problem, see notably Weithman 2010, 2015). On the other hand, however, the 'fact of reasonable pluralism' entails that no just stable equilibrium can be achieved without the fair inclusion of Muslim citizens: without the latter, stability would not be reached 'for the right reasons' but would rest exclusively on coercion and exclusion. Thus, a plausible liberal philosophical account must reconcile these two apparently conflicting dimensions of stability for the right reasons and provide at the same time the fair *inclusion* of Muslims as citizens on an equal footing and the *mutual assurance* that the social system of cooperation will be 'stable for the right reasons', and not only on the basis of a temporary compromise grounded in purely strategical considerations. In other words, such philosophical account should balance centripetal forces (which incline towards consensus, stability, and assurance) and centrifugal ones (which focus on pluralism and diversity of religious, philosophical, and moral doctrines) in a way which is consistent with liberal democracy, thus making stability for the right reasons possible.

To achieve this double aim, one must previously answer two related questions. The first concerns the establishment of a *common political identity*, which is all the more important in culturally diverse states (Kymlicka 1995, 188). One may wonder if the repeated question 'are you loyal to your country or to the Islamic *ummah*?' (a question that naturally many Muslims find quite offensive, see Ramadan 2008b: 22) originates from the lack of such common political identity. The latter may play a major role with reference to the solution of the mutual assurance problem. In fact, the difficulty is to get rid of the impasse concerning the possible temptation to preemptively defect from shared principles of social cooperation: 'if citizens are to act from their sense of justice consistently, each must have some assurance that others will consistently act justly as well' (Weithman 2010: 46–47). To preserve the very possibility of a cooperating social system based on fair terms, citizens' commitment to those terms must be a matter of public knowledge. The crucial point is that, if citizens are somehow aware of the fact that they have in common a public political identity which is morally 'thin' enough to be shared despite the 'fact of reasonable pluralism', but which is also strong enough to ground a public knowledge of their general commitment to fair terms of social cooperation, then each of them may benefit of the needed 'assurance that others accept the terms of cooperation and

[4]This lack of trust is also shown by the 2009 "Data in Focus Report: Muslims" published by the EU's Fundamental Rights Agency (http://fra.europa.eu/en/publication/2010/eu-midis-data-focus-report-2-muslims), according to which 'one in four Muslims experienced discrimination and did not report their experiences anywhere,' and which reveals that 59% of Muslims who did not report discrimination justify their silence by saying that 'nothing would happen or change by reporting' (8–9).

will not defect' (Weithman 2015: 83). Hence, a common public political identity available to all citizens as such would establish a solid basis to solve the mutual assurance problem.

The second question concerns the identification of *shared evaluative standards* for critically assessing other citizens' political claims, views, and proposals. I understand these standards as commonly held parameters and criteria for public reasoning which are available to all citizens as such and which guide the public discussion about the most fundamental political issues. Certainly, standards of this kind can be conceived in many different ways and I have presented my own characterisation of them in another work (Vezzani 2016). Here, it will suffice to consider the role of similar standards from a more general angle. In fact, shared criteria for social and political criticism must be available in public discussions if citizens are to be able to effectively reject unreasonable demands upon them, to recognise their fellows' positive political contributions, and to demand that unjust laws, policies, and institutions are reformed. In other words, it is of pivotal importance that citizens are provided with shared standards and criteria for discerning reasonable from unreasonable and legitimate from illegitimate political claims. In the passage quoted above, Tariq Ramadan maintains that the problem is not the integration of Muslims in European societies, but 'to know what their contribution is, not only for themselves, but for Europe. Europe will begin to change its perception about Islam only when it realises that Islam represents a resource and not only a problem: thus, a radical change of perspective is needed' (2008a: 326 my translation). Therefore, from this point of view the availability of shared criteria for evaluating Muslims' and non-Muslims' political contributions and demands is of paramount relevance.

Indeed, these two elements are connected. If a citizen appeals to standards that are shared, her fellow citizens are urged to listen to her. If they refuse to do this, they can be morally blamed for not recognising her political equal status as citizen. In turn, such political status as free and equal cooperating fellow citizens constitutes the basis of a common political identity. What is more, from this last point it seems plausible to conclude that the identification of shared standards of social and political criticism is a fundamental element for empowering citizens in general and members of minority groups in particular, because it is likely that their voices are more frequently neglected.

The reconstruction of this common political identity and of the standards of political and social criticism is certainly complex, and it would by far exceed the scope of this chapter. They can be devised in different ways. Elsewhere, I have argued in favour of an account based on the Rawlsian idea of public reason (Vezzani 2016): in my view, a conception of citizenship grounded in the notion of public reason can be worked out to simultaneously satisfy the two apparently conflicting demands of stability for the right reasons—namely, the solution of the mutual assurance problem and the fair inclusion of Muslims. This is so because public reason citizenship can efficaciously provide citizens with both a public political identity and shared evaluative standards for an assessment of other citizens' political views, claims, and proposals. The role of public reason is then chiefly to ground the public knowledge of citizens' shared commitment to fair terms of social cooperation so that each of them can have some 'assurance that others accept the terms of cooperation and will not defect' (Weithman 2015, 83). In my view, in doing this public reason also establishes the most profound bases for citizens' public political identity. On the other hand, public reason addresses the second horn of the problem (Muslims' fair inclusion in European societies) by identifying shared evaluative standards for critically assessing other citizens' political claims, views, and proposals from a genuinely public perspective.

In this chapter, my purpose was simply to point out the fact that a critical deconstruction of the Islamophobic narrative underlying the domestic war on terror cannot be effective in solving the problem it exposes if it is not coupled with a clear formulation of the instruments required for a theoretical reconstruction. I have also argued that such a reconstruction should represent the main task of political philosophy as reconciliation, which aims at answering both demands of stability for the right reasons: fair inclusion of Muslims and citizens' mutual assurance of their commitment to social cooperation. Only by doing this will political theory be able to reabsorb contemporary reasonable pluralism without eradicating it.

References[5]

Al-Azm, S. (2014). Times out of joint. In *Is Islam secularizable? Challenging political and religious taboos. Secularism, fundamentalism, and the struggle for the meaning of Islam: Collected essays on politics and religion* (Vol. 3, pp. 87–99). Berlin: Gerlach Press.

Allen, C. (2014). 'Tutte le differenti forme di discorsi, parole e atti': il problema della comprensione e definizione dell'Islamofobia. In A. Alietti, D. Padovan, & C. Vercelli (Eds.), *Antisemitismo, islamofobia e razzismo: rappresentazioni, immaginari e pratiche nella società italiana* (pp. 21–35). Milan: Franco Angeli.

Allievi, S. (2005). How the immigrant has become Muslim: Public debates on Islam in Europe. *Revue Européenne des Migrations Internationales*, 21(2), 135–163. Available on the REMI website, http://remi.revues.org/2497. Quotations refer to the online version.

Bowen, J. R. (2011). Europeans against multiculturalism. *Boston Review*. Available online on the *Boston Review* website, http://bostonreview.net/john-r-bowen-european-multiculturalism-islam.

Bowen, J. R., Bertossi, C., Duyvendak, J. W., & Krook, M. L. (2014). An Institutional Approach to Framing Muslims in Europe. In J. R. Bowen, C. Bertossi, J. W. Duyvendak, & M. L. Krook (Eds.), *European States and their Muslim Citizens: The impact of institutions on perceptions and boundaries* (pp. 1–25). Cambridge and New York: Cambridge University Press.

Brubaker, R. (2001). The return of assimilation? Changing perspectives on immigration and its sequels in France, Germany, and the United States. *Ethnic and Racial Studies, 24*(4), 531–548.

Cameron, D. (2011). *State multiculturalism has failed, says David Cameron*. Available on the BBC News website: www.bbc.co.uk/news/uk-politics-12371994.

Carens, J. H., & Williams, M. S. (1998). Islam, immigration, and group recognition. *Citizenship Studies, 2*(3), 475–500.

[5]Note: all websites were accessed for the last time on 25 June 2018. For publications that are available exclusively online (with no downloadable pdf version) page numbers have been omitted.

Cesari, J. (2009). *The securitisation of Islam in Europe*. CEPS (Centre for European Policy Studies) CHALLENGE Program (Changing Landscape of European Liberty and Security) research paper no. 15 (April 2009). Available on the CEPS website, http://www.ceps.eu/book/securitisation-islam-europe.

Cesari, J. (2013). *Why the west fears Islam: An exploration of Muslims in liberal democracies*. New York: Palgrave Macmillan.

Chatham House. (2017). *What do Europeans think about Muslim immigration?* Available at: https://www.chathamhouse.org/expert/comment/what-do-europeans-think-about-muslim-immigration.

European Monitoring Centre on Racism and Xenophobia. (2006). *Muslims in the European Union: Discrimination and Islamophobia*. Available on the website of the EU's Agency for Fundamental Rights, http://fra.europa.eu/en/publication/2012/muslims-european-union-discrimination-and-islamophobia.

European Union Agency for Fundamental Rights. (2009). *Data in focus report: Muslims*. http://fra.europa.eu/en/publication/2010/eu-midis-data-focus-report-2-muslims.

Glazer, N. (1997). *We are all multiculturalists now*. Cambridge, Mass: Harvard University Press.

Huntington, S. (1993). The clash of civilizations? *Foreign Affairs, 72*(3), 22–49.

Huntington, S. (1996). *The clash of civilizations and the remaking of the world order*. New York: Simon and Schuster.

Joppke, C. (2004). The retreat of multiculturalism in the liberal state: Theory and policy. *The British Journal of Sociology, 55*(2), 237–257.

Kalin, I. (2011). Islamophobia and the Limits of Multiculturalism. In J. L. Esposito & I. Kalin (Eds.), *Islamophobia: The challenge of pluralism in the 21st century* (pp. 3–20). New York: Oxford University Press.

Kundnani, A. (2014). *The Muslims are coming! Islamophobia, extremism, and the domestic war on terror*. London and New York: Verso.

Kymlicka, W. (1995). *Multicultural citizenship*. Oxford: Oxford University Press.

Kymlicka, W. (2010). The rise and fall of multiculturalism? New debates on inclusion and accommodation in diverse societies. In S. Vertovec & S. Wessendorf (Eds.), *The multiculturalism backlash: European discourses, policies and practices* (pp. 32–49). London and New York: Routledge.

Kymlicka, W. (2012). *Multiculturalism success, failure, and the future*. Migration Policy Institute. Available at http://www.migrationpolicy.org/research/TCM-multiculturalism-success-failure.

Laborde, C. (2008). *Critical republicanism: The Hijab controversy and political philosophy*. Oxford: Oxford University Press.

Lewis, B. (1990). The roots of Muslim rage: Why so many Muslims deeply resent the west, and why their bitterness will not easily be mollified. *The Atlantic Monthly*, 47–60.

Maffettone, S. (2011). From liberal multiculturalism to multicultural liberalism. *Les minorités: un défi pour les États*, Proceedings of the International Symposium. Brussels: Académie royale de Belgique, May 22 and 23, 2011), 127–162.

March, A. (2009). *Islam and liberal citizenship: The search for an overlapping consensus*. New York: Oxford University Press.

Merkel, A. (2010). *Merkel says German multicultural society has failed*. Available on the BBC News website: http://bbc.co.uk/news/world-europe-11559451.

Merton, R. K. (1995). The Thomas theorem and the Matthew effect. *Social Forces, 74*(2), 379–422. Merton quotes William Isaac Thomas and Dorothy Swaine Thomas's 1928 book *The child in America: Behavior problems and programs*. New York: Knopf.

Okin, S. M. (1999). Is multiculturalism bad for women? In J. Cohen, M. Howard, & M. C. Nussbaum (Eds.), *Is multiculturalism bad for women?* (pp. 7–24). Princeton: Princeton University Press.

Pace, E. (2004). *L'islam in Europa: modelli di integrazione*. Rome: Carocci.

PEW Research Centre (2016). *Europeans fear wave of refugees will mean more terrorism, fewer jobs*. Based on Spring 2016 Global Attitudes Survey. Available at: http://www.pewglobal.org/2016/07/11/europeans-fear-wave-of-refugees-will-mean-more-terrorism-fewer-jobs/.

Phillips, A. (2007). *Multiculturalism without culture*. Princeton: Princeton University Press.

Putnam, R. D. (2007). E Pluribus Unum. Diversity and community in the twenty-first century. *Scandinavian Political Studies*, 30(2), 137–174.

Ramadan, T. (2008a). Transcript of Ramadan's speech at the Faculty of Law, Università degli Studi dell'Insubria, May 27, 2006. In A. Ferrari (Ed.), *Islam in Europa/Islam in Italia tra diritto e società* (pp. 325–333). Bologna: Il Mulino.

Ramadan, T. (2008b). *Noi musulmani europei*. Rome: Datanews.

Ramadan, T. (2010). *The quest for meaning: Developing a philosophy of pluralism*. London: Allen Lane.

Rawls, J. (1997). The idea of public reason revisited. Originally published in *University of Chicago Law Review, 64*(3), 765–807 and now included in J. Rawls, *Political liberalism*, expanded edition (pp. 440–490). New York: Columbia University Press.

Rawls, J. (2001). In E. Kelly (Ed.), *Justice as fairness: A restatement*. Cambridge, Mass.: Harvard University Press.

Rawls, J. (2005). *Political liberalism* (Expanded edition). New York: Columbia University Press.

Said, E. (2001). The clash of ignorance. *The Nation*, October 22. Available on *The Nation* website, http://www.thenation.com/article/clash-ignorance.

Said, E. (2003). *Orientalism* (25th anniversary edition). New York: Vintage Books.

Soravia, B. (2015). Lo scontro che non c'è stato. Guerre di civiltà, guerre di parole e il Medio Oriente, 1979–2001. In *Il nuovo disordine internazionale. Conflitti politici, cambiamenti tecnologici ed evoluzioni strategiche* (pp. 171–190). Rome: Fondazione Magna Carta.

Taylor, C. (2012). Interculturalism or multiculturalism? *Philosophy and Social Criticism, 38*(4–5), 413–423.

Vertovec, S., & Wessendorf, S. (2010). Introduction: Assessing the backlash against multiculturalism in Europe. In S. Vertovec & S. Wessendorf (Eds.), *The multiculturalism backlash: European discourses, policies and practices* (pp. 1–31). London and New York: Routledge.

Vezzani, G. (2016). *European Muslims and liberal citizenship. Reconciliation through public reason: The case of Tariq Ramadan's citizenship theory*. Ph.D. Thesis. LUISS Guido Carli and Université Libre de Bruxelles, Rome and Brussels. Available at: http://eprints.luiss.it/1454/.

Weithman, P. J. (2010). *Why political liberalism? On John Rawls's political turn*. Oxford and New York: Oxford University Press.

Weithman, P. J. (2015). Inclusivism, stability, and assurance. In T. Bailey & V. Gentile (Eds.), *Rawls and religion* (pp. 75–96). New York: Columbia University Press.

Zolberg, A. R., & Litt Woon, L. (1999). Why Islam is like Spanish: Cultural incorporation in Europe and the United States. *Politics and Society, 27*(1), 5–38.

Do Populists Talk the Same? A Multilevel Analysis of the Northern League and Five Star Movements' Positions on Immigration and the European Union

Benedetta Carlotti and Stella Gianfreda

1 Introduction

During the last few years, the economic and the migration crises have challenged both the stability and unity of the European Union (EU). Some scholars argue that these two crises have contributed to the politicization of two issues, the EU and immigration, increasing their salience and divisiveness inside member states' polities (De Wilde and Zürn 2012; Hooghe and Marks 2018). Indeed, the tangible effects of such crises are visible among political parties and the public at large.

In the last rounds of European and national elections, the so-called Eurosceptic/populist parties, generally excluded from the governmental arena, were able to gain considerably high shares of votes at the expense of their mainstream counterparts (Akkerman et al. 2016; Wolinetz and Zaslove 2018). The League (former Lega Nord—LN[1]) and the Five Star Movement (Movimento Cinque Stelle, M5S) are an example of this trend.

This chapter aims at comparing how the two aforementioned Eurosceptic populist parties frame the EU and the immigration issues in two distinct political arenas: the national Parliament and the European Parliament (EP). In particular, our aim is to verify the existence of a relationship between LN and M5S's ideological identity and their positions on immigration and the EU. In doing so, this work answers the following research questions: which argumentations do LN and M5S use to talk about the EU and migration? Do they frame the two issues differently between the two arenas?

B. Carlotti (✉)
Istituto Di Scienze Umane e Sociali, Scuola Normale Superiore, Palazzo Strozzi, Florence, Italy
e-mail: benedetta.carlotti@sns.it

S. Gianfreda
Scuola Superiore Sant'Anna, Pisa, Italy
e-mail: s.gianfreda@sssup.it

[1]The party changed its name in 2017, but for simplicity, we use its former denomination throughout the chapter.

© Springer Nature Switzerland AG 2020

M. Baldassari et al. (eds.), *Anti-Europeanism*,
https://doi.org/10.1007/978-3-030-24428-6_10

The chapter starts by presenting a multidimensional reconceptualization of both the EU and the immigration issues. It then applies a computer-assisted discourse analysis (CADA) (Partington 2010) method to an original dataset of 533 speeches delivered in the national and the supranational parliamentary arenas. The comparison across the constitutive dimensions of the two issues is made according to a multilevel perspective: (1) inter-parties comparison within the national arena; (2) inter-parties comparison within the supranational arena and (3) inter-arenas comparison, between the national and the supranational parliament. The results of the analysis (conclusive section) show that LN mobilizes the EU and the immigration issues using cultural-identitarian and sovereignist argumentations. Conversely, the M5S politicizes the two issues to boost its anti-elitist claims. The work further stresses the differences between LN and M5S' Eurosceptic stances. While LN rejects the EU polity in line with its populist radical-right origin (Mudde 2007), M5S frames criticism to the EU in an elite versus people dynamic, typical of populist parties. Moreover, the chapter partially confirms the hypothesis which stresses the importance of the institutional setting—especially for the M5S, that adapts its claims to the institutional arena in which it operates.

2 Immigration, the EU and Political Competition: A Multidimensional Perspective

Issues related to immigration and European integration are complex, multidimensional, and cross-cut traditional ideological divides (Odmalm 2014). European integration produces conflict over the organization of territorial authority—from the domestic to the supranational level—to manage trans-border policy issues (Marks and Steenbergen 2002), while immigration calls into question the control of national borders and the distribution of public resources (Brubaker 2010). The following two subsections detail the conceptualization of the constitutive dimensions of both issues.

2.1 The EU Issue

Parties' positioning towards the EU is generally regarded as a Manichean phenomenon that makes a distinction between criticism (Euroscepticism) and support (Europeanism) of the European integration project (e.g. Hix and Lord 1997; Marks and Steenbergen 2002; Hooghe et al. 2002).

Indeed, researchers widely rely on the dichotomous distinction elaborated by Szczerbiak and Taggart (2001) distinguishing 'hard' from 'soft' Euroscepticism: the former implies a rejection of the very idea of the EU and European integration;

the latter encompasses criticism to both the policies and the architecture of the EU. Several typologies have been formulated to disentangle and better define the phenomenon of Euroscepticism both from a popular and from a party-based perspective (see Vasilopoulou 2009 for an extensive review). Though these efforts increase our knowledge of Euroscepticism, they 'differentiate between the degrees of the phenomenon without formulating satisfactory definitions' (Crespy and Verschueren 2009, 381).

Instead of proposing a new typology, this chapter relies on the assumption that the EU is a political system (Kreppel 2002; Brack 2018) composed by a set of *political objects* (Easton 1965, 436) that parties may support or oppose defining their overall positioning *vis-à-vis* the EU. In particular, we classify the targets of parties' positioning as the EU-elite, the EU-institutions, the EU-community and the EU-policies. As Table 1 shows, the EU issue is constituted by two broad dimensions: 'what the EU does', which identifies the *output* of the EU-political system, and 'what the EU is', which refers to the components of the EU-political system.

The EU-policies are the EU-political system's *output*: parties can express a position (support or criticism) *vis-à-vis* a specific policy, its objectives, the implied instruments, and its financial endowment. The EU-elite dimension refers to the group of 'public officials and institutional actors that exercise EU governance' (Serricchio, Tsakatika and Quaglia 2013). The EU-regime is formed by the institutions composing the EU (the EP, the European Commission, the Council of Ministers and

Table 1 EU issue's dimensions

'What the EU does'	'What the EU is'		
Policy dimension	*Elite* dimension	*Institutional* dimension	*Community* dimension
EU-policies • Objectives • Instruments • Financial endowments	EU-elite Performance and moral characteristics • Bureaucrats • Politicians • Functionaries	EU-regime Performance, values and norms • European Commission (EC) • European Parliament (EP) • Council of Ministers (Council) • Other institutions	EU- community • EU values and norms (identity) • EU-competencies (deepening) • EU-enlargement (widening) Sub-dimensions of the EU-community: territorial areas of application of some specific EU-policies • Euro-area: common monetary policy • Schengen area: protection of internal and external borders

so on), and parties can take a stance on both the performance (Krouwel and Abts 2007) and the values and norms underpinning the EU-institutions (e.g. rule of law; representativeness; democracy). The EU-community dimension is the physical community composed of member states. Parties' positioning towards the EU-community refers to: its competencies (along the national–supranational axis), its potential extension to new member states (widening), or to the country's membership to the community on the basis of identitarian or cost-benefit argumentations. The EU-community entails two further sub-dimensions identifying the two main territorial areas of application of some specific EU-policies: the Euro-area and the Schengen area (Carlotti 2017).

2.2 The Immigration Issue

Even immigration is extensively considered as a multidimensional concept (e.g. Givens and Luedtke 2005). In this chapter, we follow a widely accepted conceptualization of immigration developed by Hammar (1985), who distinguishes between 'immigration control policies' and 'immigrant policies' (Table 2).

Immigration control policies regulate the selection, admission, settlement and deportation of foreign citizens and define the degree to which a nation opens its borders to allow foreign citizens to enter and reside in the country. Whereas, immigrant policies regulate third-country nationals' socio-economic, cultural-religious and political integration in the host society and define the degree of membership there. In particular, integration is composed of three elements (Marshall and Bottomore 1992). The civic element includes the right to individual freedoms, e.g. freedom of the person, freedom of speech, freedom of expression and right to justice. The social element encompasses the right to share the welfare of the receiving society, namely access to social services, healthcare, housing, labour market, education, etc. Finally, the political element refers to the right to participate in the receiving society's decision-making process: the right to vote and to citizenship.

Table 2 Immigration issue's dimensions

Control dimension	***Integration*** dimension
Measures regulating immigrants' • Admission and entrance • Residence status • Expulsion	Measures regulating immigrants' integration • Civic rights • Socio-economic rights • Cultural and religious rights Political rights

3 LN and M5S: Eurosceptic, Populist, or Anti-immigration?

For this comparative case study analysis, LN and M5S were chosen following a most different system design (MDSD) (Przeworski and Teune 1970). LN and M5S are widely regarded as Eurosceptic and populist parties (Bulli and Soare 2018), even if they differ in terms of both their origins and ideological orientation and belong to different EP Party Groups (EPPGs).

Founded as an alliance of regionalist leagues in the North of Italy[2] in 1989, LN merged in the Northern League in 1991 (Tarchi 2002). LN's history can be summarized in three main phases: initially, the party advocated the secession of the so-called Padania (a 'mythological region' in the North of Italy) from the rest of the country. Ever since the early 1990s, the LN shifted from ethno regionalism, centred on the defence of the 'common (Northern) man' against '*Roma ladrona*' (the corrupted elite), to nativism and authoritarianism including xenophobia and law and order arguments in its rhetoric (Pirro and van Kessel 2018: 5). Furthermore, after the 9/11 terrorist attack, the party's anti-immigration claims became strongly Islamophobic in connection with an appeal to security and the defence of Italian Christianity against the 'illegal migrants (*clandestini*)'. Lastly, the party completed a process of normalization under the leadership of Matteo Salvini (from 2013 onwards), who strategically enlarged the reference community to include all native Italians, and linked the political and cultural immigration threat to the collusion of the Roman elite with EU technocrats and criminal networks penalizing native Italians (Bulli and Soare 2018: 141).

Since the 1992 Italian national election, LN holds a considerable number of seats both in the Chamber of Deputies and in the Senate. It scored its highest result in coalition with the Pole of Freedom in 1994 under the leadership of Umberto Bossi (obtaining 117 seats in the Chamber of Deputies and 60 seats in the Senate), while the lowest score was obtained by the party during the 2013 Italian national elections under the leadership of Roberto Maroni (gaining 20 seats in the Chamber of Deputies and 18 seats in the Senate). In line with the party nativist turn, since June 2015, the LN has been affiliated to the French Front National (FN) in the Europe of the Nations and Freedom EPPG. All in all, LN can be classified as a populist party belonging to the subgroup of radical-right populists combining nativism, authoritarianism and populism (Mudde 2007).

Differently, the M5S was born in 2013 as a response to the general dissatisfaction towards national politics. It mainly advocates direct democracy by turning citizens into protagonists of democracy (under the mantra of 'everyone is worth one')[3] and overcoming the mechanism of representation through the use of the Internet. Even if the party is identified under several labels—'anti-party party' (Diamanti and Natale

---

[2]The alliance was composed by: Lega Lombarda, Lega Veneta, Piemont Autonomista, Unione Ligure, Lega Emiliano Romagnola and Alleanza Toscana.

[3]This mantra is also the title of M5S' anthem as reported in the movement's official blog http://www.beppegrillo.it/movimento/2010/07/ognuno-vale-uno.html.

2013), 'anti-establishment party' (Mosca 2014), 'strange animal' or 'web-populist' (Corbetta and Gualmini 2013)—scholars agree on its populist features: anti-elitism, emphasis on direct democracy, Manichean visions, charismatic leadership, etc. (Taggart 1995; Mosca 2014).

The M5S obtained its first successes participating in local elections and winning the majority in several municipalities (the biggest one was Parma) in 2012 and, afterwards, in the regional election in Sicily, obtaining 15% of the regional vote share and becoming the largest party in the region. However, the M5S obtains its biggest success in its first national election in 2013, scoring 25.6% of the national vote share and gaining 163 seats in both Chambers (Parliament and Senate). M5S' last EP election results were described as a 'political setback' (Bordigon and Ceccarini 2014). However, in a country described in the past as pro-EU (Carlotti 2017), the party was able to score 21.2% of the vote share obtaining 17 seats in the EP. M5S became a member of the Europe of Freedom and Direct Democracy EPPG (EFDD), together with the Eurosceptic United Kingdom Independent Party (UKIP). This choice was not free from intra-party tensions as proven by its (unsuccessful) attempt, two years and a half later, to leave the EFDD and join the Liberal group (Bressanelli and de Candia 2018).

M5S's positions on immigration are not clear: while some empirical analyses suggest a discrepancy between the more conservative party leadership and the more liberal party activists (Bulli and Soare 2018: 147; Ivaldi et al. 2016), the party's official message does not contain any expressions of xenophobia or socio-cultural discrimination (Lanzone 2014: 61). Rather, it endorses an instrumental approach to immigration. In other words, opposition to immigration is not based on xenophobic, welfare-chauvinist or nationalistic arguments, as in the LN's case, but rather denounces the political mismanagement of the *res publica* and the alleged elite's collusion with organized crime (Bulli and Soare 2018: 148).

In this chapter, we hypothesize a relation between LN and M5S's ideological identity and their positions on immigration and the EU. Being a populist radical-right party, we expect the LN to use cultural-identitarian, law and order, and securitarian arguments (*H1*) when talking about immigration. Similarly, we expect this party to reject the project of European integration in the name of sovereignist claims (*H2*). On the contrary, being the M5S a pure populist party, we expect it to mobilize issues related to immigration and the EU mainly to boost its anti-elitist claims, highlighting corruption and mismanagement of the national and European elites as well as the lack of legitimacy and democratic accountability of the EU-elite (*H3*). The last formulated hypothesis (*H4*) refers to the specificities of the two considered arenas. While, at the national level, political discourse follows a government versus opposition dynamic, with peripheral parties mobilizing those issues that benefit them the most to achieve electoral success (Taggart 1998), at the supranational level, missing the government vs. opposition nexus, we expect party delegations to mobilize an opposition of principle to the EU polity, using Eurosceptic claims (Mair 2007, 15).

4 Research Design and Method

The Parliament is a privileged viewpoint being the institution *par excellence*, where political conflicts on legislation and governmental policies unfold. The national and the supranational Parliaments are decision-making institutions representing the hearth of democracy: directly elected arenas where parties' representatives work together on the same topic at the same time, having access to a public profile that is of high importance when there is media attention on some specific issues (Usherwood 2017).

The literature on the parties' position-taking in parliaments usually relies on patterns of voting behaviour as empirical datasource, even if this method is not free from problems. Some scholars show the biased nature of the studies based on Roll Call Votes—RCVs. RCVs, in fact, are only one-third of the total amount of votes and may be asked by national parties' to check for their members' loyalty (Carrubba et al. 2006). We believe that parliamentary speeches are a fine-grained and less-biased source of data to assess a party's positions (Wendler 2016). Even if, differently from votes, speeches do not result in tangible conclusions and if generally much of the real discussion concerning a policy happens in committees, participating in plenary debates represents an opportunity for parliamentarians to provide a public justification for the entirety of the legislative process (e.g. Lord 2013, 253).

This chapter analyses the speeches delivered by LN and M5S's representatives in both the Italian and the European Parliament (from now on MPs and MEPs, respectively). The time framework of the analysis ranges between May 2014 and December 2016, the first two years of the VIII EP legislature.[4] Two specific events took place during this period: the peak of the migration crisis in mid-2015 and the Brexit referendum in June 2016. Focusing on this time frame allows us to provide an in-depth description of LN and M5S' stances towards the two studied issues. Speeches were selected according to a list of keywords related to the EU and the immigration issues and retrieved from the official webpages of both the EP and the Italian Parliament.[5] The collected speeches are organized in four corpora[6]: one for each issue and level of observation (see Table 3 presenting the four corpora's descriptive statistics).

A total of 533 speeches were collected for both parties in both parliamentary arenas. The number of speeches concerning the EU issue is generally lower than the one related to the immigration issue in both analysed arenas. Furthermore, the speeches held in the EP are shorter than those held in the Italian Parliament, this is probably due to a stricter allocation of speaking time in the EP. Speeches are divided into natural sentences and codified using MaxQDA[7]—a software for mixed method analysis of texts—on the basis of a codebook that assigns to each dimension

[4]Furthermore, M5S is represented in the EP only since the last EP elections in 2014.

[5]Detailed information about speeches' selection and analysis (codebook and coding criteria) are available upon request.

[6]A corpus is a collection of texts in machine-readable format.

[7]Further information at https://www.maxqda.com/.

Table 3 Corpora's descriptive statistics

	EU issue		Immigration issue	
Party name	Total number of speeches	Speeches' average length in tokens (standard deviation in parenthesis)	Total number of speeches	Speeches' average length in tokens (standard deviation in parenthesis)
Corpora National Parliament				
M5S	44	878 (695)	112	820 (745)
LN	27	946 (1129)	137	458 (491)
Total	71		249	
Corpora EP				
M5S	47	285, 5 (145)	66	252 (103)
LN	19	282 (141)	81	192 (102)
Total	66		147	
Total overall	137	–	396	–

(detailed in Sect. 3) three categories expressing the 'directionality' of the positioning: positive, negative or neutral for the EU issue, and permissive, restrictive or neutral for the immigration issue (see Table 4).

The coding procedure recognizes the character of the expressed positioning either as principled or as pragmatic. Sentences coded as pragmatic refer to '[m]eans-ends type of rationality where actors are considered to take decisions made on calculations of utility based on a given set of interests' (Sjursen 2002, 494). On the contrary, sentences expressing a principled positioning refer to normative argumentations based on claims about values or moral standards of justice and legitimacy (Wendler 2016). The pragmatic/principled distinction is operationalized assigning to each sentence a value of 1 in case of principled character and of 0 otherwise.

The analysis assumes that parties emphasize a specific dimension of the two issues the more that dimension is important to them, while a lack of reference towards one of the specific dimensions signals a lack of saliency of that specific dimension to the party (Budge 1994; Lowe et al. 2011).

The frequencies obtained from the coding phase are used to build an additive index of parties' positioning on each of the theorized issues' targets. The index sums both the directionality (opposition or support) and the character (principled or pragmatic) of parties' positions. In what follows, we explain the two phases of index construction.

Firstly, considering the frequency of coded sentences, we assess the directionality of parties' positioning as:

$$Q = \frac{\log CX + 1}{\log N + 1} - \frac{\log CY + 1}{\log N + 1} \tag{1}$$

where *CX* represents the total number of sentences coded negatively/restrictively for each of the analysed categories; *CY* is the total number of sentences coded positively/permissively in each of the analysed categories, and *N* is the total number of coded sentences (including neutral sentences). The proposed formula is an adaptation of Prosser's re-elaboration of Lowe et al.'s 'logit scale of position' (Lowe et al. 2011; Prosser 2014) that is, in turn, an improvement of the Comparative Manifesto Project's left-right scale (the so-called RILE index).[8] The value of 1 is added to each index component to keep them consistently 0, since $\log_{(1)} = 0$ (Prosser 2014). The result is a continuous variable ranging between 1 and -1 indicating the highest opposition or the highest support for the considered targets, respectively. Whenever the variable takes the value of 0, it indicates either a lack of salience of the specific target to the party or that the same proportion of coded-negative/positive or coded restrictive/permissive sentences is present.

Table 4 Summary of the constructed codebook

Issue	Dimension	Targets	Directionality	Created category
EU	What the EU does	EU-policy	Positive	EU-policy positive
			Negative	EU-policy negative
			Neutral	EU-policy neutral
	What the EU is	EU-regime	Positive	EU-regime positive
			Negative	EU-regime negative
			Neutral	EU-regime neutral
		EU-elite	Positive	EU-elite positive
			Negative	EU-elite negative
			Neutral	EU-elite neutral
		EU-community	Positive	EU-community positive
			Negative	EU-community negative
			Neutral	EU-community neutral
		Euro-area	Positive	Euro-area positive
			Negative	Euro-area negative
			Neutral	Euro-area neutral
		Schengen area	Positive	Schengen area positive

(continued)

[8]The Comparative Manifesto Project provides researchers with parties' positioning on several issues derived from the content analysis of their electoral manifestos. Further information at https://manifesto-project.wzb.eu/.

Table 4 (continued)

Issue	Dimension	Targets	Directionality	Created category
			Negative	Schengen area negative
			Neutral	Schengen area neutral
Immigration	Control	Humanitarian migration	Restrictive	Humanitarian migration restrictive
			Permissive	Humanitarian migration permissive
			Neutral	Humanitarian migration neutral
		Economic migration	Restrictive	Economic migration restrictive
			Permissive	Economic migration permissive
			Neutral	Economic migration neutral
		Border control	Restrictive	Border control restrictive
			Permissive	Border control permissive
			Neutral	Border control neutral
	Integration	Reception	Restrictive	Reception restrictive
			Permissive	Reception permissive
			Neutral	Reception neutral
		Socio-economic integration	Restrictive	Socio-economic integration restrictive
			Permissive	Socio-economic integration permissive
			Neutral	Socio-economic integration neutral

(continued)

Table 4 (continued)

Issue	Dimension	Targets	Directionality	Created category
		Cultural/religious integration	Restrictive	Cultural/religious integration restrictive
			Permissive	Cultural/religious integration permissive
			Neutral	Cultural/religious integration neutral
		Citizenship	Restrictive	Citizenship restrictive
			Permissive	Citizenship permissive
			Neutral	Citizenship neutral

To complete the index of positioning, we include a value indicating the character: principled or pragmatic. To assign it, we look at the resulting directionality: if a party displays a positive directionality (thus denoting opposition) and if the majority of the coded-negative/restrictive sentences are principled in character (value of 1), then the party is exercising a principled opposition and vice versa. The resulting index looks like:

$$(Q \pm q) * 100 \tag{2}$$

Where Q represents the continuous variable mentioned above and q refers to the character of the expressed positioning. The formula presents the $\pm$ operator to obtain a symmetric scale of positioning: if Q is positive the value of q is added, whereas, if Q is negative, the value of q is subtracted. The index ranges between + 200 and −200 indicating the maximum degrees of principled opposition or support respectively, whereas a value of +100 or −100 indicates the maximum degree of pragmatic opposition or support, respectively. If the index takes the value of 0, it indicates a neutral position of the parties.

The obtained index is used to graphically represent M5S and LN's positioning on the two studied issues (see spider plots in Sect. 5). Furthermore, using WMatrix,[9] we performed keyword analysis allowing the identification of keywords[10] for each corpus avoiding potential biases in their selections since WMatrix objectively

[9]WMatrix is an open-source software for corpus analysis and comparison. See http://ucrel.lancs.ac.uk/wmatrix/.

[10]A keyword is 'a word which occurs with unusual frequency in a given text. This does not mean high frequency but unusual frequency, by comparison with a reference corpus of some kind' (Scott 1997: 236).

establishes the keywords according to their statistical significance or 'keyness'.[11] The keywords are used to identify and report quotes from the analysed speeches objectively, providing the reader with a qualitative hint of parties' positioning.

5 Results

This section relies on spider plots (Figs. 1, 2, 3 and 4) and compares LN and M5S' indexes of positioning. To each plots' vertex corresponds one target of positioning, while the coloured lines report—in green for the LN and in yellow for the M5S—the parties' positioning towards the observed targets. On the black continuous line (the 0 line), the index takes the value of 0. Whenever opposition to the target is present, the coloured lines are drawn in the positive side of each graph. The black patterned lines

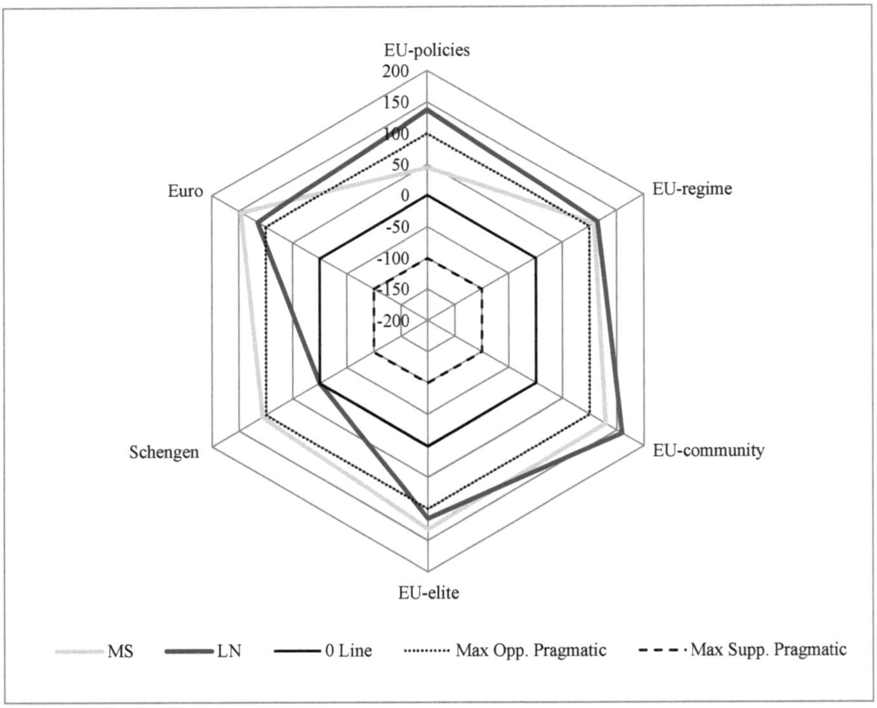

Fig. 1 Spider-plot of LN and M5S' positions on the EU issue. National arena

[11] WMatrix elaborates a word frequency list for each corpus. It then applies a statistical formula to compare each word's relative frequency in corpus A with the one of each word in corpus B. The value of statistic, or 'keyness', is proportional to the difference in relative frequencies: the higher the value of 'keyness', the more prototypical the word is for a given corpus in comparison to the other. We consider as statistically significant only those items with a 'keyness' value over 7, since 6.63 is the cut-off point for 99% confidence of significance (Rayson 2012).

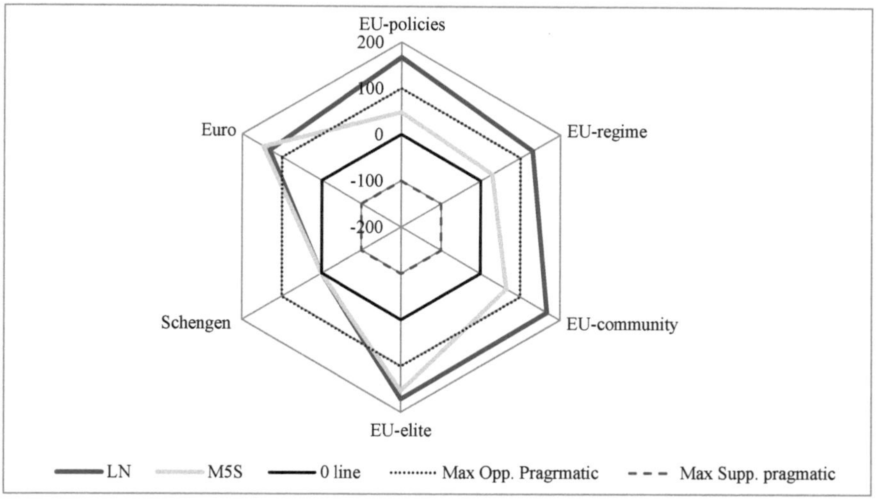

Fig. 2 Spider-plot of LN and M5S' positions on the EU issue. EP Arena

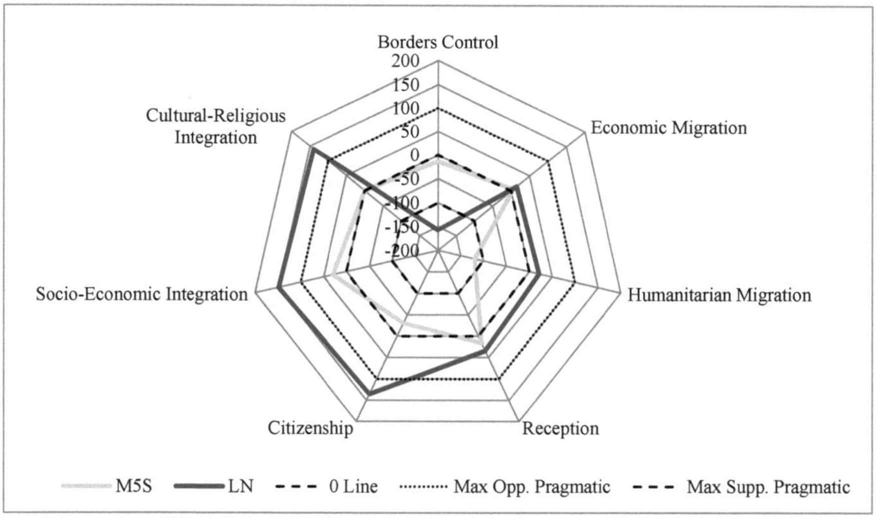

Fig. 3 Spider-plot of LN and M5S' positions on the migration issue. National Arena

highlight the distinction between the principled and pragmatic character of parties' positioning (principled positioning above ±100).

The two parties show a similar position on the EU within the national arena (Figs. 1 and 2). They both principally oppose the EU-community even if LN's index is higher (+159). The two parties are particularly different in terms of the motivations they use. LN frames its opposition to the EU-community using sovereignist, nationalist

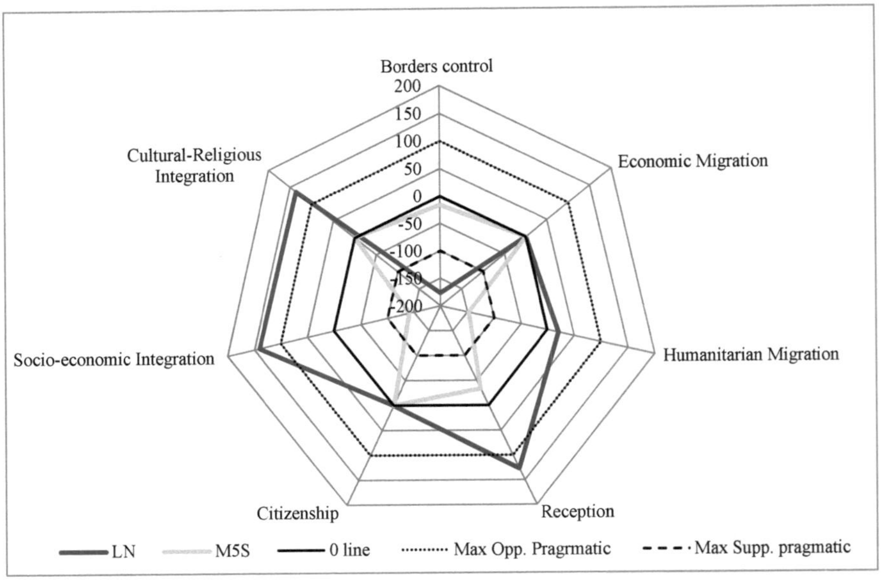

Fig. 4 Spider-plot of LN and M5S' positions on the migration issue. EP Arena

justifications (see the presence of *nazionale*—national—and *popolo*—people, among the keywords in Table 5).

> This is the problem of *democracy* […] how can we make *people,* including the ignorant ones, take part in the process of construction of the common house? […] we want *democracy*, we want the sovereignty of the people. (Giancarlo Giorgetti, LN's MP, Keywords in italics)

On the contrary, M5S focuses on three main targets: the Euro-area (+145), the EU-elite (+131) and the Schengen Area (+106). Nevertheless, the EU democratic deficit is core to M5S' criticism of the EU-community.

> The Union's *democratic* deficit must be reset […] This system has failed; it is floating but nearly drowning. The *EU* […] should be rebuilt on a solid basis, which must be distant from the Fiscal Compact, the austerity, walls, barriers and borders. […] Solidarity, cooperation, and integration: these must be the pillars at the basis of the EU. (Sergio Battelli, M5S' MP, Keywords in italics)

Interestingly, the LN does not consider the Schengen Area as a salient target but proposes a principled critique to the EU-policies (+137).

Interestingly, LN's position vis-à-vis the EU does not change much between the two levels of observation (see Fig. 2): the party shows a principled criticism towards the EU-policies (+168); the EU-community (+167) and the EU-regime (+130). LN opposes the EU-regime and the EU-community using sovereignist argumentations related both to the EU power-grab *vis-à-vis* member states and the lack of democracy at the EU-level. Furthermore, it heavily criticizes the lack of electoral accountability of the EU-regime *vis-à-vis* democratically elected national authorities.

Table 5 Top 10 keywords by Arena (EU issue). Keywords have been sorted on 'keyness'. Only items with log likelihood (LL) value ≥7 are reported

	National Arena		EP	
	Keywords	Keyness	Keywords	Keyness
M5S	*unione*	21.751	*austerità*	31.934
	piano	20.657	*europeo*	17.195
	Dublino	20.463	*sociale*	17.195
	cittadini	19.616	*crisi*	16.299
	europea	19.571	*istituzioni*	14.739
	euro	19.267	*greca*	12.282
	Europa	18.761	*mafia*	12.282
	banche	18.729	*rubato*	12.282
	Italia	18.329	*misure*	11.86
	Moneta	15.493	*politica*	11.86
LN	*problema*	32.82	*Europa*	46.867
	Europa	24.998	*qualcuno*	21.757
	popolo	22.49	*zero*	19.581
	consenso	21.62	*europea*	17.101
	immigrazione	19.727	*immigrazione*	15.877
	parte	19.258	*Isis*	15.23
	fenomeno	17.018	*commissione*	13.902
	risposte	17.018	*palazzo*	13.054
	priorità	16.239	*Turchia*	13.054
	modo	15.524	*difesa*	10.879

> This surreal debate confirms that who governs this *Europe* — the European *Commission* — are strong powers and a few dangerous subjects. (Matteo Salvini, LN's leader. Keywords in Italics)

While M5S and LN criticize the EU in a similar way in the national arena, M5S' position is different in the EP. M5S, in fact, shows a pragmatic criticism focused on the EU-policy (+49) and uses reformist argumentations to criticize both the EU-community (+65) and the EU-regime (+29). M5S highlights the EU democratic deficit stressing the need to inject democracy at the supranational level without rejecting the existence of the Union. It proposes alternatives to reform the EU-community starting from its core values (e.g. solidarity) expressed in the Treaties (see the presence of '*sociale*'—social—among the keywords in Table 5):

> We want to change: we want a different Europe, firstly and foremost in terms of treaties, agreements, and policies. We have fervently talked about treaties such as the Fiscal Compact, but we have never held a speech on the *Social* Compact or on some *social* measure of rebalancing, a subject that you obviously do not care about. (Ignazio Corrao M5S' MEP, Keywords in italics)

Both parties are equated by a similarly strong and principled criticism to the EU-elite, contesting its moral values and its alleged connections with lobbies and big financial/economic powers at the detriment of EU citizens. Furthermore, both parties reject the Euro-area geometry (scoring +130 and +146, respectively) on a principled basis, proposing to exit from it. The Euro-area is considered to be the cardinal mistake of the EU since it causes macroeconomic divergences between Member States.

> One single road is left to rebuild a Europe of peoples from its foundations: abandoning the crazy project of the euro that has accelerated its disintegration instead of reducing divergences among member states [...]. Markets have blackmailed and dismantled the *European* project that can now be rebuilt only by betting on democracy, common goods, real economy, labour and *social* welfare. (Marco Valli, M5S's MEP, keywords in italics)

Similarly to the national arena, the Schengen Area is not a salient target for the LN. On the contrary, differently from the national arena, the Schengen Area is a non-salient target for the M5S at the supranational level.

Moving the attention to the immigration issue, Fig. 3 shows that LN and M5S frame migration in two substantially different ways in the national context. LN advocates stronger border control (−157) and expresses a principled opposition towards the socio-economic (+149), cultural-religious (+140) and civic integration (+135) of migrants. For the LN, the 'immigration fluxes' are an 'invasion' threatening the national and cultural unity of the country. Indeed, words such as 'illegal migrants' ('clandestini' in Italian), 'invasion' and 'deportation' are among the top 10 keywords used by LN' MPs to talk about migration (Table 6).

The socio-economic integration of migrants is of particular concern for the LN. The party argues against the redistribution of national services that are perceived as unfairly allocated to irregular migrants at the expenses of Italians.

> To help those 4.5 million Italians that live below the poverty line [...] the Government plans to spend 600 million euro in 2016. On the contrary, to guarantee [...] an assisted *invasion* of our *country* the Government has allocated 4.2 million. These numbers show the priorities of this Executive, which in the name of political correctness [...] opens the doors to the repopulation of our *country* through uncontrolled *immigration*. (Marco Rondini, LN's MP, keywords in italics)

Differently from the LN, the M5S holds a more ambiguous position towards migration, scoring values close to 0 on all the targets with the only exception of humanitarian migration, which is endorsed on a principled basis (−119). As Table 6 shows, the word 'rights' is among the top 10 keywords in M5S' speeches, often associated with the words 'minors', 'children' and 'human'.

> We want a 'Europe' in which Italy is not left alone to manage the migration crisis, where *human rights* come before banks' needs. We want a 'Europe of people' grounded on the principles of solidarity, cooperation, welfare and direct democracy. (Sergio Battelli, M5S' MP, keywords in italics)

Another category that plays a central role in the national debate is the reception of migrants. Both parties endorse a restrictive pragmatic stance towards this category,

Table 6 Top 10 keywords by Arena (immigration issue). Keywords have been sorted on 'keyness'. Only items with log likelihood (LL) value ≥7 are reported

	National Arena		EP	
	Keywords	Keyness	Keywords	Keyness
M5S	*minori*	212.373	*membri*	31.934
	migranti	113.222	*stati*	17.195
	accompagnati	107.244	*solidarietà*	17.195
	accoglienza	89.848	*ricollocazione*	16.299
	stranieri	79.253	*equa*	14.739
	Italia	48.934	*responsabilità*	12.282
	età	48.193	*ripartizione*	12.282
	prima	43.036	*meccanismo*	12.282
	sistema	41.081	*permanente*	11.86
	bambini	40.696	*ricollocare*	11.86
LN	*clandestini*	150.191	*Europa*	46.867
	immigrazione	115.117	*immigrazione*	21.757
	immigrati	105.343	*clandestini*	19.581
	clandestina	77.066	*milioni*	17.101
	paese	72.277	*persone*	15.877
	cittadini	71.375	*politica*	15.23
	invasione	63.234	*immigrati*	13.902
	cento	59.455	*mare*	13.054
	CIE	59.119	*guerra*	13.054
	espulsione	52.413	*confini*	10.879

associating the mismanagement of the reception system to the corruption of the national political elite (Gianfreda 2018).

> Mineo[12] is the centre of illicit interests, it is the most relevant example of how the migration phenomenon can be exploited by those who want to earn from emergencies. Mineo represents the complete failure of the *reception* system, both from an economic and from a *human rights* perspective. (L'Orefice Marialucia M5S' MP, keywords in italics)

Looking at both parties' positions in the EP (see Fig. 4), we observe a substantial confirmation of LN's positioning with a strong principled endorsement of border control (−177) and a strong principled opposition to cultural/religious (+136) and socio-economic (+140) integration of migrants. LN, however, also opposes the reception of migrants in the EU on a principled basis in the EP, differently from the national arena where the party endorses a more moderate approach.

[12]Mineo is the name of a reception centre in the province of Catania (Sicily), which has been in the spotlight for corruption and human rights violations. For further details: https://www.theguardian.com/news/2018/feb/01/migrants-more-profitable-than-drugs-how-mafia-infiltrated-italy-asylum-system.

> Years and years of foolish reception, without the necessary checks, have allowed thousands of illegal migrants (*clandestini*) to enter Europe, without leaving any record. [...] *Illegal migrants* and *Islamic terrorists* wander around unhindered. (Mara Bizzotto LN's MEP, keywords in italics)

Differently from the national arena, M5S' position on the migration issue is more delineated in the EP. The M5S' delegation puts a little emphasis on immigration control (+16), while holding a positive and principled stance towards humanitarian migration (−147) and socio-economic integration of migrants (−142). Indeed, as already noticed, in the national arena, M5S often stresses the need to address the root causes of migration—namely wars and weapons trade—and enforce human rights protection across the EU.

> The socio-economic integration of *refugees* are complex processes that need to be based on the principles of *solidarity* and *fair* distribution of *responsibilities* among Member States. [...] Refugees' access to the *labour* market [...] can reduce the costs of reception [...] and contribute to the economy of host societies. (Laura Ferrera M5S' MEP, keywords in italics)

Two further considerations are noteworthy: firstly, M5S' pragmatic opposition towards the reception system at the national level (+16) is turned into a pragmatic support in the European arena (−33). Secondly, the 'citizenship' target is not salient neither for M5S nor for LN in the EP. This hints to the influence of institutional settings on the parties' framing strategies. While LN's positioning across institutional arenas seems to be driven by its ideological characterization—a radical-right populist party with nativist and xenophobic claims—M5S's framing strategies appear to be influenced by the institutional settings in which the party operates. Indeed, if at the national level, the party mainly frames immigration issues in terms of opposition to the government, in the EP, the normative arguments such as the respect for human rights prevail. Similarly, the lack of salience of the citizenship target is strictly connected to the fact that naturalization is a typical issue dealt by sovereign states (Brubaker 2010).

6 Conclusion

To conclude, we assess if the hypotheses proposed in Sect. 3 are confirmed. Starting from H1, the results of the analysis confirm our hypothesis: LN opposes immigration mainly relying on cultural-identitarian, law and order, securitarian argumentations in both the observed arenas, thus confirming itself as a populist radical-right party (Mudde 2007). Similarly, also H2 is confirmed: in fact, LN frames its opposition to the EU-community relying on sovereignist argumentation and accusing the EU to grab power *vis-à-vis* sovereign member states and authorities.

As for H3, interestingly both parties mobilize the studied issues to boost their anti-elitist claims. In the national parliament, M5S and LN use the two issues to attack mainstream governing parties, thus following a government versus opposition dynamic as expected. On the contrary, lacking a government versus opposition distinction, the supranational arena forces parties to behave differently. While the M5S mobilizes the EU issue and proposes a principled attack to the EU-elite also at the supranational level, the LN translates its positioning in a direct attack to the EU-elite, the EU-regime, and the EU-community constituting a sort of anti-systemic opposition to the EU. In connection to this last assertion, while H4 is confirmed for both parties' positioning within the national arena, the same dynamic is not observable for the M5S within the EP. Even if M5S is critical to the EU-community and the EU-regime, its criticism shows a pragmatic character relying on reformist motivations. On the contrary, LN confirms its rejectionist position *vis-à-vis* the EU.

In general, it is noteworthy that LN shows a constant opposition between the two observed levels (national and European), while the M5S adapts itself to the institutional setting in which it operates. Furthermore, the results of our analysis show marked differences between LN and M5S' Euroscepticism. While the former sees the EU as a threat to the national territorial/cultural unity, the latter stresses the lack of democracy and democratic accountability of the EU-elite highlighting the elite vs. people distinction typical of a populist party (Mudde 2007).

The two parties object of this study managed to form a yellow-green governmental alliance after the last Italian election (March 2018). On the basis of previous findings (van Spanje 2010), we hypothesize that LN will have a contagion impact on the M5S, thus shifting Italian immigration policies towards the right of the ideological spectrum. Further research is needed to assess this hypothesis.

References

Akkerman, T., de Lange, S. L., & Rooduijn, M. (Eds.). (2016). *Radical right-wing populist parties in Western Europe: Into the mainstream? Routledge studies in extremism and democracy*. London; New York: Routledge.

Brack, N. (2018). *Opposing Europe in the European parliament*. London: Palgrave Macmillan UK. https://doi.org/10.1057/978-1-137-60201-5.

Bressanelli, E., and de Candia, M. (2018). Love, convenience, or respectability? Understanding the alliances of the Five Star Movement in the European Parliament. *Italian Political Science Review/Rivista Italiana Di Scienza Politica*, 1–24. https://doi.org/10.1017/ipo.2018.5.

Brubaker, R. (2010). Migration, membership, and the modern nation-state: Internal and external dimensions of the politics of belonging. *Journal of Interdisciplinary History, 41*(1), 61–78. https://doi.org/10.1162/jinh.2010.41.1.61.

Budge, I. (1994). A new spatial theory of party competition: Uncertainty, ideology and policy equilibria viewed comparatively and temporally. *British Journal of Political Science, 24*(04), 443. https://doi.org/10.1017/S0007123400006955.

Bulli, G., & Soare, S. C. (2018). Immigration and the refugee crisis in a new immigration country: The case of Italy. *HKJU-CCPA, 18*(1), 127–156.

Carlotti, B. (2017). The odd couple: Analyzing United Kingdom Independence Party (UKIP) and Italian Five Stars Movement's (FSM's) European Union (EU)-opposition in the European Parliament (EP). *Italian Political Science Review/Rivista Italiana Di Scienza Politica*, 1–24. https://doi.org/10.1017/ipo.2017.24.

Carrubba, C. J., Gabel, M., Murrah, L., Clough, R., Montgomery, E., & Schambach, R. (2006). Off the record: Unrecorded legislative votes, selection bias and roll-call vote analysis. *British Journal of Political Science, 36*(04), 691. https://doi.org/10.1017/S0007123406000366.

Corbetta, P., & Gualmini, E. (Eds.). (2013). *Il partito di Grillo*. Bologna: Il mulino.

Crespy, A., & Verschueren, N. (2009). From Euroscepticism to resistance to European integration: An interdisciplinary perspective. *Perspectives on European Politics and Society, 10*(3), 377–393. https://doi.org/10.1080/15705850903105793.

De Wilde, P., and Zürn, M. (2012). Can the politicization of European integration be reversed?: Can the politicization of European integration be reversed? *JCMS: Journal of Common Market Studies, 50*, 137–153. https://doi.org/10.1111/j.1468-5965.2011.02232.x.

Diamanti, I., & Natale, P. (2013). *Grillo e il movimento 5 stelle: analisi di un fenomeno politico*. Bologna: Il Mulino.

Easton, D. (1965). *A systems analysis of political life*. New York: Wiley.

Gianfreda, S. (2018). Politicization of the refugee crisis? A content analysis of parliamentary debates in Italy, the UK, and the EU. *Italian Political Science Review/Rivista Italiana Di Scienza Politica, 48*(01), 85–108. https://doi.org/10.1017/ipo.2017.20.

Givens, T., & Luedtke, A. (2005). European immigration policies in comparative perspective: Issue salience, partisanship and immigrant rights. *Comparative European Politics, 3*(1), 1–22. https://doi.org/10.1057/palgrave.cep.6110051.

Hammar, T. (Ed.). (1985). *European immigration policy: A comparative study*. Cambridge [Cambridgeshire], New York: Cambridge University Press.

Hix, S., & Lord, C. (1997). *Political parties in the European Union*. New York: St. Martin's.

Hooghe, L., & Marks, G. (2018). Cleavage theory meets Europe's crises: Lipset, Rokkan, and the transnational cleavage. *Journal of European Public Policy, 25*(1), 109–135. https://doi.org/10.1080/13501763.2017.1310279.

Hooghe, L., Marks, G., & Wilson, C. J. (2002). Does left/right structure party positions on European integration? *Comparative Political Studies, 35*(8), 965–989. https://doi.org/10.1177/001041402236310.

Ivaldi, G., Lanzone, M. E., and Sozzi, F. (2016). Eurosceptic Parties and the EU: MEPs' attitudes in the roll-call votes on immigration policies. A cross-country analysis (Italy, France and UK). *Presented at the 66th PSA Annual International Conference, Brighton, UK*.

Kreppel, A. (2002). *The European parliament and supranational party system: A study in institutional development*. Cambridge, New York: Cambridge University Press.

Krouwel, A., & Abts, K. (2007). Varieties of Euroscepticism and populist mobilization: Transforming attitudes from mild Euroscepticism to harsh Eurocynicism. *Acta Politica, 42*(2–3), 252–270. https://doi.org/10.1057/palgrave.ap.5500187.

Lanzone, M. (2014). The "Post-Modern" populism in Italy: The case of the five star movement. *The many faces of populism: Current perspectives* (Research in Political Sociology, Vol. 22, pp. 53-78), Emerald Group Publishing Limited.

Lord, C. (2013). No representation without justification? Appraising standards of justification in European Parliament debates. *Journal of European Public Policy, 20*(2), 243–259. https://doi.org/10.1080/13501763.2013.746123.

Lowe, W., Benoit, K., Mikhaylov, S., & Laver, M. (2011). Scaling policy preferences from coded political texts: Scaling policy preferences from coded political texts. *Legislative Studies Quarterly, 36*(1), 123–155. https://doi.org/10.1111/j.1939-9162.2010.00006.x.

Mair, P. (2007). Political opposition and the European Union. *Government and Opposition, 42*(1), 1–17. https://doi.org/10.1111/j.1477-7053.2007.00209.x.

Marks, G., & Steenbergen, M. (2002). Understanding political contestation in the European Union. *Comparative Political Studies, 35*(8), 879–892. https://doi.org/10.1177/001041402236297.

Marshall, T. H., & Bottomore, T. (Eds.). (1992). *Citizenship and social class*. London: Pluto Press.

Mosca, L. (2014). The five star movement: Exception or vanguard in Europe? *The International Spectator, 49*(1), 36–52. https://doi.org/10.1080/03932729.2013.875821.

Mudde, C. (2007). *Populist radical right parties in Europe*. Cambridge: Cambridge University Press. https://doi.org/10.1017/CBO9780511492037.

Odmalm, P. (2014). *The party politics of the EU and immigration*. London: Palgrave Macmillan UK. https://doi.org/10.1057/9781137462510.

Partington, A. (2010). Modern diachronic corpus-assisted discourse studies (MD-CADS) on UK newspapers: An overview of the project. *Corpora, 5*(2), 83–108. https://doi.org/10.3366/cor.2010.0101.

Pirro, A. L., & van Kessel, S. (2018). Populist Eurosceptic trajectories in Italy and the Netherlands during the European crises. *Politics, 38*(3), 327–343. https://doi.org/10.1177/0263395718769511.

Prosser, C. (2014). Building policy scales from manifesto data: A referential content validity approach. *Electoral Studies, 35,* 88–101. https://doi.org/10.1016/j.electstud.2014.05.004.

Przeworski, A., & Teune, H. (1970). *The logic of comparative social inquiry* (p. 153). New York: Wiley. Fleming, W. G. (1970). *American Political Science Review, 64*(04), 1255–1256. https://doi.org/10.2307/1958372.

Rayson, P. (2012). Corpus analysis of key words. In C. A. Chapelle (Ed.), *The encyclopedia of applied linguistics*. Oxford, UK: Blackwell Publishing Ltd. https://doi.org/10.1002/9781405198431.wbeal0247.

Scott, M. (1997). The right word in the right place: Key word associates in two languages. *AAA—Arbeiten Aus Anglistik Und Amerikanistik, 22*(2), 239–252.

Serricchio, F., Tsakatika, M., and Quaglia, L. (2013). Euroscepticism and the global financial crisis: Euroscepticism and the global financial crisis. *JCMS: Journal of Common Market Studies, 51*(1), 51–64. https://doi.org/10.1111/j.1468-5965.2012.02299.x.

Sjursen, H. (2002). Why expand?: The question of legitimacy and justification in the EU's enlargement policy. *JCMS: Journal of Common Market Studies, 40*(3), 491–513. https://doi.org/10.1111/1468-5965.00366.

Sørensen, C. (2008). *Love me, love me not… A typology of public Euroscepticism*. Sussex European Institute.

Szczerbiak, A., & Taggart, P. (2001). *Parties, positions and Europe: Euroscepticism in the EU candidate states of Central and Eastern Europe*.

Taggart, P. (1995). New populist parties in Western Europe. *West European Politics, 18*(1), 34–51. https://doi.org/10.1080/01402389508425056.

Taggart, P. (1998). A touchstone of dissent: Euroscepticism in contemporary western European party systems. *European Journal of Political Research, 33*(3), 363–388. https://doi.org/10.1111/1475-6765.00387.

Tarchi, M. (2002). Populism Italian style. In Y. Mény & Y. Surel (Eds.), *Democracies and the populist challenge* (pp. 120–138). London: Palgrave Macmillan UK. https://doi.org/10.1057/9781403920072_7.

Usherwood, S. (2017). How has Brexit changed British Euroscepticism? *Political Insight, 8*(2), 42–43. https://doi.org/10.1177/2041905817726907.

van Spanje, J. (2010). Contagious parties: Anti-immigration parties and their impact on other parties' immigration stances in contemporary western Europe. *Party Politics, 16*(5), 563–586. https://doi.org/10.1177/1354068809346002.

Vasilopoulou, S. (2009). Varieties of Euroscepticism: The case of the European extreme right. *Journal of Contemporary European Research, 5*(1), 3–23.

Wendler, F. (2016). *Debating Europe in national parliaments: Public justification and political polarization*. Palgrave Macmillan.

Wolinetz, S. B., & Zaslove, A. (Eds.). (2018). *Absorbing the blow: Populist parties and their impact on parties and party systems*. London, New York: Rowman and Littlefield International Ltd.

Paths of Critical Europeanism: From Blockupy to Neo-municipalism

Maurilio Pirone

1 Contentious Politics and European Integration

The main theoretical approaches frame the European integration as a functionalist or interstate federalist or social embedding process (Rosamond 2000; Bergmann and Niemann 2013). By the time, these approaches based on a top-down perspective or on institutional actors have been challenged by phenomena that could not be easily considered as parts of a progressive path of integration. More and more, the European project—with its decision-making rules and institutions, political geographies and social policies—has been so far contested to threat the existence of the Union itself (Balibar 2016). Considering this, it would be interesting to propose other theoretical approaches in order to grasp the ongoing transformations. The contentious politics approach emphasises the role of conflicts and non-institutional actors in producing power configurations (Tarrow 1994, 2005). I will adopt such approach in order to show how in recent years other actors, as well as institutional ones, have drawn alternative European geographies that have sometimes clashed and sometimes overlapped with the official ones (FitzGibbon et al. 2017). In fact, with regard to the policies and institutional system of the European Union, social movements have often taken positions that can be described in terms of critical and radical Europeanism (Della Porta 2006a, b; Della Porta and Caiani 2007), distant from both nationalist claims and the forms in which European integration has historically taken place.

Following one of the most influential scholars of social movements—Donatella Della Porta—we can distinguish three main macro-aptitudes towards Europe:

> Eurosceptics, who want to limit European competences and are critical of the EU's specific policies; critical Europeanists, who want more competences for Europe, but are dissatisfied with its present policies; and identity Europeanists, who are in favour of the extension of the EU's competences and satisfied with the Union's current policies. (Della Porta 2006b: 16)

M. Pirone (✉)
University of Bologna, Bologna, Italy
e-mail: maurilio.pirone2@unibo.it

© Springer Nature Switzerland AG 2020
M. Baldassari et al. (eds.), *Anti-Europeanism*,
https://doi.org/10.1007/978-3-030-24428-6_11

On the basis of this repartition, Della Porta includes social movements within the second group:

> Social movements appear in this frame as critical Europeanists, in favour of deeper integration but with policies very different from those that have so far characterised the so called "negative integration" dominant in the EU. The stability pact in particular is criticised as one of the main examples of the neo-liberal policies privileged by already privileged groups, which reduce welfare for the poor and disadvantaged. They do not call, however, for a return to the nation state, but for a process of Europeanisation from below. (ibid)

I will therefore try to take up Della Porta's analytical scheme—that she built on the basis of a research on movements participating in the Social Forum in the first half of the 2000—problematising some aspects in the light of some transnational campaigns of recent years. I believe, in fact, that there is a fundamental critical point in this categorisation, namely how much the concept of "another Europe from below"—which is still central to some of the transnational social movement paths of recent years—can be reconciled with current EU policies.

In general, we can see how this definition of "critical and radical Europeanism", rather than surrounding a specific programme or organisational model, brings together a series of political mobilisations and experimentations—even very different ones—which in recent years have combined opposition to EU policies with a transnational attitude. It should also be noted that, while the so-called radical left is historically characterised by an internationalist vocation, on the other hand it has experienced various difficulties in acting on a supranational level as certain geographical, historical, and economic differences still seem to weigh (Pietiläinen 2017).

In particular, I intend to focus on two paths promoted in recent years: the anti-austerity mobilisation of Blockupy (Neumayer et al. 2016a, b) and the experiences of neo-municipalism that arose first in Spain, and then spread throughout Europe. I will initially try to briefly outline some of their features (political composition, counterpart, goals) and then highlight some common points with regard to the European field of intervention.

2 Blocking the ECB

On three occasions (2012, 2013 and 2015), many different German and European political formations met in Frankfurt—conceived as a global city and as the European financial centre (Nehemiah 2016)—to block the construction works and the opening of the European Central Bank (ECB), considered to be both the symbolic and real place for the organisation of austerity policies imposed within the framework of the economic crisis. The latter has been interpreted not only as an effect of the neo-liberal economic policies that led to the financial crash of 2007/2008, but also as a political process designed to encourage the concentration of wealth in the hands of a few and to impose measures to cut welfare, privatise public services and reform labour market national legislations through the leverage of public debt:

> As the cost of the Euro crisis was imposed on the states, the economic crisis moved into the political systems, inducing a severe crisis of public debt. This crisis was used by the German hegemonic bloc to switch cause and effect: the crisis of public debt was no longer perceived as an effect of the economic crisis, but was reframed as being caused by poor fiscal governance. In this situation, austerity measures, coordinated by the Troika and conducted in the form of authoritarian statism, were positioned as appropriate. (Mullis et al. 2016: 52)

From an organisational point of view, Blockupy can be described as a process or as a network system (Gutierrez 2014) rather than a subject. As Mullis et al. state, "the place-based, multi-scalar and networked character of the early Blockupy protests was central to its ability to infuse a radical position" (2016: 51). The multi-scalar aspect of the network lies in the fact that it was organised, at the same time, both on a German and European level through meetings of activists. The aim was to create a space of political feasibility in which to bring together a plurality of actors (parties, collectives, unions, associations) to implement actions of civil disobedience regulated by a conduct code (action consensus) endorsed by all participants.

In 2015—the year in which the ECB opened its new headquarters—the movement met in the streets of Frankfurt in March while an arm wrestling match between the Greek government of Alexis Tsipras and the so-called Troika (ECB, European Commission and International Monetary Fund) was taking place. The discussion regarded the adoption of a plan of measures to reduce the national debt, accused of imposing *de facto* an extraordinary administration of Greece. We could draw a line of symbolic continuity between the days of mobilisation in March organised by Blockupy and the consultative referendum of 5 July organised by the Greek Government with regard to a critical Europeanism approach that aimed to transform the EU from within. The signing of the agreement between Tsipras and the international creditors on 13 July of the same year was described by many of the actors involved in the Blockupy network as a "capitulation", or a "negotiation with the knife to the throat", if not a real "betrayal", and led to the breakdown of faith in the possibility of reforming the EU. It is no coincidence that after 2015 Blockupy no longer had the strength to repeat mobilisation appointments and has exhausted its political mission.

3 City Air Makes You Free

After this period of extraordinary crisis management, the refusal of EU neo-liberal policies seems to have moved to a more local level. According to Dardot and Laval (2016), the crisis itself has become a real form of government: the policies of welfare cuts, the privatisation of public services, and debt reduction for the relaunch of productivity and the containment of public expenditure have been standardised, embedded in the national constitutions, and implemented through a reduction in democratic decision-making spaces. The leverage of debt has thus shifted from states to cities, which in turn are subject to stability constraints that have affected their ability to offer services and pursue effective public policies. From a political point of view, the implementation of these measures had as its objective "to systematically deny any space of territorial self-government, and to reduce the local autonomies to dependent variable, subordinate and purely executive function in a centralized and hierarchically induced project of containment of public expenditure" (Caccia 2016).

The term neo-municipalism acts as an umbrella to indicate a range of political experimentations spread throughout Europe (Shea Baird 2015; Russell and Reyes 2017) that aim to empower (Harvey 2015) the multiple urban experiences of social engagement (Mayer 2013). This wave of "bottom-up" urban political experiences "starts from a significant political fact: the results of the Spanish local elections of May 2015, which saw the establishment of mayors and express lists from *plataformas ciudadanas*" (Caccia 2016). In this case, there was a convergence between different experiences, albeit connected: on the one hand, the legacy of the 15-M movement of 2011 with all its production of political spaces, decision-making processes and practices of mutualism; on the other, the formation of a new party like Podemos, founded in 2014 by some activists linked to the 15-M movement. The formation of local coalitions between social activists and Podemos—such as Ahora Madrid and Barcelona en Comù—has led to the victory of some of these lists at the 2015 local elections in some of Spain's major cities including Madrid, Barcelona, Zaragoza, La Coruña, Pamplona, Cadiz and Santiago de Compostela. In the wake of this success, many similar experiences have arisen around Europe (in Italy, e.g. the Civic Coalition for Bologna). In all cases, we can identify a general tendency towards the creation of networks and coalitions between subjects who define themselves through the practice or the appeal to more participative decision-making processes, and push for forms of cooperation and solidarity as an alternative to market competition or neo-liberal policies.

As already explained, these neo-municipalist political groups primarily identify the urban space as a field of action. On the one hand, they denounce the effects of real estate income on urban transformations, the social consequences of cuts and privatisation on public services, as well as the restriction of forms of participatory democracy. On the other hand, they identify the city as the ground on which political responses to the effects of austerity policies can be tangibly tested, as well as forms of urban trade unionism against evictions, practices of mutualism that have given rise to a proximity welfare system, and opposition to large-scale infrastructural projects. The Spanish civic platforms were the first to embed the claims of these social and urban movements into political formations which, through the electoral process, aimed to take over the government of the city.

In comparison with Blockupy, therefore, there is no unified process or path of shared mobilisation. The European dimension remains a central issue but in less direct ways: on the one hand, the EU is identified as the entity responsible for imposing neo-liberal economic policies that would widen the gap of social inequalities, and vertical governance processes that would transform political decision into technocratic rationality. On the other hand, the different experiences of municipalism have immediately initiated forms of networking between them. The attempt to build a network of cities (described from time to time as "rebellious", "fearless" and so on) has given rise so far to several meetings—the most important, probably, has been that of the Fearless Cities held in Barcelona from 9 to 11 June 2017—but it has not found ways to translate on a more markedly organisational level yet.

4 Alternative European Geographies

At this point—after having highlighted some of the main aspects of the two paths of European mobilisation—I would like to try to define a common attitude among them with regard to the European dimension. Academic literature and politicians generally consider protests and social movements as parts of a dialectical process that leads to the evolution and improvement of political systems. Although the European Union has been often perceived as "opaque, distant, irresponsive, and inefficient" (Diez Medrano 2003, Chap. 2) or "bureaucratic, inefficient, and insufficiently transparent" (Le Torrec et al. 2001, 8), it has long been believed that (a) more participation (Eichenberg and Dalton 1993), (b) the recognition of material advantages (Carey 2002) and (c) the contribution of critical positions would have allowed greater cohesion and an improvement in the functioning of the European institutions.

This process of integrating the bottom-up forces within the political system can be described in neo-functionalistic terms as a spillover effect (Schmitter 1971):

> Acquiring competences, the EU institutions attracted protest, and during the organization of protest, social movement organizations from different countries developed Europe-wide organizational networks and common visions about Europe. (Della Porta 2006b: 11)

Indirectly, therefore, the EU would be "legitimised by social movement organisations that recognise its competencies by addressing at the European level claims of various types" (Della Porta 2006b: 12).

In my opinion, nevertheless, both the Blockupy network and the experiences of municipalism partially call into question the possibility of integrating these bottom-up forces into the current institutional set-up of the EU. In both cases, Europe—understood as a transnational area of cooperation from below as well as of contentious politics—is distinct from the Union—represented as a centralised and oligarchic institution (Skærlund Risager 2017). The criticism of the process of European integration by these movements goes hand in hand with the intention of building confederate forms of expansive democracy on a local basis (Caccia 2016) or through coalitions (Genschel 2014). In other words, the European social movements of recent years have articulated themselves according to irreducible political cartographies, both to some of the modern political categories (such as those of state and sovereignty), but also to forms of functionalistic or top-down integration.

Therefore, a field of tension is generated where these experiences aim at acting to reorganise society within and against the crisis and austerity policies, in order to invent new forms of political participation and social inclusion. Within this field, there are pushes which are articulated according to the moment and which can incline towards a reform of the EU as well as towards a radical adversity. It is, therefore, a new critical and radical Europeanism which is never totally and definitively embedded or completely separated or disruptive from the institutions of the Union.

References

Balibar, E. (2016). *Crisi e fine dell'Europa?* Bollati Boringhieri.
Bergmann, J., Niemann, A. (2013). Theories of European integration and their contribution to the study of European Foreign Policy. *Paper prepared for the 8th Pan-European Conference on International Relations, Warsaw 2013.*
Caccia, G. (2016). Europa der Kommunen. Von Bürgerplattformen zu rebellischen Städten. LuXemburg. *Gesellschaftsanalyse und Linke Praxis, 2,* 68–73.
Carey, S. (2002). Undivided loyalties. Is national identity an obstacle to European integration? *European Union Politics, 12*(3–4):387–413.
Dardot, P., & Laval, C. (2016). *Ce cauchemar qui n'en finit pas*. La Decouverte: Comment le néolibéralisme défait la démocratie.
Della Porta, D. (2006a). *Quale Europa? Europeizzazione, identità e conflitti*. Bologna: Il Mulino.
Della Porta, D. (2006b). Social movements and the European Union. *Policy paper 22*, Notre Europe.
Della Porta, D., Caiani, M. (2007). Europeanization from below? Social movements and Europe. *Mobilization: An International Quarterly, 12*(1), 1–20.
Diez Medrano, J. (2003). Framing Europe. Attitudes to European integration in Germany, Spain and the United Kingdom. Princeton University Press.
Eichenberg, R. C., & Dalton, R. J. (1993). Europeans and the European community: The dynamics of public support for European integration. *International Organization, 47*(4), 507–534.
FitzGibbon, J., Leruth, B., Stratin, N. (2017). *Euroscepticism as a transnational and a Pan-European Phenomenon*. Routledge.
Genschel, C. (2014). *Blockupy and beyond*. https://www.tni.org/en/article/blockupy-and-beyond. Accessed 15 Nov 2018.
Gutierrez B (2014) Network movements and the new 'social atmosphere'. https://www.tni.org/en/article/network-movements-and-new-social-atmosphere. Accessed 15 Nov 2018.
Harvey, D. (2015). Consolidating power. *Roar Magazine*, 269–282.
Le Torrec, V., et al. (2001). *Framing Europe: News coverage and legitimacy of the European Union in five countries*. Paper presented at the European Community Studies Association, Madison, Wisc. May 31–June 2.
Mayer, M. (2013). First world urban activism. Beyond austerity urbanism and creative city politics. *City: Analysis of Urban Trends, Culture, Theory, Policy, Action, 17*(1):5–19.
Mullis, D., et al. (2016). Social protest and its policing in the heart of the European crisis regime. The case of Blockupy in Frankurt. *Political Geography, 55,* 50–59.
Nehemiah, Y., et al. (2016). Convergence as organization. Blockupy against the ECB. *International Journal of Sociology and Social Policy*, 36.
Neumayer, C., Rossi, L., Karlsson, B. (2016a). When the police hijacked #Blockupy Frankfurt. In: *Democratic public sphere: current challenges and prospects* (pp. 405–431). Aarhus University Press.
Neumayer, C., Rossi, L., Karlsson, B. (2016b). Contested Hashtag—Blockupy Frankfurt in social media. *International Journal of Communication*, 10.
Pietiläinen, J. (2017). What is left in Europe: a comparative analysis of survey data on left self-location. In: Baier, W., Müller, W., Himmelstoss, E. (Eds.), *The left, the people, populism: Past and present*. Transform Europe Yearbook.
Rosamond, B. (2000). *Theories of European integration*. New York: St. Martin's Press.
Russell, B., Reyes, O. (2017). Fearless cities: The new urban movements. *Red Pepper*, Aug 2017. http://www.redpepper.org.uk/fearless-cities-the-new-urban-movements/. Accessed 15 Nov 2018.
Schmitter, P. C. (1971). A revised theory of regional integration. In L. N. Lindberg & S. A. Scheingold (Eds.), *Regional integration: Theory and research*. Cambridge: Harvard University Press.
Shea Baird, K. (2015) Rebel cities: The citizens platform in power. *Red Pepper*, Dec 2015. http://www.redpepper.org.uk/rebel-cities-the-citizen-platforms-in-power/. Accessed November 15, 2018.

Skærlund Risager, B. (2017) Mobilizing for a 'Europe from below': network, territory, and place in the anti-austerity Blockupy movement. *Space and Polity, 22*(1), 67–85.

Tarrow, S. (1994) *Power in movement. Social movements and contentious politics*. Cambridge University Press.

Tarrow, S. (2005). *The new transnational contention*. Cambridge University Press.

Conclusions: Opposition to Europe, Past and Future

What clearly emerges from the chapters that are collected in this edited volume is that, since the foundation of the European communities almost seventy years ago, opposition to Europe has been a persistent phenomenon (Usherwood and Startin 2013), a sort of corollary of the integration process (Taggart 1998: 363). Both at the level of public opinion and among political parties in European countries, criticism has frequently been raised towards those agreements that were gradually being ratified and against supranational bodies that were emerging with them. It is well known that several political parties, especially those belonging to the left and to the radical right, took a firm stand against the Europeanist perspective from its very outset in the years following the Second World War, and that they maintained this attitude for a long time, fueling in the population of member countries a latent opposition to the perspective of a common European homeland. Once the first European institutions had been established, it did not therefore take long for the techno-bureaucracy in Brussels to be considered by many as an obstacle to the economic, social and cultural development of European countries and for the political bodies in Brussels and Strasbourg to represent an odious authority interfering with the sovereignty of each state, and therefore of its citizens.

Europe, its bodies, its rules and often also its protagonists have always been the subject of controversy and discussion. The public debate on Europe has often been marked by the tendency to emphasize the limits and the failures that have characterized and still characterize the path of Europe, rather than to highlight its successes and achievements. Even for many of those who shared the European dream and saw in the choices that gradually gave shape to the European project, in fact, communitarian institutions continued (and still continue today) to be perceived as distant, undemocratic and heavily bureaucratic. Many citizens of the continent, undoubtedly, have looked and continue to look with hope and with a sense of belonging—if not pride—at the European institutions. But this does not detract from the fact that, since their inception, those institutions have had to deal with the bitter controversy of their critics and with feelings of distrust, mistrust and adversity equally rooted among the population.

To be sure, these feelings have taken on different forms and degrees, just as different in content and intensity were the critical positions expressed by

© Springer Nature Switzerland AG 2020

M. Baldassari et al. (eds.), *Anti-Europeanism*,
https://doi.org/10.1007/978-3-030-24428-6

intellectuals and political forces in Europe. Over the last two decades, several scholars have proposed to distinguish and define, by type and intensity, the different forms of opposition to Europe, which is to be intended as a neither binary nor absolute phenomenon. According to the seminal work by Taggart (1998: 366), two main forms of Euroscepticism can be distinguished: a "principled opposition" to Europe and to the integration process (hard Euroscepticism) and more contingent, "qualified forms of objection" to the EU, ranging from the opposition to its economic policy to the criticism of its future trajectories (soft Euroscepticism). Kopecky and Mudde (2002: 300) offered a more precise distinction between support for the European integration and for the EU "as it is and as it is developing", identifying Eurosceptic, Europragmatist and Eurorejectionist attitudes, while in a later work, Szczerbiak and Taggart (2003) identify six possible gradations of opposition to the EU (from harder to softer attitudes: *rejectionism*, *revisionism*, *minimalism*, *gradualism*, *reformism* and *maximalism*). Despite these different definitions, most studies agree that Euroscepticism is independent from party family (Taggart 1998), although it can be determined by party ideology (with radical parties that are more likely to share anti-European attitudes) as well as by party positioning and by their role in the political spectrum (with opposition parties that tend to be more Eurosceptic than those supporting the government, see Conti 2003). In sum, Eurosceptic positions seem to be widespread in new emerging, peripheral and radical parties, while few mainstream parties show a negative attitude towards Europe (Hooghe and Marks 2017: 14).

In the light of the essays presented in this volume, it seems evident that negative attitudes towards the European Union can be divided into at least three broad categories. First, *anti-Europeanism*, i.e. the approach of those political and cultural forces that, over the decades, have opposed and are now more or less openly opposed to the very principle of European unity, by implicitly rejecting the historical, ideal, political and economic reasons of the Union or simply by opposing any transfer of sovereignty to the EU level. This is the way of looking at the European institutions of those who see in them, to paraphrase a famous definition by Ronald Reagan, "the problem, not the solution of the problems". A second form of opposition to Europe is *Euroscepticism*, i.e. the point of view of those, politicians, intellectuals or ordinary "men in the street", who, although not opposed in principle to the transfer of sovereignty to a supranational authority, believe that European institutions are doomed to failure, because they are irreparably inadequate for their task and unable—for various reasons—to effectively reform themselves. Third, *Eurocriticism*, i.e. the way of thinking of those who do not oppose the European ideal, but who are against "this Europe", its institutions, its structure and its bureaucracy. Under this view, opposition to Europe may range from the critiques towards supranational policies to its failure to reflect the interest of member states or even for being insufficiently integrationist or democratic (Szczerbiak and Taggart 2003). This last approach is more positive and open than the two previous ones, but it is nevertheless marked by a strong detachment from Europe, not only from a theoretical point of view but also, and perhaps above all, in its practical impact, envisioning a mixture of disillusionment, pessimism and indifference.

All three of these ways of dealing with the European project have always existed, and of course, they have intertwined and sometimes overlapped. There is no doubt, however, that over the last ten years all those three forms of opposition to Europe have progressively acquired space and importance in the European public arena. In some instances, it seems that they have become even prevalent in some member states. It is not easy to explain this sudden spread of feelings and arguments of rejection, opposition and distrust. However, the hypothesis that it seems possible to advance in the light of recent studies—starting with those presented in this volume—is that anti-Europeanism, Euroscepticism and Eurocriticism have been amplified by the multiple crises that Europe has had to face over the last decade (Pirro and Taggart 2018; Fabbrini 2019): the 2008 financial crisis, which soon prompted a debt crisis in some member states as well as a crisis of the single currency; the migration crisis, which reached its peak in 2015 and is still producing its effects upon European countries, showing the lack of a common European strategy in some key areas of domestic political affairs; and the security crisis, which was mainly the consequence of the series of terrorist attacks carried out in France, Germany, Belgium and in the UK between 2014 and 2018. The Brexit referendum in June 2016 was only the litmus test of an overall crisis of legitimacy that is still undermining popular support for the European project.

It is also evident that, over the last ten years, Eurosceptic tendencies have been combined with two related processes: on the one hand, the very idea of liberal democracy has been questioned, a trend that is witnessed by the emergence of populist forces occupying an increasingly significant space on the European political scene (Mény and Surel 2002); at this regard, the challenge to democratic governance has been recently accompanied by the attempt to propose more or less credible and viable forms of "sortitive" democracy (Van Reybrouck 2018) or, on the opposite side, "epistocracy" (Brennan 2016). On the other hand, there is an increasingly widespread tendency in Europe to challenge the representative nature of democratic regimes, questioning the traditional allocation of political authority in the sense of either "who" should rule (the people vs. elite debate) or "where" should sovereignty lie (the local–supranational-level debate). In both instances, popular sovereignty in the form of direct democratic rule and the devolution of the decision-making process to the local level are increasingly identified by European citizens as a way to build a more genuine form of democracy.

Opposition to Europe is thus a multifaceted phenomenon, which has recently intertwined with multiple crises and trends. It would be therefore useless, if not impossible, to identify its causes. However, a focus on its possible roots may be a useful theoretical exercise to sketch some possible scenarios for the future. Overall, we may say that the literature in this field has pursued several paths in the last two decades, advancing at least three broad sets of hypotheses: the party strategic positioning hypothesis, the cleavage hypothesis and, more recently, the Great Recession (or economic) hypothesis. The first two groups of hypotheses tend to stress structural and endogenous causes (the first focuses on the domestic side, while the second has a more transnational dimension); the third one is a conjunctural hypothesis, stressing exogenous causes.

The strategic positioning hypothesis (Sitter 2002) has been mainly supported by the European Parties Elections and Referendums Network (EPERN) of the Sussex School on party-based Euroscepticism (Mudde 2012). According to this hypothesis, attitudes towards Europe depend on the party's position in the domestic political spectrum: more radical and peripheral parties will adopt a stronger Eurosceptic position for strategic reasons (i.e. differentiating themselves from mainstream parties). Under this view, opposition to Europe may be considered just a party-based phenomenon, with domestic institutions (i.e. whether they are dominated by just one party or by a multiparty coalition) and electoral systems (i.e. whether they are majoritarian or based on proportional representation) both influencing parties' tactics and strategic positioning. In a recent essay, for example, Brigevich (2018) has stressed that new radical parties can even clue negative attitudes towards Europe in their voters, thus shaping their preferences. As this hypothesis suggests, radical and populist parties in Europe have exploited the multiple crises of the 2010s as an opportunity to gain electoral consensus, typically by stressing more their pre-existing Eurosceptic messages. In some cases, this has induced mainstream parties to adopt a less enthusiastic attitude towards the European Union (Pirro et al. 2018). A corollary of this hypothesis, of course, is that Eurosceptic attitudes may turn more positive when parties are involved in the government for the evident reason that they will be also involved in EU political bodies.

The social cleavage hypothesis starts from opposite assumptions, namely that changes in voters preferences shape party positioning in the political arena. This hypothesis has been mainly supported by the North Carolina School on party-based Euroscepticism (Mudde 2012), which has underlined the role of ideology and cultural change to explain opposition to the European Union. Building upon the theory originally put forward by Lipset and Rokkan (1967) and Inglehart (1977), works in this field of research contend that social cleavages are still shaping European party systems, with old cleavages (such as the Church–State cleavage, or even the Capital–Labor cleavage) losing their salience and new political movements emerging from more recent social conflicts. This new conflict has been referred to as an integration–demarcation cleavage (Hutter 2014; Kriesi et al. 2006, 2012) or, more broadly, as a communitarianism–cosmopolitanism divide (Zürn and De Wilde 2016). According to this hypothesis, party systems emerging from this new cleavage are structured around a GAL-TAN dimension, with Green, Alternative and Libertarian parties showing open and cosmopolitan views, and Traditional, Authoritarian and Nationalist parties having a more communitarian ideology (Marks and Wilson 2000; Hooghe et al. 2002). As Hooghe and Marks (2017: 6) have argued, this cleavage "proved to be strongly associated with support for Europe" (i.e. GAL parties tend to be more Europhile and TAN parties more Eurosceptic), though there are some significant differences between European countries.

The economic hypothesis points to an exogenous, conjunctural cause like the Great Recession started in 2008 as a consequence of the financial crisis in the United States. This hypothesis assumes that economic globalization tends to produce both "winners"—benefiting from increased competition—and "losers", who tend to be weakened by increased competition (Kriesi et al. 2006) and concludes that this divide has broadened with the impact of the economic crisis in the first years of the 2010s, producing discontent towards EU institutions—in particular towards the EU Commission and its management of the debt crisis—and thus more opportunities for populist, Eurosceptic parties (Kriesi and Pappas 2015). Under this view, domestic politics is determined by the business cycle, since voters "reward or punish incumbents [and therefore pro-European parties] according to the economic situation" (Hernàndez and Kriesi 2016: 203). This has been especially true in Western Europe, where people have been less accustomed to economic hardship than in Central and Eastern European countries. As a result, radical left parties in Western Europe have criticized Europe for its neoliberal agenda and its austerity measures (Pirro et al. 2018: 380), while radical right parties—whose opposition to Europe had always been for cultural and nationalist reasons—have incorporated economic grievances in their Eurosceptic discourse (Pirro and Van Kessel 2017).

If support for Europe determines the trajectories that the Union will undertake in future, we may conclude that its destiny will probably depend on all the above-mentioned political, sociocultural and economic variables. However, its actual impact on the integration process may vary depending on which hypothesis (whether structural or conjunctural) will eventually prevail. Indeed, if negative attitudes towards the Union are the mere result of strategic competition among political parties in member countries, this will not constitute a fundamental challenge for the European Union since national variations may compensate and balance each other (i.e. some governments turning more Europhile while others more Eurosceptic at the same time). If opposition to Europe is just an aspect of a deeper, transnational cleavage emerging in European societies, on the contrary, the future of Europe seems more unpredictable, because it will depend on the conflict between cosmopolitan and communitarian views and on its eventual outcome (not only in Europe but, more broadly, in all Western societies). If hard anti-Europeanism has a more conjunctural (i.e. cyclical) nature, opposition to Europe is likely to decrease as soon as member countries will recover from the economic recession. In this case, however, the European Union should be ready to cope with economic crises in future, finding new ways to manage exogenous economic shocks and, above all, their natural political consequences. Over the last seven decades, Europe has been able to deal with its critics, making *creative efforts proportionate to the dangers* that have threatened the integration process (echoing what Robert Schuman envisioned in 1950). Of course, this does not mean that Europe will be able to overcome the current crisis. It only means that current opposition to Europe should not be underestimated by its leaders and that addressing its political, economic and cultural roots should be among their main priorities.

References

Brennan, J. (2016). Can epistocracy, or knowledge-based voting, fix democracy? *LA Times*, August 28, 2016. Available at https://www.latimes.com/opinion/op-ed/la-oe-brennan-epistocracy-20160828-snap-story.html.

Brigevich, A. (2018). Cueing the radical voter: The impact of economic, immigration and integration cues on public fear of the EU. *Party Politics*. https://doi.org/10.1177/1354068818808324.

Conti, N. (2003). *Party attitudes to European integration: A longitudinal analysis of the Italian case*. EPERN working paper 70. Guildford: European Parties Elections and Referendums Network.

Fabbrini, S. (2019). *Europe's future: Decoupling and reforming*. Cambridge: Cambridge University Press.

Hernández, E., & Kriesi, H. (2016). The electoral consequences of the financial and economic crisis in Europe. *European Journal of Political Research, 55*(2), 203–224.

Hooghe, L., & Marks, G. (2017). Cleavage theory meets Europe's crises: Lipset, Rokkan, and the transnational cleavage. *Journal of European Public Policy, 25*(1), 109–135.

Hooghe, L., Marks, G., & Wilson, C. J. (2002). Does left/right structure party positions on European integration? *Comparative Political Studies, 35*(8), 965–989.

Hutter, S. (2014). *Protesting culture and economics in Western Europe: New cleavages in left and right politics*. Minneapolis: University of Minnesota Press.

Inglehart, R. (1977). *The silent revolution: Changing values and political styles in advanced industrial society*. Princeton: Princeton University Press.

Kopecky, P., & Mudde, C. (2002). The two sides of Euroscepticism. Party positions on European integration in East Central Europe. *European Union Politics, 3*(3), 297–326.

Kriesi, H., Grande, E., Dolezal, M., Helbling, M., Höglinger, D., Hutter, S., et al. (2012). *Political conflict in Western Europe*. Cambridge: Cambridge University Press.

Kriesi, H., Grande, E., Lachat, R., Dolezal, M., Bornschier, S., & Frey, T. (2006). Globalization and the transformation of the national political space: Six European countries compared. *European Journal of Political Research, 45*(6), 921–956.

Kriesi, H., & Pappas, T. S. (Eds.). (2015). *European populism in the shadow of the great recession*. Colchester: ECPR Press.

Lipset, S. M., & Rokkan, S. (1967). *Party systems and voter alignments: Cross-national perspectives*. New York: Free Press.

Marks, G., & Wilson, C. J. (2000). The past in the present: A cleavage theory of party response to European integration. *British Journal of Political Science, 30*(3), 433–459.

© Springer Nature Switzerland AG 2020

M. Baldassari et al. (eds.), *Anti-Europeanism*,
https://doi.org/10.1007/978-3-030-24428-6

Mény, Y., & Surel, Y. (2002). The constitutive ambiguity of populism. In M. Canovan, Y. Meny, & Y. Surel (Eds.), *Democracies and the populist challenge* (pp. 1–21). London: Palgrave Macmillan.

Mudde, C. (2012). The comparative study of party-based Euroscepticism: The Sussex versus the North Carolina school. *East European Politics, 28*(2), 193–202.

Pirro, A. L. P., & Taggart, P. (2018). The populist politics of Euroscepticism in times of crisis: A framework for analysis. *Politics, 38*(3), 253–262.

Pirro, A. L. P., Taggart, P., & van Kessel, S. (2018). The populist politics of Euroscepticism in times of crisis: Comparative conclusions. *Politics, 38*(3), 378–390.

Pirro, A. L. P., & Van Kessel, S. (2017). United in opposition? The populist radical right's EU-pessimism in times of crisis. *Journal of European Integration, 39*(4), 405–420.

Sitter, N. (2002). *Opposing Europe: Euro-scepticism, opposition and party competition*. Sussex: Sussex European Institute.

Szczerbiak, A., & Taggart, P. (2003). *Theorising party-based Euroscepticism: Problems of definition, measurement and causality*. Paper prepared for presentation at the 8th Biannual International Conference of the European Union Studies Association Conference, Nashville, March 27–29.

Taggart, P. (1998). A touchstone of dissent: Euroscepticism in contemporary Western European party systems. *European Journal of Political Research, 33*(3), 363–388.

Usherwood, S., & Startin, N. (2013). Euroscepticism as a persistent phenomenon. *JCMS: Journal of Common Market Studies, 51*(1), 1–16.

Van Reybrouck, D. (2018). *Against elections*. New York: Seven Stories Press.

Zürn, M., & De Wilde, P. (2016). Debating globalization: Cosmopolitanism and communitarianism as political ideologies. *Journal of Political Ideologies, 21*(3), 280–301.

MIX
Papier aus verantwortungsvollen Quellen
Paper from responsible sources
FSC® C105338

If you have any concerns about our products,
you can contact us on
ProductSafety@springernature.com

In case Publisher is established outside the EU,
the EU authorized representative is:
Springer Nature Customer Service Center GmbH
Europaplatz 3, 69115 Heidelberg, Germany

Printed by Libri Plureos GmbH
in Hamburg, Germany